T8

Suzanne
Best Wishes
Neil Moloney

COPS,

CROOKS

&

POLITICIANS

Revised Edition
by
NEIL W. MOLONEY

with a Foreword by Governor John Spellman

Published by

PEANUT BUTTER
PUBLISHING

Seattle, WA

Copyright© 1993 by Neil W. Moloney

ISBN: 0-89716-510-1

PRINTED IN CANADA

8 1.5 7 3

Cover Design: *Kerri Eden*
Editor: *Donaleen P. Saul*
Typesetting / Design: *Bob Banner*

Revised Edition 1994
Library of Congress Number: 94-065893

Peanut Butter Publishing
226 2nd Ave. West
Seattle, WA 98119

CONTENTS

Acknowledgements iv

Foreword vi

Introduction vii

1. The Robbery 1

2. The Investigation 19

3. The Canadians 43

4. Corruption Within 61

5. Political Response 95

6. The Informant 113

7. A Return To Canada 145

8. Informant Revisited 171

9. The Interviews 185

10. The Business Connection 213

11. The Indictment 235

12. Extradition 251

13. The Trial 263

14. The Aftermath 283

15. Epilogue 313

    Appendices 331

Acknowledgements

The author is indebted to many people who were willing to share their experiences and information relative to the events described in this story. There were several colleagues of this writer who, as Seattle Police Department officers, either played a major role in this investigation or were instrumental in helping to gather the facts of this case for publication. These included Chief of Police Robert L. Hanson; Deputy Chief of Police Charles A. Rouse; Assistant Chief of Police Michael D. Brasfield; Inspector of Detectives William J. Walsh; Captain Michael Slessman; Detective Lieutenant Austin Seth; Major Raymond L. Carroll; Detective Sergeant Charles K. Waitt; Police Records Manager Judy de Mello; Officer Vernon R. Chase; Detective Eugene F. Ivey; Detective Robert Waitt; Officers Fred Keenan, Glenn Rouse, and Michael Johnson. There were others in Seattle who supported the author's search as well, including Mrs. Vernon (Joyce) Chase, Kenneth McElhaney, Mrs. Frank (Rolene) Hardy, Mrs. Charles (Willa) Waitt and many more.

This writer is also indebted to FBI Agents Dean C. Rolston, Alfred G. (Alf) Gunn, and Chet Crisman who were the lead FBI agents involved in this investigation. They were, by Bureau policy, precluded from responding to the author's specific inquiries relating to the FBI's role in this case, which was very significant throughout the course of the investigation. These dedicated professional law enforcement officers undoubtedly did more than any other persons in pursuit of a solution to this case.

The author is also indebted to many others who helped in preparing the manuscript, including Ann Rule who read the first draft of this narrative and gave the author the encouragement to continue the pursuit of this story. He would also like to acknowledge Assistant Chief of Police Clayton E. Bean and Major Harry Schneider, retired

Seattle Police Department Officers, particularly for their recommendations which clarified the actual events which took place both in Canada and in the U.S. during the investigative phase of this case, and for their honest and objective analysis of the story relative to both the events which occurred in Seattle, Washington and of the Seattle Police Department's investigative role in this case.

The author is indebted to several kind and considerate Canadian citizens who assisted in the extensive search for much of the statistical and historical data discussed in this book, including the lengthy search for the pictures and background information on several of the key players in this story. These included Kate Abbott, Pacific Press librarian and Trudy Driver, Curator of the Vancouver Police Centennial Museum (in Vancouver, British Columbia); Jan Papageorgis and Richard Trudeau of Statistics Canada in Vancouver, British Columbia and in Ottawa, Ontario; and from the ladies from the Vancouver, British Columbia Public Library, including Margaret Ford, Head of the Sociology Division, Susan Bridgeman, Head of Historical Photographs Division, and Laurie Robertson and Carolin Kowpak of the Historical Photograph Section. The profile of Canadian bank robbers and much of the historical data on Canadian robberies was made available to the author by Michael E. P. Ballard, Vice-President, Security Canadian Bankers Association and David Pollock, Regional Director British Columbia and Alberta Canadian Banker's Association.

Retired Vancouver Police Detective Dan Brown assisted the author in the identification of many of the principals involved in the story. At the Museum of History and Industry in Seattle, Rick Caldwell Librarian and Assistant Librarian Carolyn Marr were of great assistance in locating for the author several of the photographs utilized in this book.

A special thanks is owed to Dorothy Moloney and Traci Ann Hollingsworth for transforming my many grammatical errors into understandable sentences and paragraphs and to Heidi Joan Riedeman for her tremendous clerical support in preparing the multiple drafts of the original manuscript. Also, thanks to Donaleen Saul for her editing transformations and Bob Banner for his typesetting and production capabilities.

Foreword

I was honored to be asked to write the foreword for Neil Moloney's *Cops, Crooks, and Politicians*. Moloney has always been the epitome of an honest cop. A quiet spoken, confident professional, Chief Moloney improved every police unit on which he served or lead. He emerged from the troubled times of police corruption described in this book as a skilled investigator and administrator.

In *Cops, Crooks, and Politicians*, Moloney relates the story of the attempts made to bring a group of Canadian criminals to justice. However, the political manipulation of the police organization by corrupt and incompetent elected officials for their personal benefit thwarted these efforts. As the story unfolded dozens of local police officers, politicians, and businessmen were indicted for criminal offenses. Their actions and offenses were indicative of the epidemic of corruption and ineptness of public officers within the criminal justice agencies in Western Canada and in the Northwestern U.S. at the time.

As a first-hand witness to these events, Moloney is able to provide a descriptive account of the investigative processes utilized by the police. He is also able to reveal the impact that political corruption had upon that investigation and the police officers themselves.

In 1981, I appointed Neil Moloney to command and revitalize the Washington State Patrol. Then he was Chief of the Port of Seattle Police and he'd had a distinguished career with the Seattle Police Department. Moloney's no nonsense approach to improved police services and accountability in the self-satisfied highway patrol caused waves from the union and politicians. The positive impact of the Moloney years continued to be felt even after he had left his position.

Cops, Crooks, and Politicians is the product of Moloney's thorough investigation and critical analysis of the Greenwood Bank robbery and killings. This *true and factual* story of bungling, political posturing, neglect, and corruption teach a powerful lesson.

— *Governor John Spellman*

Introduction

This story has its beginnings in the depression years of the mid thirties on the prairies of Western Canada. This era spawned a group of young criminals who committed a series of bank robberies and other felony crimes throughout Western Canada for a period of over 30 years. Many efforts were made by Canadian law enforcement officials to put a stop to this, but through a series of circumstances, not the least of which involved corruption of several Canadian criminal justice and political leaders, these criminals were not held accountable for many of their crimes. The end result of such corruption and the lack of action to curtail these unlawful activities was the widening of these criminals' territory to include the western United States.

The incident which aroused the interest of this author began as a robbery in Seattle, Washington in 1954 which ultimately led to the murder of a young police officer and the permanent disabling of two others who responded to a bank robbery-in-progress call in the city. This incident was followed by a ten-year investigation, the resolution of which was never really achieved. The primary reason for this failure can be traced directly to more than a dozen City of Vancouver Police officers, Royal Canadian Mounted Police officers, as well as some politicians and judges in British Columbia who entered into a conspiracy with one or more of the participants in these crimes, or who failed to carry out the duties of their elected or appointed office.

The story outlines a series of events which led to this crime, describes how it was carried out, identifies the perpetrators, and provides the details of how the crime was solved. This would have been a relatively easy accomplishment, yet as the story unfolded it became evident that the forces that were at play here precluded the mere telling of a crime story. For as the author explored the circumstances surrounding the crime, the information began to paint a much broader picture of crime within the political framework of the City of Vancouver, and within the City of Vancouver Police Department and the Royal Canadian Mounted Police.

A close reading of the story may well give the reader the impression that the author was overly critical of the actions of the police and political leadership of the law enforcement agencies within the City of Vancouver (and in Seattle, Washington). If that is the case, the author offers no apology, for the illegal actions of these politicians, judges and inept or corrupt police officials led directly to the death of a young police officer. Although the majority of the men and women working within their respective criminal justice agencies both in Canada and in the U.S. are highly principled and dedicated individuals, when some of their members fail to do their job properly, not only does the general public suffer but the street officer often becomes the real target of criminals who are allowed to continue unabated in their predatory activities.

As this crime story and the subsequent investigation was unfolding in the U.S., through a series of quite unrelated events in Canada, a glimpse of the corruption within the Vancouver Police Department was being exposed by several of their own people and was soon to became front page news throughout the country. The organizational integrity of the entire police force was brought into question when it was discovered that the Chief Constable and others within the Vancouver police force were participating in a widespread scheme to protect several people involved in illegal activities within the city, activities which included providing protection for hard-core criminals. And such activities were being carried out with the knowledge of those elected officials who had the responsibility to oversee the operations of the police. Upon public disclosure of these activities one high ranking officer committed suicide, a detective shot himself and the Chief Constable fled the country to avoid prosecution.

So it is this backdrop of 1954 that one should think of when reading this book; for in Seattle, as well as in Vancouver corruption within the police department was widespread, but in Seattle it had not yet surfaced publicly. The Seattle Department however was understaffed and the officers underpaid, poorly equipped, trained and supervised. The end result was evident. A group of young officers, some of whom had never been to the Police Academy, nor received anything more than a few hours of on-the-job training in the field, responded to the scene of a bank robbery in North Seattle, where three officers were shot, one fatally, by one of three Canadian bank robbers. All three criminals escaped, even though more than two dozen officers responded to this robbery within minutes of the crime, with at least five arriving before the suspects left the scene of the crime. The three holdup men from Vancouver, British Columbia would return to their homes in Canada where they would continue their crime spree, but they would never be held accountable for their crimes in the U.S.

Chapter

1

The Robbery

In 1954 Kenneth McElhaney, at age 36, was one of the youngest bank managers in the huge Seattle First National Bank Corporation, having begun his career with the firm as a bank messenger and part-time clerk in 1940. His service to the bank was interrupted by the war when he enlisted in the U.S. Navy, but resumed again with his discharge in 1945. McElhaney was a Seattle native, a Queen Anne High School graduate and former University of Washington student. He loved his position as the manager of one of the company's largest satellite locations and he was very active socially with his colleagues and within the North Seattle Community of Greenwood, where his branch was located. He was described by his associates as a bright, level-headed, hardworking manager, who was well-respected within the banking family. At corporate headquarters it was expected that within the year he would be moved up to fill a soon to be vacated senior vice president's position.[1]

The Greenwood Branch of the Seattle First National Bank was located on the northeast corner of North 85th Street and Phinney Avenue in the Greenwood District, a large business and shopping center in the northwest part of the City of Seattle. The bank faced south, with the front entrance opening onto North 85th Street and a side entrance located on the east side of the building, for entry to and from the parking lot which bordered the entire east and north sides of the bank. This small L-shaped parking lot had a one-way traffic pattern from north to south, with the entrance on Phinney

Avenue, on the north side of the building and an exit onto North 85th Street at the southeast corner of the bank. Immediately to the east of the bank on North 85th Street was located the Greer-Thomas Lumber Company, and directly across the street from the south exit of the parking lot stood the Kraabel Medical Clinic. The bank was a contemporary one-story building of red brick construction with large windows with lower panes of frosted glass. Visibility from the outside, in daylight, was severely restricted due to these windows. Both entrances had double glass doors with a small vestibule between the inner and outer doors. The building itself was about 70 feet wide by 100 feet long. The bank officers' desks were across the oval-shaped lobby from the tellers' cages. There were eleven cages in tellers row, on the north side of the oval.

At 10:50 A.M. on March 12, 1954, McElhaney, while sitting at his desk in the bank, looked up, his attention directed toward two men approaching the officers' section of the bank from the lobby. The shorter of the two remained outside the low railing surrounding the officers' desks and the other strode directly toward the bank manager. This man was a tall slender Caucasian man, about forty years old, with dark swarthy skin. What surprised McElhaney was that he and his accomplice were wearing false rubber noses and horn-rimmed or plastic glasses. The man yelled, "You," and again, "You, get up off the chair. I mean you!" McElhaney started to laugh, thinking that some of his business friends in the district were clowning with him. Then the man yelled, "God damn it, I'm not fooling. Get the hell up out of there!" By this time the man was leaning over Kenneth McElhaney's desk, pointing a shiny blue .45 automatic pistol, which he held in his right hand, a few inches away from the bank manager's chest. McElhaney was now convinced that this was no gag. With his left hand, the man raked back the action on the weapon to full cock, letting the slide snap forward which chambered a bullet. In response, McElhaney bolted out of his chair and the man stepped back and said, "Let's go to the vault." As the manager moved toward the vault through the officers' section, he noticed the stickup man put on a pair of imitation suede leather gloves; this action appeared to be very difficult for the man to accomplish. He also noticed that the second man, who was much shorter entered through the lobby gate and followed them through the officers' section toward the vault. The first man said to the second one, "Okay George, come on." Halfway to the vault, McElhaney paused, only to have the gunman jam him in the back with the automatic. He then moved quickly toward the vault, with the gunman following closely behind.[2]

The stickup man took long quick strides, like a military strut, as if "on parade," the former navy man thought. As they approached the vault, the man saw that the bookkeeping office, adjacent to the vault, was filled with employees. "Get those people out of here," he said. The bank manager quietly asked the employees to come out and stand behind tellers' row. They were then told by the tall dark-haired man to turn around and face the wall.

During this time the two stickup men completely ignored Florence Hageland, the bank switchboard operator. Ms. Hageland had worked at the bank for eight years and there were few occasions when the normal business routine of the bank was disrupted. However, this morning the woman was alerted when she heard shouting coming from the direction of the manager's desk. She heard, then saw, a tall dark-complexioned man say to McElhaney, "Get up, I told you." Shortly afterwards, the manager walked past Florence's station, followed by the tall man. As they went by, she saw what she thought was an automatic pistol held by the man, pointed directly at the bank manager's back. As the two men passed her position, she pressed the alarm button on the switchboard which was wired directly into the north precinct of the Seattle Police Department. It was 10:51 A.M.

Meanwhile, a second man, with a gun in his hand, was following the first man across the bank lobby. The first was at least 6 feet tall and immaculately dressed, whereas the second was quite small, under 5' 7" and older. The telephone operator's first impression was that he was at least 45 or 50 years old. He reminded her of a comedian whose clothes were too big for him. He had on a large fake nose and horn-rimmed glasses, as did the first man, and wore an overcoat that hung nearly to the floor.

Ms. Hageland was not the only one to sound the alarm this morning. Harry Edwards, a counterman at the bank, was talking to a customer but did not see the stickup men enter the bank. Edwards was soon to learn that something unusual was occurring when he saw two people approach his counter from the bank lobby. The first man said in a low voice, "This is a stickup." Edwards didn't immediately realize what was happening as he was distracted by the comical appearance of both men with their horn-rimmed glasses and over-sized red rubber noses. The men walked past Edwards toward the bank manager's desk, with the first man telling everyone to be quiet. Shortly afterward, as McElhaney and the two stickup men headed toward the vault, Edwards pushed an alarm button which was concealed under the counter.

Assistant Manager Harry Strong also sounded the alarm; Strong had been talking on the telephone to Harold Logan at the Main Office Credit Department in downtown Seattle. He had asked Logan to hold the line and laid the telephone receiver on his desk to check a name in the files behind him. As he got up from his chair, he noticed a man standing at the counter nearby. The man was wearing horn-rimmed glasses with a false rubber nose and a moustache; he was also carrying what appeared to Strong as a .38 revolver. The assistant manager also thought that one of the local merchants was pulling a gag on him and thus continued toward the files behind his boss's desk where he came face-to-face with the number one man who was holding the .45 automatic, now pointed directly at Strong. His first impression was that this was part of the show being staged at the counter; and he looked close at this number one man, trying to determine who he was.[3] The stickup man told Strong, "Sit down." McElhaney, interjecting himself into the conversation, said, "You'd better sit down, Harry," for the bank manager was now fully aware of the robber's intentions and he was "... scared as hell" that either a customer or a member of his staff would do something "dumb" which would lead to the injury of an innocent party.[4] Strong returned to his chair. Shortly after the manager and the two men left the officers' section and approached the vault, Strong whispered to Edwards, "Push the alarm." He then picked up the telephone receiver and told Logan at the downtown branch, "We're being robbed, call the police." After looking around and not seeing anyone watching him, he repeated, "I'm not kidding, call the police."

There was no doubt during this time that the tallest of the two stickup suspects was fully in charge of this robbery. After McElhaney had asked all of the bank employees to come out of the back office, the tall man said to him, "God damn it, open the vault!" With this stern admonition the bank manager, now in fear for his own life, called the head teller, Robert Swaggert, to come over and open the vault. Swaggert had been working at window nine, in the middle of tellers' row, some distance from the vault, and it was necessary for McElhaney to call twice before Swaggert responded. Upon his arrival, the stickup man again told him to open the vault. He had to repeat himself until finally Swaggert opened the vault door and all three men entered. The manager, upon direction from the stickup man, told Swaggert to open the inner safe door. This was already unlocked and all the head teller had to do was throw the handle, and the door opened.

While the tallest of the two robbers was trying to command both the actions of the bank manager and the head teller in the vault, it was obvious he was having problems getting his partner, "George," to clean out the tellers' cages. The man became noticeably irritated with George, who acted as if he didn't know what to do and most of the time either followed or stood behind the tall man, as if waiting for directions. They weren't long in coming; he ordered his partner George, "Get those cages." Whereupon the short robber began to clean out the top drawers of the tellers' cages, taking only paper money and placing it in a large shopping bag.

McElhaney asked the tall man where he wanted to put the money from the inner safe. The man responded by throwing a folded shopping bag at the bank manager, who unfolded it and held it as Bob Swaggert began filling it with bundles of money taken from the safe. When this was completed, the stickup man looked into the safe and noted that a small inner safe, located in the top of the larger unit, was not open. The man ordered that this be opened. This compartment contained the only large bills kept by the bank. Swaggert was so nervous by this time that it took three separate attempts for him to work the combination. During this time the tall man kept walking in and out of the vault, trying to keep an eye on both customers and employees in the area close by. There were approximately twenty customers in the bank and thirty employees on duty at the time.

After the head teller had opened the inner safe, he took out the only large bank notes present, three $500.00 bills, which he handed to the bank manager. As McElhaney placed these in the shopping bag, the stickup man asked him what he had. The manager replied, "Five hundreds and thousands." The man appeared to be satisfied with this. He took the bag from McElhaney, giving him another and ordered him to proceed down tellers' row and, "Get all the cash". As the manager started down the inside of tellers row, the tall robber returned to the lobby of the bank, following McElhaney from the lobby side, cage by cage. Swaggert, for some reason unknown even to himself, followed behind McElhaney, watching his boss, until the employee found himself face-to-face with one of the stickup men, who ordered him to turn and face the wall.[5]

It was obvious to the bank manager at this time that George, didn't know where to look for money within the tellers' cages. He was banging the drawers open and closed, causing considerable noise and confusion. When the manager and the tall gunman reached the last teller's cage, the stickup man leaned over the counter and noticed that the manager was only taking small bills out of the center drawers of the cages, whereupon he said, "God damn it, open all those drawers." He then reached through the cage pulling open one of the lower drawers, which contained a large amount of currency. He cursed McElhaney again saying, "God damn it, why haven't you been opening those drawers?" He then yelled at George, "Get the big stuff in the bottom drawers." McElhaney called Dorothy Potter, the teller who worked in this last cage, to come over and unlock the lower drawers. Mrs. Potter however, in her excitement, placed her key in the lock for the top drawer instead of the bottom. She had difficulty working the key out of the lock, but finally got it out and unlocked the bottom drawer. She then laid her key on top of the counter. The tall man reached in through the window, opened the top drawer, and then tried the bottom drawer, which readily opened. Looking into the drawer and seeing a large amount of currency, he again ordered George, "Get the lower drawers." He told Mrs. Potter to step back and face the wall, away from the tellers' cages. She complied.

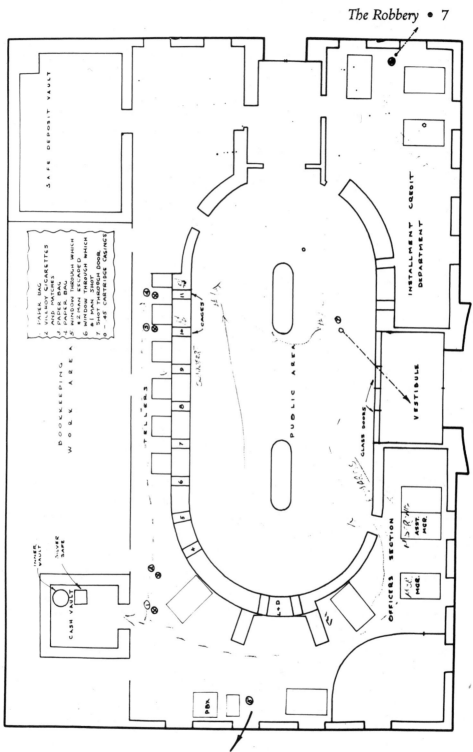

Sketch of interior of bank and path the robbers traveled within the Seattle First National Bank, Greenwood Branch during the robbery

George was observed by Beatrice Ekloff, teller in cage seven, as he entered the cage next to hers, ordered this teller out of the cage, and removed the money from the top drawer. At this time, the tall man ordered everyone to face the wall, but Miss Ekloff remained as she was, frozen by the activity that was swirling about her. George then entered her cage, took her gently by the shoulder, turned her around and reminded her she was to face the wall. She noticed George was carrying a shopping bag as he tried to open the lower cash drawers, but they were still locked. George then went back to window number five and returned shortly carrying a long, yellow-handled screwdriver which he used to force open the drawers in her cage, then moved on to cage number eight dropping the screwdriver into the bag containing the money.

Although the bank manager was aware that a third stickup man was present in the building, his attention was centered on the tall man, who not only directed the entire stickup operation, but continued to stay with McElhaney, ordering his every movement in gathering up the bank's money.[6] But not so with Harold Sanford. Sanford was employed as the Installment Credit Department Manager and during the robbery was at his desk in the Consumer Credit Department in the southeast corner of the bank. He was talking on the telephone to Alan Shaw of the Commercial Credit Corporation in downtown Seattle when he first noticed a man standing in front of his desk pointing a .38 caliber revolver at him. The man ordered Sanford to hang up the phone, which he did; then he was ordered to take the receiver off the hook. Instinctively, the junior manager raised it to his ear, only to discover that he was still connected to Shaw. He finally laid the receiver on this desk. The man kept his gun pointed in the general direction of Sanford and told him to put his hands on his desk and keep them there. The robber stayed near Sanford and in the vicinity of the Consumer Credit Department, at the east entrance, as customers continued to enter through this door. As they entered, he ordered each of them to go to one of the counters in the middle of the lobby, directing them to remain quiet and to place their hands on the counter. One customer standing in line at a teller's cage first became aware that a stickup was in progress when she heard a command behind her, given by the third man, whereupon she removed $500 in cash, which she was carrying in a bank deposit bag along with several checks for deposit, and placed the money inside her blouse.

By now, it was obvious to Sanford that the third man was the "lookout." Throughout the robbery, he remained quiet and paced back and forth in the lobby, never venturing too far from the east entrance. Sanford would be one of a few witnesses who could later accurately describe this man to police and FBI agents, even though the robber had been observed by nearly fifty persons in the bank at the time of the robbery. This man too was over 6 feet tall, weighing about 200 pounds; he was about 45 years old and well-dressed. What Sanford noticed most about the man was a scar on the left side of his face in the form of a question mark, curling at the top and then running vertically, parallel to the hair line on the side of his face. Other witnesses would be unable to later describe the robber except in a general way, but they too noticed the scar on the man's face and each described its configuration in the same manner. Later, all would claim that the bandit tried to cover the scar with his coat collar which was turned up, and that he held his left hand to the side of his face in an apparent attempt to hide his disfigurement.

As the bank holdup alarm sounded in the Seattle Police Department's north precinct station, the desk clerk on duty immediately relayed it via intercom to the Seattle Police Headquarters radio communications room. The radio dispatcher pressed a button on his radio console which caused the emission of a high-pitched tone signal on all police radio frequencies, the signal broadcast to all police units in "holdup" cases. North precinct units 213, 215, 216, 223, 224, 226 and 252 responded initially to the alarm, and notified the dispatcher of their location and that they were moving toward the bank.

Officer Vernon Chase, operating patrol unit No. 213, was at North 50th Street and Phinney Avenue, about 35 blocks away at the time the alarm was broadcast, and was the first officer to arrive. Chase had been with the police department nine months. He had graduated from the Police Academy in November, 1953; he was 24 years old, a slim wiry man of medium build. He parked his patrol car at the southwest corner of the bank with the back of the car protruding out into the line of traffic on North 85th Street. As he exited his patrol vehicle, he pulled his shotgun out and headed toward the front entrance of the bank on 85th Street. As the officer approached the front of the bank, he was met by Sergeant Howard Slessman, the district supervisor, who was assigned to car No. 252. Slessman had been at 12th Avenue Northwest and North 88th Streets, 17 blocks away and had arrived seconds after Chase. He double-parked his patrol car directly across the street from the main entrance to the bank on North 85th before meeting Chase at the front door. Slessman ordered Chase to take the east entrance. Then, working the action on his shotgun and carrying the weapon pointed toward the ground, he started through the outer glass doors of the bank.[7]

Both Slessman and Chase were seen almost immediately upon their arrival by several persons inside the bank, including the bank manager and the number three stickup man. As McElhaney was placing currency from cage number 11 into a shopping bag, he glanced up and saw Sergeant Slessman heading for the front door and a second officer approaching the east door from the parking lot. McElhaney's action alerted the tall man with the automatic, and the robber with the scar on his face, who was standing in the center of the lobby, half way between each entrance, yelled "They're here!" The dark-complexioned man responded, "Some son-of-a-bitch turned on the alarm!"[8] He then walked directly over near the third man and stood just to the east of the front door. As Sergeant Slessman pushed his way through the outer door, the stickup man calmly raised his weapon, taking a shooter's stance, and shot the sergeant, the bullet passing through the inner glass doors, striking the officer in the neck. The impact drove him back to the outer doors where he turned, fell to the ground with his body holding the outer doors open, and lay on his stomach with the shotgun underneath him. As Slessman went down, the first man walked over, momentarily stood over him, pointing his automatic at Slessman's head, saying, "Stay down there you son-of-a-bitch," and then proceeded out the front door.

Upon hearing the gun shot, Officer Chase returned to the front of the bank at the southeast corner, where he saw his supervisor lying in the doorway. Seeing Chase, the first man fired one round at him. This bullet missed, burying itself in a 4" by 4" post in the corner of the Greer-Thomas Lumber Company behind Chase. The man then went back into the bank and yelled at his partners, "Take care of the east door". The third man headed for the east exit, but stopped short of the door and crouched behind the railing by the Installment Credit Department as if trying to remain unseen by those outside the building. The leader of the group of stickup men then moved quickly from the center of the lobby by the front door, through the Installment Credit Department officers section toward Chase, whose movements in the parking lot could be seen easily from the interior of the bank.

After having been shot at in front of the bank, Chase again proceeded around the corner of the bank to the east side of the building and backed toward a cement planter-box at the end of the parking lot. Facing the east side of the building, he was able to see movement inside, but not well enough to determine what was happening. The tall dark-complexioned man with the automatic had, by this time, walked to the window directly opposite the young officer and again, taking careful aim, shot him. The bullet struck Chase, driving him back, where he collapsed on the sidewalk just outside the parking lot entrance.[9]

With the firing of the first shot inside the bank, George, who was still having difficulty opening the money drawers and was now in cage number 10, dropped the sack of money he had gathered and ran to the west end of the bank, climbed on a desk and tried to break a window with his shoulder. Failing this, he took the butt of his gun, broke out the window and jumped out, landing in a flower bed. He ran across the street and headed north through the parking lot on the east side of Phinney Avenue. While running, George was seen removing some of his outer clothing, including his top coat and hat. He ran in a slow gallop and appeared to tire rapidly. He soon disappeared between two houses on the west side of Phinney Avenue. This turned out to be a dead end and seconds later he was seen by witnesses returning to the street minus his hat and top coat. George then ran between the next two houses in that block and was not seen again by witnesses.

Shortly after Chase had been gunned down, Officer Frank W. Hardy, who had been working patrol car No. 223 just north of the Greenwood District, arrived at the scene. Hardy, a 30-year-old patrolman and recent graduate of Seattle University, had been with the Department for two years. He and his wife of eight years, Rolene, had a five-year-old daughter and Mrs. Hardy was expecting their second child.[10]

Hardy, parking his patrol car about 30 feet east of Chase's vehicle, exited his car carrying a shotgun and walked toward Chase from the vicinity of the Greer-Thomas lumber yard. By this time, the dark-complexioned robber and the man with the scar on his face had left the bank by the east door, both walking toward a late model dark-green Oldsmobile parked a short distance from the exit. The man with the scar got in the driver's side of the vehicle and started the motor as the other man turned and fired two rounds at Hardy, then disappeared between parked cars in the bank parking lot. Hardy went down on one knee near Chase, raised his weapon to his shoulder and hollered, "Stop fellow, stop." The dark-complexioned man then walked out from in between two parked cars with both hands at his side, walking towards Hardy. As he reached the middle of the parking lot, he again raised his weapon and fired one round, the bullet striking Hardy in the forehead at the hair line. The officer pitched forward on his face. He died instantly.[11]

The dark-complexioned gunman then turned and quickly walked back across the parking lot toward the driver's side of the getaway car where the driver was heard to say, "Ease down, ease down." Seeing his partner behind the wheel, the bandit walked around the front of the car, got in the passenger side and the vehicle left through the north entrance of the lot.

Shortly after the shooting occurred in the parking lot, several police units arrived at the bank. Witnesses began to direct officers to the robbers' escape route. However, when the shooting occurred, most of the witnesses had ducked for cover, thus not seeing the entire movement of the suspects. Officers Gerald Boyer and William Pope were the first to arrive after Hardy. Boyer, although having had no police training, had the presence of mind to park his car so that it partially blocked the Phinney Avenue exit from the bank. When he

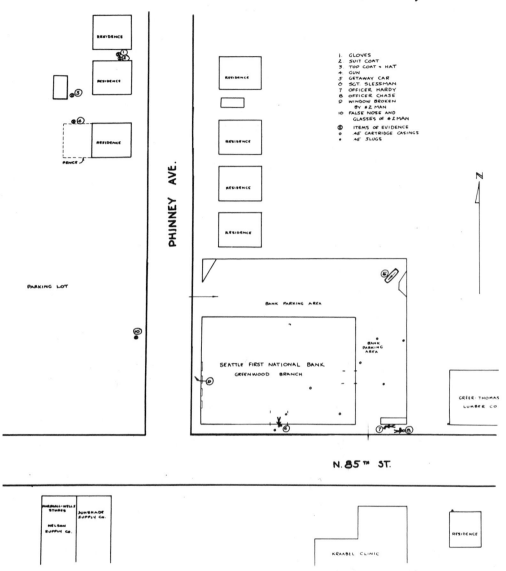

Diagram of the Seattle First National Bank, Greenwood Branch and surrounding area.

exited his vehicle, a witness told him that one of the bandits had fled on foot behind the houses on the west side of the avenue. Boyer yelled to Pope, who had just parked in the intersection of 85th and Phinney, to cover the rear of the houses and he would take the front. As the two officers headed across the parking lot toward the houses,

Boyer saw a green Oldsmobile going north on Phinney at a high speed. He lost sight of the vehicle as it passed the first house north of him. He then ran to the street where he again saw the vehicle; a door on the right side of the car was open and Boyer could see a man's leg protruding from the car as the car sped north on Phinney Avenue. Boyer ran to his police patrol car yelling to Pope about the Oldsmobile, then raced after the escape car. But the stickup men had too much of a head start and soon disappeared from Boyer's sight.[12]

As officers Boyer and Pope returned to the bank, other north precinct patrol units soon reached the area and were quick to notify the radio dispatcher of the situation at the scene of the robbery. Boyer had, in the meantime, broadcast the direction of travel of the stickup men and of the fact that he had lost sight of the car on North 90th and Phinney Avenue.[13]

The radio dispatcher sent over a dozen additional police units to the area and several young officers who were working traffic enforcement units were moved into the north precinct. These officers, who were assigned to Headquarters precinct, had been with the Department for only two months and many had a difficult time in locating the robbery scene. Although each was eventually assigned a search area by the radio dispatcher, several of the officers, having never worked in the north precinct, found it necessary to stop and find the location of the stickup on a city map before proceeding. One young traffic officer was overheard on the police radio asking "Where the hell is that stickup location?"[14]

After hearing the description of the getaway vehicle, two of these men proceeded to the north city limits and, working as a team, began stopping every late model dark-colored Oldsmobile seen in the area; neither realized that their method of stopping and questioning potential suspects was not conducive to continued good health or longevity. They would take turns pulling over a suspect car, with the other parking his police car in front of the stopped car and walking back to it, where he would meet and question the driver and passengers, with both officers standing on the roadway side of the stopped vehicle. Reflecting back on this, they were sure that they had certainly not encountered the robbers as both were alive at the end of the day.[15]

NOTES

Author's note: Crime in Seattle at the time of the incident which is narrated here, in stark contrast to Vancouver was considered to be, by most police managers, at an "acceptable level," probably because of the marked reduction in crime following the war years 1942-1945, and this trend would continue for another few years. Yet in 1954, in comparison to the 17 U.S. cities of 500,000 population and over, Seattle had one of the highest crime rates in the U. S. In the intervening years, little has changed. In 1990 only six other major cities in the U. S., in this population group had a higher incidence of reported crime per 1000 population.

In 1955, Seattle's 1.56 per capita police employees per 1,000 population, was also the lowest of the 17 cities in their population group in the U.S. (Although that figure had increased substantially by 1992 to 2.31). See 1990 Annual Report, Seattle Police Department, Seattle, Washington pp. 26-27 and the 1955 Annual Report, Seattle Police Department, Seattle, Washington, p. 1.

In the 1950's, Vancouver and other parts of western Canada were plagued by crime. Bank robberies were occurring almost daily and the related drug wars in Vancouver were at a fever pitch. Forty years later, little has changed in the city. And as we enter the 1990's, the city, now nearly as large as Seattle with a population approaching one-half million people and a mushrooming metropolitan area, continues to have a high crime rate. In a community where the metropolitan population is still less than half of Seattle, and in a country which has some of the most restrictive firearms prohibitions, the rate of violent crime in Vancouver is considerably higher than in Seattle. (Violent crime reported, 1988-Vancouver-7399 cases; Seattle-6778 cases per 100,000 population). See Canadian Centre For Justice Statistics, Crime in Canada, Statistics Canada Advisory Services, Pacific Region, Vancouver, B. C. Canada, 1988 Preliminary Crime Statistics, p. 41.

While much of the information used by the author to compile the sequence of events surrounding the robbery of the Greenwood Branch of the Seattle First National Bank and the shooting of the three Seattle Police officers on March 12, 1954 came from official Seattle Police Department and Federal Bureau of Investigation case files, first-hand accounts of what transpired during and after this robbery came both from personal participation of the author (in an admittedly minor role) and through direct interviews of those closest to the case as it evolved over a ten-year period following this crime.

The Vancouver Municipal Library staff were extremely helpful to the author in gathering the necessary newspaper articles, pictures and background data on the principals involved in this crime and in the follow-up investigation. But the first-hand data must (and did) come from the participants who were willing to contribute their time so that the author could question them and record their recollections. It should be noted that several FBI Agents, following Agency guidelines, were reluctant to provide first-hand information on their investigative activities associated with this case and Canadian officers refused comment. However, unless otherwise specified, the following citations refer to interviews or conversations with the author by these participants or are directly attributable to a police department, newspaper or other official report obtained by the author through research.

In order to protect the privacy of persons who played only a peripheral role in this case, fictitious names have been used by the author to identify several characters in this story. The names Jackie Brown (Talbot) Bailey, Charles Bailey, Donna Clearidge, Kris McRay, Paul McRay, Bonnie Murphy, Allen Peters, Mary Peters, Joe Richard, Bobby Smith, Peggy Teller and Junita Warren are fictitious and any similarity to actual persons living or dead is purely coincidental.

1   Kenneth McElhaney, interview with the author, June 18, 1974.
2   Seattle Police Department, (S.P.D.) Case Report, *Seattle First National Bank, Greenwood Branch, Bank Robbery/Murder*, Case No. 288527, March 12, 1954, pp. 19-24.
3   Ibid., pp. 25-28.
4   McElhaney, op. cit., June 18, 1974.
5   S.P.D. Case Report No. 288527, op. cit., pp. 19-24.
6   McElhaney, op. cit., June 18, 1974.
7   S.P.D. Case Report No. 288527, op. cit., pp. 113-114.
8   McElhaney, op. cit., June 18, 1974.
9   Vernon Chase, interview with the author, January 29, 1975.
10   Rolene Hardy, interview with the author, May 5, 1974.
11   S.P.D. Case Report No. 288527, op. cit., p. 222. Also see Autopsy Report of Coroner John P. Brill, Jr. Autopsy performed by Gale E. Wilson, M.D. March 13, 1954.
12   Gerald Boyer, S.P.D. Case Report No. 288527, statement of March 17, 1954.
13   Harry L. Schneider, conversations with the author, November 7, 1991. In 1954 many North Seattle streets were dirt or gravel and Officer Boyer, although having lost sight of the getaway vehicle, was able to determine its direction of travel by the dust clouds raised during this very high speed exit from the crime scene. He was aided at one intersection in this pursuit by a lineman atop a telephone pole who pointed out to the officer the direction of travel of the robbers. Boyer cursed the patrol vehicle he was driving, an eight year old, six-cylinder Plymouth sedan, for it was no match for the Oldsmobile driven by the suspects.
14   On January 2nd, 1954, the City of Seattle hired 75 men as police officers, most of whom were unfamiliar with specific street locations within the city, yet

all of these officers were put to work in uniform and were assigned to street duties after only one day of training. This training consisted of firing six rounds of ammunition through the Department service revolver at the police range, a lecture on uniform requirements, and a short dissertation on writing traffic citations.

Even with the death of officer Frank Hardy, the wounding of Sergeant Howard Slessman and Officer Vernon Chase, and the killing of more than a dozen Seattle police officers over the next twenty years, the practice of assigning newly hired police personnel with little training to the street continued. Each year, a succession of police chiefs, encouraged by Department management staff, unsuccessfully attempted to persuade the Mayor and Council to provide funds for the construction of a modern and professionally-staffed police training facility for Seattle police officers. The community had provided two classrooms and a gymnasium within the city's Public Safety Building and a staff of two officers for police training; however, most of the basic instruction was carried out by line personnel, many of whom were ill-equipped to fulfill that role. For a police department of nearly 1000 personnel, the training staff could do little more than provide recruit personnel with a crash course on basic police methods. No continuing in-service training or refresher training was ever offered to Seattle Police personnel, and for many of the officers who responded to the Greenwood bank robbery, it had been years since they had set foot in a police training classroom.

Over the next several years, as other city departments grew in size, there were continuing demands for alternative use for the space within the city's Public Safety Building and soon the two training rooms and gymnasium were taken for other uses. Between 1965 and 1992, the Department training program, now consolidated with the State, would be shuttled from one abandoned school house or other publicly owned and discarded building to another. In one unusual move, over the strong objections of the Department staff, for a period of four years, the training program for the City Police was assigned to an unused school building some twenty miles outside the city, in a building formerly used by the Catholic Church to educate and train nuns.

Finally by 1993, the city of Seattle found a solution to this very difficult problem of training their police officers; the city's answer was to let someone else do it. And the Mayor and City Council did just that by entering into an agreement with The Washington State Criminal Justice Training Commission where officers would be trained by the State not the City. The Commission, originally charged by the State Legislature with the responsibility for training members of the judiciary, county prosecutor's, law enforcement and correctional staffs, but is now best known for its ability as a latent political force in the State Capitol, for it has long been dominated by small city police chiefs and elected county sheriffs. It has also become a haven for a staff of instructors who in general lack teaching experience, have little knowledge of large city police problems and frequently meet no standard of performance within the professional police service. The Commission eventually became so ineffective that the State Prosecutors and members of the judiciary severed their relationships with the Commission and even the State of Washington refused to require the State Police to participate in ongoing Commission sponsored police training programs. It has been used repeatedly to sway members of the State Legislature into supporting several dubious law enforcement proposals and is considered by many professional police managers to be incapable of training either recruit or veteran police officers. Commission members however are able to influence elected officials at the state level in the allocation and distribution of public funds for police services. So the City of Seattle has been able to wash its' hands of this whole problem of using local tax dollars for police training. Thus Seattle has become the first major city in the United States to completely abdicate its responsibilities in the training of their own police personnel. (In re-examining the issue of police training, the Director of the State Training Commission vigorously defended his agency from the author's criticism, stating, "the State provides the best possible training for Seattle Police officers." In 1994 however, when the author re-interviewed members of the Seattle Police command staff on this issue, they reiterated that training provided by the State for Seattle officers today, was "at best mediocre.")

Annual Report, Seattle Police Department, 1955, pp. 4-5 and *History of the S.P.D. Training Acalcmy,* 1965. Also see *The History of the Seattle Police Department,* from an unpublished manuscript by Michael Johnson, 1974, pp. 143-145.

[15]   Harvey H. Noot, conversation with the author, March 12, 1954.

Chapter

2

The Investigation

Shortly after the full extent of the circumstances surrounding the Greenwood Bank robbery were known at Police Headquarters, over two dozen detectives and half as many FBI agents were on the scene. Chief of Police H. J. "Jimmie" Lawrence responded, as did FBI Special Agent in Charge of the Seattle office, Richard D. Auerbach. The responsibility for coordinating and supervising the investigation which was to follow was passed principally to Seattle Police Homicide Captain Charles A. Rouse and FBI Special Agents Dean C. Rolston and Chet Crismann; they did not realize at the time that they were to spend several thousand hours over the next ten years working on this case.[1]

The investigation disclosed that George, the No. 2 man, had discarded his glasses and false nose in the parking lot west of the bank, and his top coat, hat, gloves and suit coat, between the residences in which he fled. He dropped at this same location a long barrelled Colt .38 Special revolver. The investigators assumed that George had thought that he would be left behind and had tried to change his appearance in order to mix with the gathering crowd without being identified.

The license number of the getaway car had been incorrectly identified by witnesses as a Washington license 58-148A, but it was close enough that when Margaret Dimak, wife of Seattle detective Steven Dimak, heard the description of the suspect vehicle on commercial radio at 11:30 A.M., she notified authorities about a green Oldsmobile. It was parked some 70 blocks away in a parking lot at North 56th and 24th Avenue Northwest, with the license number 51-148A.

In the meantime, part of the getaway route was traced and it was learned that instead of continuing north on Phinney Avenue, the suspects had turned east at North 92nd Street, seven blocks from the robbery scene and proceeded east for three blocks at a high rate of speed to Fremont Avenue, then south on Fremont, crossing North 85th Street just three blocks from the bank. The suspects were seen three more times by witnesses after they crossed North 85th and finally a fourth time before pulling into the parking lot where Mrs. Dimak spotted the empty vehicle at 11:45 A.M. Witnesses remembered the erratic manner in which the suspects drove, first at a very high rate of speed, then as they got farther away from the bank, witnesses stated that the driver appeared to be lost and not familiar with the city. Other witnesses observed the suspects changing clothes in the car as they traveled. However, once the suspects left the car in the parking lot, there was no further trace of them.

The investigation disclosed that the Oldsmobile was stolen on the night of March 10th, two days before the robbery, from an

Seattle detectives, FBI agents and spectators gather around the Greenwood bank robbers getaway car, a dark colored Oldsmobile discovered within an hour of the robbery, in a northwest Seattle grocery store parking lot by the wife of Seattle Detective Steven Dimak. (Photo courtesy: Seattle Police Records Archives)

apartment garage on East Union street in downtown Seattle, the theft having been reported to the police by the owner at 9:45 A.M. on March 11th. At that time, the car bore its correct license of 126-310A. However, it was later learned the license plates now on the car were stolen from a 1937 Packard, due to be scrapped, and parked on the street in front of Nix Auto Wrecking yard, just a few blocks from where the car was recovered. The owner of the Packard was not aware that his plates were missing. The legal license plates for the getaway car were found under the front seat. But what definitely tied this car to the robbery was a .45 automatic shell casing, found in the front seat, which matched the shell casings found at the bank.

At the scene, investigators found two shopping bags full of money on the floor of the bank, one dropped by George as he dashed from tellers' row to the window and the other in cage No. 11, thrown there by the bank manager when the shooting started. These two bags contained $90,855.00 in cash. The robbers got away with only seven thousand dollars: three $500 bills and fifty-five hundred one dollar bills from the bank vault. Through McElhaney's delay and stalling tactics, the stickup men missed nearly $36,000 in the lower drawers of cage 10 and 11, and no attempt at all was made to clean out cash drawers in cages 1, 2 and 3 in the Loan and Discount tellers' section, nor any of those in the Installment Credit Department. Had the robbers been successful in this venture, they could have obtained nearly a quarter of a million dollars in the stickup. Of the money that was taken, the serial numbers were known on only one thousand of the one dollar bills.

During the robbery and shortly after the shooting began, patients of the Kraabel Clinic who were attracted by the noise, yelled to the two doctors working in the examination room. Upon seeing three officers on the ground near the bank, Doctors Donald Kraabel and John Kangley rushed from the clinic to the officers' aid. Officer Chase and Sergeant Slessman received medical attention almost immediately, which meant that one or possibly both of their lives were saved. Both men were quickly taken to local hospitals where they underwent extensive surgery. The bullet that struck Chase entered his body just below the sternum and traveled upward through the liver where the metal casing separated from the lead slug; the slug, continuing, buried itself in the chest wall. The shot that hit

Slessman struck him just above and to the left of the right collar bone where the shoulder meets the neck, causing extensive tissue and bone damage.[2]

Seattle Patrol Sergeant Howard Slessman lies on his back in the doorway of the Greenwood bank after being shot by Clifford Dawley March 12, 1954. (Seattle Post-Intelligencer/Seattle Police Records Archives)

On March 13th an autopsy was performed on Officer Frank Hardy by Dr. Gale E. Wilson, the County Medical Examiner; in attendance were Seattle Police Detective George F. Donnelly and Special Agent Jonathan H. "Pat" Harrington, the local FBI - Police Department liaison officer. (Harrington would work closely on this case with Seattle Police detectives for the next ten years.) The bullet that struck Hardy entered his forehead at the hair line, base first, indicating that it was a ricochet with its first contact being traced back to the hood of a car parked in the south end of the bank parking lot, directly in line with Hardy and the position where the number one stickup man stood, in the center of the lot.[3]

Seven .45 caliber shell casings were recovered at the scene. The casings, including the one recovered in the getaway car and the bullets that were taken from the officers' bodies, were all fired from the same gun. Although a live shotgun shell was found on the sidewalk in front of the bank and witnesses stated that both Chase and Hardy had fired at least one round from their shotguns, the investigation disclosed that no shots were fired by any of the officers present. (No other live rounds of ammunition were found inside or in the immediate vicinity of the bank; thus investigators assumed the number one suspect who first confronted the bank manager with a loaded .45 caliber automatic pistol, did so with a weapon which did not have a bullet in the chamber.) Slessman, Hardy and Chase's revolvers were still in their holsters and all three shotguns were still fully loaded, but Hardy and Slessman's shotguns were on full cock when taken from them.[4]

In addition to the clothing and gun abandoned by George in his flight and the .45 caliber shells and bullets, some of which fragmented upon entering the officers' bodies, over 200 separate pieces of physical evidence were recovered from the scene and from the getaway car, including twelve 32.20 cartridges and two .32-20 caliber special cartridges found in George's discarded suit coat. Some partial fingerprints were recovered from the shopping bags and from the automobile, but none would later identify any of the stickup men.[5]

During the next few weeks, agents of the FBI and Seattle Police detectives would pursue over seven hundred different leads without success. Although the serial numbers of one thou-

Seattle Police Patrolman Frank Hardy, slain by bank robbers in Seattle, Washington March 12, 1954. (Seattle Police Records Archives)

Seattle First National Bank, Greenwood Branch — crowd gathers shortly after the robbery of March 12, 1954. (Seattle Post-Intelligencer Collection Museum of History & Industry)

sand of the one dollar bills taken in this robbery were known, none were ever located. In hopes of finding some of these, the local newspapers ran the serial numbers of some in their "Lucky Dollar" columns, where cash prizes were given each week to the holder of a "Lucky Dollar" winning number. It was hoped that someone would come across one of the stolen bills and report it, but this did not happen.

In the early evening of the same day of the robbery, a conference with the top FBI and Seattle Police officials was called to piece together the evidence obtained thus far in the investigation and to assign investigative responsibilities to detective-agent teams who would continue the follow-up investigation. This required locating and interviewing over one hundred witnesses, many of whom did not realize that their observations might add something to the case. By evening, a composite description of the three robbers had been put together; and at 8:15 P.M. the following teletype was sent throughout the eleven western states and Canada, adding the three robbers' description to earlier messages:

ADDL: BANK ROBBERY MAR 12-54. 8:15 P.M.
CS#288527 N-3809
CAPT C.A. ROUSE
SPD
REPORTS
ADDL: DESC: #1 35-40 YRS, WHT. MALE, 5-10, 6-2, THIN FACE WITH SMOOTH OLIVE COMP., DK BRN EYES, DK BRN HAIR. THIS MAN WAS LAST SEEN WEARING A PLAIN BRN SUIT, WHITE SHIRT, BRN SHOES, WITH EITHER A BROWN FELT OR DARK RAIN- TYPE HAT. HE IS DESCRIBED AS BEING WELL BUILT AND WELL DRESSED. WAS ARMED WITH A .45 CALIBER AUTOMATIC.

SUSP. #2 45-50 YRS, WHT MALE, 5-5, TO 5-8", 140#, DK HAIR, GREYING AT TEMPLES, SLIGHT BUILD, HEAVY BLUE BEARD THAT WAS CLEAN SHAVEN, ROUND SHOULDERED, HAS A WEATHER BEATEN FACE WITH LARGE

Seattle Police Patrolman Frank Hardy's funeral, Seattle, Washington March 17, 1954.
(Seattle Post-Intelligencer Collection Museum of History & Industry)

PORES, CHEEKS ARE SUNKEN. LAST SEEN WEARING DARK TROUSERS, AND MAY HAVE RUBBER SOLED SHOES. THIS MAN MAY BE ARMED WITH A 32-20 PISTOL.

SUSP. #3 30-40 YRS, WHITE MALE, 6-1, to 6-2, 190 TO 220#, HAS SCAR ON LEFT TEMPLE IN FRONT OF SIDEBURN, LIGHT BROWN HAIR, DOUBLE CHIN. DESCRIBED AS BIG, HEAVY SET MAN. LAST SEEN WEARING SNAP BRIM HAT, LIGHT BRN TOPCOAT, DK BRN SLACKS, ARGYLE SOCKS, BROWN SHOES, WHITE SHIRT. TOP COAT MAY HAVE FAINT BLUE HORIZONTAL STRIPES. THIS MAN WAS ARMED WITH 32-20 OR 38 CALIBER REVOLVER.

CC ALL

INIT REP CAPT ROUSE

TT JW AT 8:20 PM

By the end of the day, Captain Rouse had the name of the number one suspect. Before the joint dinner-hour strategy meeting began on the case with FBI supervisory and police command staff members, Homicide Sergeant Paul C. Lee had received a call from Vancouver, British Columbia, City Police Superintendent John C. Horton regarding this case. After hearing of the Seattle robbery, Vancouver detectives, who had been investigating a whole series of bank robberies in the Canadian city, were not long in matching the method of operation of the three Seattle robbers with several Canadian criminals who had been operating in the Vancouver metropolitan area. Horton told Lee that the circumstances of the robbery most clearly followed those robberies committed both in Vancouver and throughout Western Canada by Clifford Dawley and his associates. He described Dawley as a "vicious criminal, capable of anything." Dawley had escaped from Vancouver General Hospital on March 7th, five days earlier. He had been held at the Oakalla Prison Farm in Burnaby (a Vancouver suburb), where he was awaiting trial for assaulting a Royal Canadian Mounted Police Officer. He was soon to be charged as a Habitual Criminal, a charge which carried a life sentence. Dawley had supposedly fallen down a flight of stairs at the Penitentiary and injured his back and had been taken under guard to Vancouver General where he escaped. His description matched the number one man in the robbery. Lee passed this information on to Captain Rouse. Two days later, the Department received the following letter from Vancouver Chief Constable Walter H. Mulligan[6]:

CITY OF VANCOUVER
POLICE DEPARTMENT
W. H. Mulligan 236 Cordova Street East
Chief Constable Vancouver 4, B.C.

VIA AIRMAIL-SPECIAL DELIVERY
 March 13th, 1954
J. N. Lawrence, Esq.,
Chief of Police
Seattle, Wash., U.S.A.

Dear Sir:
With reference to the telephone conversation last evening between a member of your Department and Superintendent Horton of this

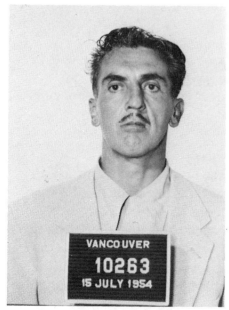

Clifford Eugene Dawley — picture taken after his capture in Montreal and return to Vancouver. (Seattle Police Records Archives)

John Wasylenchuk, wearing a toupee, from an early photograph taken by Vancouver Police. (Seattle Police Records Archives)

Department in regard to your recent bank holdup, I am enclosing herewith two copies each of photographs of suspects known to members of this Department.

Nick Novak, @ Meloff, Vancouver 12431;
Clifford Dawley, Vancouver 10263;
Frank Douham, Vancouver 13756;
Ronald Smith, @ Ryan, Van. Local 10400;
John Douham, @ Wm. Smith, Van. 12922;
Ernest Dennis, deserter from the Canadian Army

For your information, Clifford Dawley is an escapee from custody in this city. He was in a hospital, pending appearance in Court, and was to be charged with "Habitual Criminal". Dawley is dangerous, and his associates are Nick Novak and Steve Polanski.

Ernest Dennis is a deserter from the Canadian Army and, for your added information, I am attaching hereto a copy of a report from the Provost Corps. In a bank holdup in the City (of Vancouver) on December 24th, 1953, the photo of Dennis was picked by a witness but unfortunately we have no further evidence, nor have we been able to locate him.

Faithfully yours,

W. H. Mulligan
Chief Constable

jmpm
encls.

One needed only a quick glance at Dawley's record, which arrived the following day, to confirm Horton's description that Dawley was a "vicious criminal." Dawley was born on April 6, 1911; in 1924 at the age of thirteen, he received a suspended sentence for highway robbery in North Bay, Ontario and was ordered returned to his home in Esquimalt, British Columbia, where his father was Chief of Police. Between 1924 and March 7, 1954, he had been arrested 25 times on a variety of charges, including robbery, assault, burglary, theft and escape from custody. In September, 1930, he was arrested in San Francisco, where he had fled after escaping from the Penticton, British Columbia, city jail. He was later deported to Canada. This was the first of several escapes.[7]

Dawley's "mug shot," along with "mug shots" of several other criminals from British Columbia were shown to bank employees and to several customers who were in the bank at the time of the robbery but no positive identification was obtained from any of these witnesses. However, some hesitated when looking at Dawley's picture and commented that his general appearance reminded them of the tall dark-complexioned man in the robbery.

With the death of Hardy, political ramifications began almost immediately and these would be evident throughout the investigation. Chief Lawrence held a press conference on March 13th where he criticized the lack of adequate funds which would enable the police department to operate around-the-clock with two-man patrol units instead of with one-man cars. Lawrence said that two-man patrols might have prevented the slaying of Hardy and the wounding of Chase and Slessman. Mayor Allen Pomeroy, now placed in a defensive position by his chief, deplored the fact that the Department was undermanned. He said he had always opposed the use of one-man patrol cars and that the shooting proved that they were not adequate for the job; however, because of a lack of personnel on the force, he said it was the best the police department could do at the time. He continued: "In order to avoid a repetition of the tragic shooting at the bank, the city must have more policemen so that each police car could be manned by two officers." When questioned about this by the press, he stated he planned no immediate action, but said he would request more men in the next police budget.[8]

Two City Councillors, David Levine and Robert Harlin, criticized the mayor's remarks regarding the proposal to increase the police budget but failed to suggest how to raise the money to do this. Harlin said that nobody, least of all the mayor, should glibly tell Council to spend more money than the city could afford without an increase in taxes.[9]

During the next twenty years, each time an officer was killed in the line of duty, it was interesting to hear a succession of new mayors repeat almost the same identical statement as made by Pomeroy.

The ironic part of it, however, was the police officers never expected, nor for that matter believed, that it was necessary to operate in every part of the city with two-man patrol units, but it made good copy for the press. However, what was more difficult to understand was that there was no mention made of the fact that the majority of the officers who had responded to the robbery that day had received little or no prior training on proper police patrol tactics nor were there adequate plans or comprehensive guidelines for officers to follow in responding to bank robbery alarms in the city. In the case of the older officers, most had received little or no training since completing the academy which, in some cases, was twenty years prior to this incident.[10]

On Tuesday, March 16, 1954, funeral services for Hardy were held in Saint James Cathedral, while Chase remained on the Critical List in King County Hospital. Hardy was the thirty-ninth Seattle police officer killed in the line of duty. Four days later, the City Council passed an ordinance offering $1,000.00 reward for the arrest and conviction of Hardy's killers.[11]

In the days following the robbery, FBI agents and detectives continued to question witnesses and examine the physical evidence collected. The crime was re-enacted at the scene, and witnesses who were at the bank returned and each was walked through the role they played during the actual robbery. Some remembered a few additional details of the crime, but little else was gained in this laborious procedure.

Several "suspicion arrests" of "known hoods" were made by Seattle Police officers, most through shear desperation, as the officers appeared to be grasping at straws with little more justification for the arrest than the fact that the person was a known stickup man. In some cases the officers, in responding to anonymous tips, made an arrest "Just to be sure", but frequently without supporting evidence.[12] Dozens of queries from other police departments were received, either supplying additional information on potential suspects from their jurisdiction, or seeking information which could possibly tie this case to one that had occurred in their city.

Within a week of the stickup, Captain Rouse and FBI supervisors were convinced that the three suspects in this case were probably not "local hoods" and that they would not be found in the Seattle area. A great deal of publicity had been given the case as a result of the death of Officer Hardy and the shooting of Officer Chase and Sergeant Slessman. Rouse was sure that after such wide media coverage, the three stickup men could not have been known or have been "operating" locally without some trace of their activities coming to light. Eight days after the robbery, on March 20th, he prepared a Special Bulletin which was sent, over the Chief of Detective's signature (as was the custom in large police departments), to all major Canadian and American city, state and federal police agencies describing the "mode of operation" (M.O) of the robbers in this case. Included in the report (bulletin) was the physical description of the three robbery suspects, with the hope that some officer would recognize one or more of the subjects and their "M.O."

Case 288527

March 20, 1954

To: All Law Enforcement Agencies

Subject: MURDER OF POLICE OFFICER

On March 12, 1954, at 10:55 A.M., the Greenwood Branch of the Seattle First National Bank was held up by three men. The suspect that we shall refer to as #1 shot three police officers, one of them fatally.

SPECIAL NOTE: The #2 man carried a .38 calibre Colt Police Revolver, 4" barrel, #402140, which he discarded immediately after leaving the bank. Please *check your files* for the above number, and forward us any information you may have.

In addition to the description of the three suspects, the following points are important regarding the #1 man:

1. From his actions and the result of his shooting it is apparent that he had extensive firearms training.

Witnesses stated that he stood with his feet apart, set himself, and took deliberate aim. His actions were those of a person who had spent considerable time on a target range. He used a .45 calibre automatic. We have recovered seven shell cases.

2. The #1 man was the leader. He had command ability.
   He ran the show. His speech was gruff, vulgar, sharp,
   and commanding. He told everybody what to do and got
   them to do it.
3. He was physically trim and fit. He was well built.
   He had a flat stomach.
4. He was well-dressed.
5. This man was cool and sure. He was deliberate.

The following M.O. items are worthy of note:

1. All three suspects wore plastic noses and glasses,
   all three of which have been recovered.
2. They used an Oldsmobile car, which they had stolen.
3. They took paper shopping bags into the bank and forced
   the bank employees to carry and fill these bags.
4. The #2 man carried a .38 calibre Colt Police Positive
   Revolver, 4" barrel, #402140, which he discarded
   immediately after leaving the bank, along with his
   topcoat and suit coat.
5. A number of .32-20 cartridges were found in the pockets
   of his suit coat.
6. The #3 man carried what is believed to be a .38 calibre
   revolver, make unknown.
7. The #2 and #3 men did not seem to be very capable. They
   did not seem to have good control, and were nervous and
   uncertain. . . . .

H. J. LAWRENCE, Chief of Police

CAPT. C.A. ROUSE   V.L. KRAMER
Homicide/Robbery   Detective Division
Chief
Case #288527   SEATTLE POLICE DEPARTMENT

In discussions with his supervisors, Rouse surmised that his best
hope of solving this crime lay in directing the investigative effort of
the Department toward the Canadian suspects. Though witnesses at

the bank had failed to identify any of the suspects through the "mug shots" sent to the Department by Vancouver authorities, for now, this was Rouse's principal lead.[13] In 1953 and 1954, western Canada, particularly southern British Columbia, was being rocked by a wave of bank robberies. Banks in the Vancouver metropolitan area were the prime targets, but New Westminster, Burnaby and North Vancouver were target cities also. Calgary, Edmonton and several smaller cities in the three western provinces were being plagued by bank stickup men. However, Rouse soon discovered that the imaginary line that separated the United States and Canada presented one of many road blocks which would hamper the investigation. Although Vancouver and Seattle were only 150 miles apart, the Department found itself in a tenuous position in trying to "go it alone" in conducting an investigation in a foreign country.

Unfortunately, Rouse was also soon to find that for the most part the higher ranking officers of the Canadian police would be uncooperative in this investigation for reasons not fully understood by his officers at this stage of the investigation.[14] Fortunately, the assistance of a few extremely competent Vancouver and Royal Canadian Mounted Police (RCMP) mid-level officers was obtained early on, at least in part due to previous favorable relationships that had developed between the American and Canadian officers, otherwise the Canadian aspect of this case may never have been uncovered. At this time, the Vancouver Police Department and other Canadian governmental agencies were being rocked with charges of internal corruption, involving payoffs to high police, judicial and other public officials in British Columbia by gangland figures involved in prostitution, narcotics and bank robberies in the Vancouver metropolitan area. As a result, formal investigative assistance from the Vancouver Police Department was to be minimal and many top RCMP officials were less than enthusiastic in their support. An investigation of the Vancouver Department by a Royal Commission from the provincial government was about to get underway. This would eventually lead to the resignation and flight to the United States of Walter H. Mulligan, the city's Chief Constable.[15]

This Royal Commission-Investigative Task Force was soon to uncover widespread corruption within the Vancouver City Police

Officer Vernon "Bud" Chase and Patrol Sergeant Howard Slessman receiving police service awards from Chief of Police H.J. "Jimmie" Lawrence subsequent to their return to duty after being wounded at the Greenwood Bank by robbers. (Seattle Police Records Archives)

Seattle Police Headquarters 2nd Watch Patrol and Traffic Squads (circa late 1950's) with Patrol Sergeant Art Drovetto. (Seattle Police Records Archives)

Seattle Police on parade. (Seattle Police Records Archives)

Seattle Police Officers pay homage to their dead on Memorial Plaza, Public Safety Building Seattle, Washington. (Seattle Police Records Archives)

Department. Ironically, their findings were to parallel similar findings of another investigative body of the same agency, just twenty years earlier. And corruption within the force had also been raised again in 1947 when the then Chief Constable, the Deputy Chief Constable and six other ranking officers were removed from leadership roles within the police department. This shakeup within the organization lead to the selection of Walter Mulligan as the new Chief Constable on January 7, 1947.[16] Yet because of the flagitious actions of the city's political leadership, who either condoned or in many cases supported corrupt police practices within the Vancouver Police Department, many members of the force continued on into the 1950's operating outside the law.

Captain Charlie Rouse never guessed, however, that in just a few short years, he too would be swept up in a similar investigation of corruption of Seattle Police Officers and local and state public officials in his home city for a widespread political and police payoff system was soon to be uncovered by Seattle Police Department Detectives, the initial evidence being discovered accidentally through a police vice raid. The irony of it all was that in the Seattle investigation, many of the officers who were involved in the payoff system would later flee to Canada, Mexico or to Europe to avoid prosecution, mimicking the actions of Vancouver's Chief Constable Walter Mulligan.[17]

Notes

[1] Sergeant Charles K. Waitt, conversations with the author 1962-1965. Also see S.P.D. Case No. 288527 Op. Cit., Investigator's Report March 12, 1954.
[2] Jerome B. Jacobs, M.D., attending physician's report, April 6, 1954. Also see Detectives Larry W. Webb and John F. Larsen, Case No. 288527 Op. Cit., Investigator's Report, March 12, 1954.
[3] S.P.D. Case Report No. 288527, Op. Cit., p. 222.
[4] Detective Sergeant W. H. Paust, S.P.D. Case No. 288527 Op. Cit., Investigator's Report, March 12, 1954 and Detective Sergeant W. H. Paust, Detective Steven J. Dimak, Investigator's Report, March 16, 1954.
[5] Collection of physical evidence at the scene of this crime was neither properly coordinated, nor was the search carried out systematically by the officers. The large number of physical evidentiary items coming into the Evidence Room,

collected by more than fifty officers, overwhelmed the Department's single crime laboratory physical evidence specialist Detective Sergeant Max M. Allison. Some of the material was forwarded to the FBI for processing, but the failure of the Department to place responsibility for the collection of physical evidence on trained specialists or to train police officers in the proper techniques for collecting and preserving evidence at a crime scene often resulted in overlooking evidence at the scene of a crime or in the contamination of collected evidence by the field officer.

Over a dozen Seattle Police officers involved in the collection of physical evidence at the crime scene, violated Department regulations in the collection and preservation of that evidence. Several items of evidence, where a laboratory specialist should have been able to recover identifiable fingerprints, were too crudely marked and packaged for identification purposes. And in some cases there was little thought given to the recovery of identifiable finger prints of the suspects from the object.

In quoting from both official S.P.D and FBI reports of this case: A citizen finding a .45 caliber shell casing in the bank parking lot, had presence of mind to insert a pencil into the casing and gave it to one of the most senior detectives at the scene. This officer took the casing in his hand, "made eight marks on the cartridge casing with a knife blade and in addition to S.A. [Special Agent] - - -, placed his initials and the date 3/12/54 on the cartridge case," then turned the casing over to SA Agent - - -. Another citizen, Alden R. Heitman turned over to Officer - - - a .45 caliber empty cartridge that he found in the parking lot adjacent to the bank. The officer had Mr. Heitman initial the inside of the cartridge case and the officer also initialed it. The initials of both Mr. Heitman and Officer - - - were also written on a small piece of paper which was jammed inside the cartridge." Another cartridge case was "found at the scene of the bank robbery by Mr. James Livingston, who turned it over to Detective - - - who initialed the case H. J. T. on the side of the case near the open end."

And notwithstanding that all three disguises, i.e. false plastic noses, horn-rimmed glasses, including one with a black mustache attached, were recovered along the robber's get-away route within minutes of the crime, no reasonable steps were taken by the officers to preserve possible fingerprints on these items. One disguise found by a 12-year-old girl, Janis Lyon, on the parking strip in front of her home "was taken to King County Deputy Sheriff - - - who turned it over to Seattle Police Officer - - -, who placed it into evidence. The nose had been initialed by Janis Lyon, by Deputy Sheriff - - - and by Officer - - - ." In all three cases (even though in one instance, a Seattle Police officer was the first to discover this item of evidence), "these were not sent to the Laboratory [FBI] inasmuch as they had been handled to the point where they were valueless so far as latent fingerprints were concerned."

Although FBI agents for the most part followed accepted procedures in the collection of physical evidence, their indiscretions were no less noteworthy. The fourteen bullets recovered from the pockets of the coat worn and then discarded during George's flight from the bank, were marked with an Agent's initials on the side of the cartridges at the scene and never submitted to the laboratory for fingerprints. And this robber's gun, a Colt .38 Special revolver, located by a local resident, after photographing and measuring its location in the accepted manner, was retrieved by Seattle Police Detective Donald Sprinkle. The officer placed a pencil through the trigger guard to protect any evidence which may have been on the weapon. Within minutes of recovery, the weapon was taken into custody by a Federal Bureau of Investigation Agent who inserted a pen in the muzzle to keep from smearing the fingerprints. Unfortunately for this agent, the picture of him taking custody of the weapon in this manner was recorded by more than a half dozen press photographers who had complete access to the area where this evidence was recovered. (The Seattle Times, March 13, 1954 p. 2.).

A corollary problem in the evidence chain also frequently arose because the Police Property Room (along with Communications and City Jail Divisions) was a "dumping ground" for the Department's alcoholics. Theoretically these officers who could not be trusted on the street would receive closer supervision in these assignments. Unfortunately it was a "Catch-22" case as their supervisors were reassigned to these duties for the same reasons as their subordinates. Under the circumstances it was not unusual for high value items to simply disappear from the Property Room. Over the years, items of evidence found their way into the possession of the Mayor, members of City Council, the City Attorney and the Chief of Police. In an audit conducted in the 1960's by Police Lieutenant James J. McCarthy, at the direction of the newly appointed Chief of Police Frank Ramon, the Lieutenant found that over 1600 firearms had simply disappeared from the Property Room.

[6] Walter Hugh Mulligan, born in 1904, was appointed a patrolman in the Vancouver Police Force in 1927. He rose through the ranks rapidly and was appointed Chief Constable on January 24, 1947. He would soon leave office after the American officers began their extensive investigative inquires into the Greenwood case in Canada. He was granted a leave of absence from office on January 24, 1955 and was fired shortly thereafter by the Board of Police Commissioners. His termination from office was only indirectly related to the investigation of the Greenwood case in Canada by both Canadian and American authorities.

[7] R.C.M. Police, (RCMP), Identification Branch F.P.S. No. 120004, Ottawa, Ontario August 11, 1971, p. 3.

[8] Seattle Post Intelligencer, March 15, 1954, p. 1.

[9] Ibid.

[10] The fact that all three officers who were shot at the scene as they were either approaching or entering the bank was stark evidence of the failure of the administration to even suggest that basic tactical training for street officers was important in life threatening crimes. Nor was any thought given to apprehension of a suspect who would flee the scene of such a crime. No perimeter searches were established; rather, each officer chose his own tactics. Quite often this resulted in an entire patrol watch responding directly to the location of the crime, only to arrive long after the suspects had fled the scene. Within days of the robbery, however, the Chief of Police issued a General Order outlining a crime scene tactical response guideline for Department personnel.

Prior to the Greenwood Bank robbery, only the very basic tactical plans were in place for S.P.D patrol officers who responded to crime scenes in the city. Officers were instructed to :

1. Hurry to the scene.
2. Do not announce presence.
3. Play hunches, if they knew the area well.
3. Cover all exits.
4. Wait for a sergeant, and
5. The sergeant will enter the bank with a shotgun upon arrival.

These procedures were revised in April 1954 when officers were instructed:

1. The radio operator has floor plans with entrances and exits located, plus parking lot and adjacent street diagrams, for all banks in the city.

2. Condition one: Assume robber(s) are still in the bank-cover all exits.

3. Condition two: Assume robber(s) have left the bank on foot-cover all exits.

4. Condition three: Assume robber(s) have left the scene in a vehicle-cover all exits.

5. All officers not assigned to an exit will receive assignment from the radio operator.

6. Officers not on assignment will approach no closer than four blocks of the bank, unless directed to do so by the radio operator.

7. After all exits covered, the officer on post No. one will enter the bank. Shotguns will not be taken into the bank.

8. Radio operator shall initiate quadrant search areas under condition one and two.

[11] Seattle officers who had been involved in a long-standing labor dispute with the City Council over salaries, accepted the reward notice as a not-too-subtle hint of the value placed upon their lives by this parsimonious group in Council Chambers.

[12] The reader should keep in mind that prior to the 1960's it was common practice for the police to arrest felony suspects on charges of "Suspicion," or to hold suspects for "Investigation," for extended periods of time (10 days or more) without filing formal criminal charges with the Prosecuting Attorney's

Office. The Uniformed Crime (statistical) Report for 1965 identified over 75,000 arrests made by the police on "Suspicion" charges in the U.S. In most American communities, it was not unusual to find that between five and fifteen percent of all felony arrests made by the police were of this nature. These activities were soundly condemned in the 1968 report on the police by The President's Commission on Law Enforcement and Administration of Justice (See Task Force Report: The Police, Chapter 6); but it was not until the United States Supreme Court intervened, beginning in the late 1950's that such practices came to an end. See:

Mallory v. United States, 354 U.S. 449, (1957), "—detention in Violation of . . . prompt arraignment rules."

Mapp v. Ohio, 367 U.S. 643 (1961), "The Fourth Amendment is applicable to the states through the Due Process Clause of the Fourteenth Amendment."

Haynes v. Washington, 373 U.S. 503, (1963), "—prisoner held in a technically . . . incommunicado status."

Terry v. Ohio, 392 U.S. 1, (1968), "—'frisk' may be justified when its purpose is . . . to discover guns, knives, (etc.)."

In Canada, police records of the 1950's indicate that the percentage of those arrested on "suspicion" charges was much greater than in the U.S. from 1950 to 1955, the City of Vancouver Police arrested an average of 1450 persons each year for serious/felony offenses. Of these, most were "Held for Investigation," yet nearly half were later released without being charged with a criminal offense.

	1954	1955
Total Held For Investigation	833	1289
Total Number Charged	406	774
Total Number Released	427	515

See Vancouver Police Department Annual Report, Vancouver, British Columbia, Canada 1955, p. 25.

[13] Charles A. Rouse, conversations with the author, 1973.

[14] Ibid.

[15] The Vancouver Province, May 15, 1954 P. 1. Also see The Province July 13, p.1; August 5, p. 1; October 25, 1955 p. 1; May 12, 1956 p. 1 and The Vancouver Sun February 29, 1956 p. 1.

[16] The Vancouver Province, January 25, 1947 p. 1.

[17] The Vancouver Province, February 8, 1956 p. 1.

The Vancouver Province
A Dependable Newspaper
FRIDAY, JUNE 24, 1955

Result of police inquiry

Mounties will probe corruption charges

Bonner answers Tupper

Hearing waits for Len Cuthbert

Detective shoots self

Bonner acting to end boiling police crisis

Missed heart

Mayor Hume awaits word

Attorney-General Robert Bonner said today he would take "major action" within the next few days to cope with a major crisis in police administration which has boiled up in Vancouver.

Continued from Page 1

Bonner will act in city police crisis

Cuthbert

The Vancouver Province
A Dependable Newspaper

Mulligan accused of part in bookmaking bribe plot

Accuser

Detectives talk at police probe

Accused

Chief to

Mulligan to take stand 'to deal with accusers'

Fred Hume **RUSSIA UNCENSORED** will go 'if asked'

Mounties will report to Bonner for action

A Mulligan allowed to fly

Georgi j at party

The Vancouver Province
A Dependable Newspaper

B.C. convict Cliff Dawley captured by Toronto police

Fugitive free 18 months

For Israeli-Arab peace

EDEN

Russians dominate Olympics

The Vancouver Province
A Dependable Newspaper
SATURDAY

Cuthbert describes hours before his suicide attempt

Court hears dramatic tale

The Vancouver Province
A Dependable Newspaper

Key figure in police probe

Supt. Whelan kills himself

n'49

Full details of city police probe

Top detective officers first witnesses heard

Gunmen hold up bank clerk in car, escape with $3600

Senior police officers appear at probe

Whelan tells police probe of meeting with Cuthbert

Reliability questioned

Never showed his notes

Chapter
3

The Canadians

By July, 1954, both Seattle Police Department and FBI investigations indicated that the "Canadians" were the most logical suspects in this case. In a meeting with Captain Rouse, Federal Bureau of Investigation Special Agent in Charge Richard Auerbach, and Chief

Homicide Detective Captain Charles A. Rouse (right) and colleagues talking to Rouse's boss Inspector of Detectives William J. "Bill" Walsh seated. (Photo courtesy: Glenn Rouse)

Lawrence, it was decided to send a team of investigators which included Agents Dean Rolston, Alfred G. (Alf) Gunn and Chester C. (Chet) Crisman, and Homicide Detective Eugene F. Ivey to Vancouver to pursue the investigation in Canada.

Arriving in Vancouver, Detective Ivey and Special Agent Rolston and the other Bureau agents were quick to learn that a great deal of local investigative effort, by Vancouver and Royal Canadian Mounted Police officers, had been directed towards Clifford Dawley and his associates over the preceding years for crimes committed throughout Western Canada. Dawley was still actively being sought, not only for escape from custody, but also as a suspect in several recent bank robberies in the British Columbia lower mainland, New Westminster, and other suburban cities. He was also a suspect in at least five other bank robberies in western Canada, the first occurring in 1927 when Dawley was sixteen years old, at which time a British Columbia police officer was murdered.[1] In addition to the names of Dawley's associates in Vancouver, which were furnished earlier by Superintendent John "Jack" Horton to Chief Lawrence, John Wasylenchuk and Maurice "Bobby" Talbot were identified as running-mates of Clifford Dawley. Both men had extensive criminal records, Talbot being convicted of bank robbery in 1943 and Wasylenchuk, twice convicted in Canadian courts for a similar offense, the first time in 1938.[2] (Both Wasylenchuk and Dawley, when not in prison, would continue their criminal careers throughout the life of this investigation.)

On July 6th, Detective Ivey and Agents Rolston, Gunn and Crisman met with the local RCMP Detachment commander, George Archer, to discuss this case and to request his assistance in locating Clifford Dawley. Archer assured the officers of his command's complete cooperation and said he would assign one of his best men to work with the Americans. He introduced Corporal Ernest Nuttall and his supervisor, Sergeant Edward Murton, to Ivey and the three Agents. Corporal Nuttall was assigned to work with the officers.[3] During the remainder of the day, the law men discussed in detail the aspects of the case. Although the American officers received a warm reception from the Mounties' command personnel, they were struck by Corporal Nuttall's apparent lack of enthusiasm for the assignment. Outwardly he was friendly, and as the officers began to zero in on specific information about Dawley's associates and movements, the Mountie appeared to be evasive in his responses. Finally, after considerable questioning, he came up with the names and addresses of Dawley's wife Rose and several others who reportedly were very close to the "stickup artist." But they were still concerned, for earlier they had seen this same attitude in other officers at Vancouver Police Headquarters. There the American officers received a cool reception from several Vancouver P.D. homicide detectives. At that time they chalked it up to the fact that they were not only outsiders but were from the States as well. To Detective Ivey this was inexcusable. Never before had he been unwelcome in another police department. This attitude seemed all the more strange when one realized that the Canadian officers should have been as interested in locating Dawley as they were; after all, he was a British Columbia prison escapee and an accomplished stickup man, specializing in Canadian bank robberies, and was believed to have participated in the murder of a Canadian police officer.[4]

During this first meeting, Corporal Nuttall told the officers he had been to the Dawley residence shortly after the suspect's escape in March and had found a letter from John Wasylenchuk to Rose, the suspect's wife, indicating that $2,500.00 had been paid to the "right people" and that "Cliff would soon be out." Hearing this, Ivey had an uneasy feeling that Nuttall knew more about Clifford Dawley than he was willing to admit.

The following day the American officers, accompanied by Corporal Nuttall, located Barbara Olson in Vancouver, a friend of Clifford Dawley's wife. The Olson woman told them that her friend was in Montreal, Quebec with her husband and gave the officers the address where they were staying. With this information, Corporal Nuttall placed a call to the RCMP Detachment at Montreal, which quickly resulted in the escapees' arrest. Two days later, on July 9th, Nuttall left for Montreal and soon returned the stickup artist to Vancouver. Upon his return, Clifford Dawley was interviewed on July 15th by the American officers in the Vancouver City Jail where he gave Detective Ivey and the Bureau agents a story concerning his activities after his escape of March 7th.

The prisoner admitted that he had feigned the back injury at the Oakalla Prison Farm in order to arrange his escape from Vancouver General Hospital. He fled in his hospital gown and was to have been picked up outside by his friend, Steve Polanski. Unfortunately for him, Polanski was observed outside the hospital by Vancouver Police patrol officers, who detained him after finding several items of clothing in his vehicle, which were obviously too large for Polanski. Although Polanski was released by the police, he was then unable to find his colleague who had fled the hospital.

The suspect said, after making good on his escape he made his way to a friend's boat and was later picked up by Charles and Maurice "Bobby" Talbot. He hid out in the Talbot's apartment until March 14th and then traveled to Millardville, British Columbia, a Vancouver suburb, where he stayed in a motel with the Talbots until March 24th. He claimed he was then taken to New Westminster and boarded a Canadian National Railway train for Montreal. After this interview, the officers questioned approximately two dozen individuals in the greater Vancouver area in a effort to unravel the prisoner's alibi. They were only partially successful, in that they were able to establish that he had stayed with the Talbots until either March the 10th or 11th, 1954 but not, as claimed by Dawley, that he stayed with these friends until March 14th. But there was no witness except Rose Dawley who would "place" Dawley in Canada on March 12th.[5]

On July 20th, the officers made arrangements with the RCMP and the Vancouver City Police to conduct an identification line-up of the suspect, for the Greenwood Bank Manager, Kenneth McElhaney, his secretary and several others who had witnessed the robbery. The prisoner learned of the proposed show-up and protested to City Magistrate Oscar Orr[6]. Orr, who was presiding in a Police Court preliminary hearing on Dawley's escape, ordered the RCMP escort officers not to place Dawley "on exhibition" (the Canadian term for an identification line-up) for the American witnesses. This order came after the Prosecutor announced that Dawley would also be charged as a Habitual Criminal and with the crime of burglary in the City of Nanaimo, British Columbia. This instruction to the Mounties was issued after Justice Orr heard a plea from the prisoner, who said he was without counsel and was to be placed in the line-up by the FBI on a murder charge, where he feared he could be mistakenly identified. He claimed to be a working man and no gangster, with a wife and family to support. He was not against cooperating with the Americans he said, and would be willing to take a lie detector test to clear his name. Following this plea, Justice Orr prohibited the line-up.

Upon hearing this, the American officers were shocked and expressed their feelings to Nuttall. It had taken considerable time and effort to arrange for the witnesses to be brought to Canada for this line-up and now a city magistrate, fully aware of both the circumstances of the crime and Clifford Dawley's past criminal history prohibited "exhibition" of the prisoner.

The suspect was returned to the Vancouver City Jail. In the meantime, Kenneth McElhaney and the other witnesses were taken by Detective Ivey and Agents Alf Gunn and Dean Rolston to an outer corridor of the jail where the escort officers, on a pretext, and at Detective Ivey's request, "paraded" the prisoner past the group. Upon seeing the prisoner, both the bank manager and his secretary tentatively identified him as one of the robbers, another witness was positive that this was the man she had seen standing outside the bank before the robbery and later inside wearing a false nose and horn-rimmed glasses. As the prisoner walked past the witnesses, he realized the purpose for which he had been taken down the outer corridor and immediately began to arrogantly berate Corporal Nuttall and the escorting officers. Ivey, who was an old-time homicide detective, was present during this tirade and said to the Mounties, "Let me have the son-of-a-bitch alone for five minutes." Ivey was a powerfully built man with broad shoulders and a heavy frame. He had a reputation of not being the "most gentle" homicide cop on the force, and was the type that could be depended upon in any physical encounter. However, the escorting officers returned Dawley to his jail cell without comment.[7]

On July 27th, the officers learned that the suspect was to appear in court again, thus avoiding any possible interference from Justice Orr. The officers made arrangements for several of the witnesses to attend the court hearing. McElhaney was present, but still he was not positive in his identification of Clifford Dawley. Some of the other witnesses present were of the opinion that quite possibly they too might never be able to identify the suspect as one of the robbers, but all agreed that he fit the physical description and his mannerisms were nearly identical to the number one robber. During an earlier interview that the officers had with the prisoner, they noted that his left hand appeared to be physically impaired; and when asked to don a pair of gloves, he did so with some difficulty. This tended to confirm one of Kenneth McElhaney's main observations about the number one man during the robbery, but unfortunately it was not sufficient to identify the prisoner and the robber as being the same person.

The officers next located John Wasylenchuk, a close friend of Dawley's, who was living in Burnaby, British Columbia. This man lived well. He drove expensive cars, owned a boat and was supporting four people, which was rather remarkable since he had only a part-time job. He tried to avoid discussing this however during the interview, and was extremely evasive and nervous with the officers during the interview. Corporal Nuttall had told the officers on an earlier occasion that after hearing of the Seattle robbery at Vancouver Police Headquarters on March 12th, at about 11:30 A.M., he thought that Wasylenchuk would be a potential suspect, so immediately drove to the suspect's home where he found the ex-con working on a boat in his back yard.

It was because of this visit by this Mountie that this man's "mug shot" had not been included in Chief Constable Mulligan's letter to Chief Lawrence on March 13th. Superintendent Horton's records showed that the "Mounties found Wasylenchuk to have been in Burnaby, British Columbia, at the time of the robbery." For similar reasons, the Talbot brothers' "mug shots" were not included in Chief Constable Mulligan's letter, although the Talbots and Wasylenchuk were known to be close associates of Clifford Dawley. Shortly after hearing of the robbery in Seattle, Vancouver City Police Inspector Peter Lamont reported that he suspected the Talbot brothers of this crime and began an immediate search of their known hang-outs. He reported back to Superintendent Horton that he had located both Charles and Bobby and both had been gambling in downtown Vancouver at the time of the robbery, thus ruling them out as suspects.

Vancouver Detective (Staff Sergeant) Peter Lamont. It was Lamont who reported to his police superiors that he conducted an investigation in Vancouver, B.C. on March 12 and 13, 1954 in which he located Maurice and Charles Talbot in Vancouver about 2: A.M., March 13, 1954. They claimed to have been in Vancouver all day and he claimed his inquiry tended to verify their story thus eliminating them as possible suspects in the Greenwood robbery case. (Photo courtesy of Vancouver Public Library)

During this interview, Wasylenchuk was quick to point out to the officers that Corporal Nuttall, who was not present, would support his alibi. He told the officers he did not like Clifford Dawley and had not seen him for several months. (This was later disproved when the officers visited with Mark Adams, the Assistant Warden at Oakalla Prison. Prison records indicated that John Wasylenchuk visited Clifford Dawley on several occasions at Oakalla before the prisoner escaped on March 7th).

The officers next interviewed the Talbot brothers. Bobby Talbot attempted to substantiate Dawley's alibi relative to his movements between March 7th, when the suspect escaped and March 24th when he claimed to have left for Montreal by train. Talbot's story varied so much from Dawley's statements that the officers were convinced Talbot was lying. Bobby's older brother Charles Talbot's story, was different; he opened up to the officers and discussed Dawley freely. He said Cliff Dawley was the top man in criminal activity in western Canada and John Wasylenchuk was second only to his partner. Charles said that on the day the prisoner escaped from Vancouver General, he gave Wasylenchuk $200.00 which was to be delivered to the escapee and that both Wasylenchuk and Cliff Dawley were out of Vancouver by March 9th or 10th. When he heard of the robbery in Seattle on March the 12th, he called Mrs. Wasylenchuk and she told him that John was out of town and would not be home for several days. Talbot claimed that the reason he had called was that at 1:00 P.M. that day the Mounties "checked him out," he assumed because of the robbery in Seattle; and he wanted to notify John that the "heat was on because three cops were shot in the robbery." Talbot said he next heard from "the Farmer," (as Wasylenchuk was frequently referred to) on the 14th of March.

Charles Talbot's story was the first that the officers found which was in direct conflict with that of the two now principal suspect's, and they were curious why Talbot would place Clifford Dawley in jeopardy. Talbot responded by opening his shirt front and showing the officers an old wound which he claimed was inflicted by Dawley. He said he and Dawley made a "big score" on a drug sale and he cut Dawley out of his share. When Dawley caught up with him, he shot Talbot, seriously wounding him in the shoulder. Talbot claimed that Dawley was a killer, and it was just luck that he survived. He said he hoped that the officers would, "get that son-of-a-bitch."[8]

After several days of interviewing witnesses and potential suspects in this case, the officers split up and began the arduous task of tracing the source of the physical evidence picked up at the scene of the robbery which could have originated in Canada. Bureau agents covered every tailor and cleaning establishment in the Vancouver metropolitan area, looking for someone who could identify the suit coat abandoned by George at the robbery scene. All the tailors contacted felt that the coat, which was of English weave, was tailor-made in Canada but by an unknown craftsman. The cleaning mark was traced to the Fairview Cleaners in Vancouver. This mark had been used about four years earlier, but the records of the customer had long since been destroyed. Similar results were obtained with the .38 calibre revolver. Although the manufacture's initial sales record of the weapon was located dating back many years, the retail sales record search was not successful.

Weeks went by. The three agents continued their investigation in Canada as time permitted, but Detective Ivey had returned to Seattle on Captain Rouse's order, after being briefed on the officer's progress during the initial phases of the Canadian connection. Rouse felt that the FBI was better equipped to carry on the investigation outside the country than was the Seattle Police Department and he had complete confidence in the agents assigned to the case. He was aware that the FBI had nearly unlimited funds and could "buy" much information not readily available through normal investigative procedures. The Seattle Department's resources were scarce; investigative funds for informants, such as they were, were generally limited to vice cases. Any information on major criminals was obtained by detectives "buying" information with money out of their own pocket or by "squeezing" a suspect for information after catching the individual in a criminal act. Occasionally, if the information was valuable enough, the officer would "front" for the suspect with the Prosecuting Attorney, requesting a reduced charge or with a recommendation to the sentencing judge for a lighter than normal sentence. Several Seattle city councillors would never understand that criminals, and many "respected citizens" for that matter, would not talk to the police unless there existed for them an opportunity for gain, financial or otherwise; thus, each year, they would resist the payment of investigative monies to police informants.

In Canada FBI Agents were successful in locating three ex-convicts who were willing to talk. Besides the potential of receiving a cash payment from the FBI for worthwhile information, the "cons" were now well aware of the reward which was being offered for information leading to the arrest and conviction of the three stickup men. In addition to a $5,000 reward offered by the Seattle First National Bank, the State Banking Association and others had contributed to the reward fund until, by mid-1954, the reward had climbed to a total of $13,000.[9]

One informant advised the agents that he had known the two suspects for several years and was well aware of their recent activities in regard to bank robberies in Western Canada. He claimed Clifford Dawley was a very capable stickup man and that he would not hesitate to go on any "bank job" which had been "cased" by Wasylenchuk. And further, that Dawley would use The Farmer both as a look-out and driver of the getaway car on all his jobs. The informant advised that Wasylenchuk had pulled at least six bank robberies in Canada during the summer and fall of 1954 and that the method of operation in the Greenwood case followed the general pattern of these robberies.

A second informant was even more explicit; this man who claimed to be very close to the two criminals stated that the modus operandus of the robbers in the Seattle case was nearly identical to those cases in which the informant knew John Wasylenchuk to have been involved in Canada, either as the man who planned the robberies or both planned and participated in them. He stated that Wasylenchuk either pulled the Greenwood job or set it up for his associates. The informant believed that Cliff Dawley, or John McCluskie, as he called him, (one of the robber's many aliases) was undoubtedly the number one man in the stickup, and the use of the Oldsmobile as the getaway vehicle, left little doubt that Wasylenchuk was along as the "wheelman." The informant knew both men well and claimed that Wasylenchuk owed Dawley a favor and would try to repay it by a "big score" in the States. He claimed that when Dawley or "John" as he called him was arrested in Duncan, British Columbia, in December, 1953, he and his colleague had been interrupted by the Mounties before they could pull off a robbery there. Wasylenchuk deserted his partner when a fight ensued between Dawley and the police. This is the incident which later lead to Dawley being charged as a Habitual Criminal for assaulting the arresting officer, RCMP Constable S. R. Langdon at Duncan, B.C. The men had stolen an automobile on the morning of December 7, 1953, which belonged to a local doctor well known to Langdon. Upon seeing the vehicle on the street at 2:00 A.M. with two men in it, the officer stopped to check them out. As he approached the vehicle Clifford Dawley threw a whiskey bottle at the officer, and his "unknown" passenger, who turned out to be Wasylenchuk, fled the scene on foot. Langdon seized the bottle thrower and in the ensuing fight both men were injured, but the officer was able to subdue his prisoner. Later a screwdriver and a pry bar were found in the car which lead to Dawley being charged with possession of burglary tools.

This same informant also advised the agents that Wasylenchuk had invited him to participate in a "big score" across the border, and that he had shown the informant false noses and horn-rimmed glasses which they would use to hide the features of some of the gang members, particularly those of Cliff Dawley who had outstanding facial features. This informant also claimed that Wasylenchuk had access to several guns, that he would have no problem obtaining a .45 caliber automatic and that the stickup man frequently used the name John Wesley when "capering" in the United States.[10]

Meanwhile in Seattle, Homicide detectives were questioning David Robert Auld, a twenty-three-year-old Canadian stickup artist and drug trafficker. Auld had been recently released from the British Columbia Penitentiary[11] after serving three and one-half years of a five-year sentence for Armed Robbery. He was being held by United States Immigration and Naturalization Service Inspectors for violation of the immigration laws. Upon learning of Auld's background, Immigration Officials, who were well aware of the Canadian involvement in the Greenwood Bank robbery and of the death of Officer Frank Hardy at the bank, notified Seattle Homicide Detectives, and Detective Ivey was assigned to interrogate the man.

Auld began his criminal career in 1948 at the age of sixteen, when he was caught stealing the seats out of sports cars in Vancouver. He graduated to armed robbery that same year and received a twenty month sentence in British Columbia Correctional Center for Young Offenders. In 1951, at the age of nineteen, he was doing time in the penitentiary with some of Canada's toughest criminals. Auld was proud of his past, particularly his association with and knowledge of the activities of men like Clifford Dawley and John Wasylenchuk. He was a willing subject for Ivey's interrogation.

Auld, in response to questions by the detective, stated that he was a frequent visitor to Steve Polanski's "bootlegging joint" in Vancouver, that this was a meeting place for Cliff Dawley and his friends including The Farmer, the Talbots, Bobby Lewis and several other stickup artists. He said that, since the 1954 robbery, Polanski and others frequently discussed the "Seattle caper" as they called it; Polanski claimed to have obtained the guns for the job and transported them to Seattle where he met the two principals of this investigation. Auld said that Polanski claimed he was a friend of Cliff Dawley, but in fact he was afraid of him and thus acted as his errand boy and did whatever the man told him to do. He said that Polanski frequently discussed the robbery and said that The Farmer set it up and his partner Cliff Dawley did all the shooting at the bank. When asked who the third man in the robbery was, Auld said it was probably Bobby Lewis, as he had been on several prior bank jobs with the two men. When asked where Lewis was now, he responded that he was in custody in Vancouver, as he and Lewis were both picked up just two weeks earlier by Canadian authorities and held for an identification line-up. After this arrest in Vancouver, David Auld was released, but the police held Lewis on a bank robbery charge. Auld was questioned about the circumstances surrounding Dawley's latest escape from Oakalla Prison Farm[12]. He responded that he knew nothing about it except word was out that the escapee hid out inside a stack of truck tires at a garage in Burnaby owned by Alex Decker and was there when the police came looking for him. He claimed the man stayed there for three days.[13]

Later another associate of John Wasylenchuk and Clifford Dawley was located in Canada by the FBI. For a price, this man was willing to talk to the agents. He claimed to have known the two stickup men for several years, having served time with them in the British Columbia Penitentiary. This was later verified by the agents. He claimed, "Dawley's a killer and capable of anything, and his partner is a greedy bastard. The Farmer has cheated so many of his associates that few of the old time stickup men, other than Dawley, will have anything to do with him."[14] The informant stated that a mutual friend of the two suspects, whom he knew for a fact had hid Dawley out after his March 7th escape, told him that Dawley and his partner were later bragging about their "big score in the States." The informant stated that it was common knowledge among Vancouver ex-cons that these two Canadian cons were the gunmen in the Seattle robbery.

But time was running out for the FBI Agents. Vancouver officers were enmeshed in a corruption scandal which would rock the entire department from the Constable on the beat to the Chief Constable's office and beyond. The city detectives had other problems to worry about and were not concerned about a bank robbery "across the line." Crime in the city in 1954 was at an all-time high and continued to rise in 1955.[15] Politicians and citizens alike were demanding action from the Police Department, and City Government and the Department were being roasted by the press. Even former supporters were now demanding that the Department do something to lift the cloud of suspicion which hung over each man wearing the blue uniform.

Notes

[1] Detective Eugene F. Ivey, S.P.D. Case No. 288527 Investigator's Report, Op. Cit., July 11, 1954. Vancouver Police records indicated that Clifford Dawley was a participant in at least five and possibly as many as seventeen bank robberies in Western Canada between 1927 and 1954; (He was also involved in an assault in San Francisco on September 18, 1930, where, at the age of nineteen, he was shot in the left arm by a San Francisco Police Officer). Other crimes included:

(1). Robbery of a bank in North Bay, Ontario in 1924.

(2). Robbery of The Royal Canadian Bank of Vancouver-1927.

(3). Robbery of The Royal Canadian Bank of Vancouver-1940, where over $50,000.00 was taken by the robbers.

(4). The Oak Bay Bank, Vancouver Island-1953.

(5). Bank of Edmonton, Edmonton, Alberta-1953.

During this period, Clifford Dawley, with aliases Bert Norton, John McCluskie, William Duggan, Clifford Frassier and Clifford Dixen was arrested and/or charged in over two dozen separate felony crimes in Canada. See Vancouver City Police Department, Criminal Identification Bureau Record No. 10263 and RCMP Identification Branch F.P.S. No. 120004

[2] City of Vancouver Police Department, Criminal Identification Bureau Record No. 15095 and No. 12515. John Wasylenchuk, also known as John Wesley or "The Farmer" born in 1913, was first arrested at the age of 19 in 1931 for theft in Calgary, Alberta. Subsequent arrests followed for Possession of Stolen Property, Auto Theft, Burglary, Possession of Explosives (for purposes of breaking into a safe), Obstruction of a Peace Officer, Armed Robbery and Escape From Custody.

[3] Ivey, Op. Cit., July 11, 1954.

[4] Eugene F. Ivey, interview with the author September 3, 1974.

[5] Ibid.

[6] " Magistrate Orr Warns 'No Lineup,'" The Province, July 20, 1954, p. 1. In response to a plea from Clifford Dawley to prevent him from standing in a "line-up" for the American witnesses to the Greenwood Bank robbery, the Magistrate told Dawley: "I am not sure what your rights are, until you are tried by me, however, you are in my custody. I don't want you placed on exhibition."

[7] Kenneth McElhaney, interview with the author June 18, 1974. In this interview the former Seattle First National Bank Branch Manager claimed that FBI Agent Alf Gunn was disciplined and later reassigned by the FBI to Houston, Texas for participating in the ruse which allowed the robbery witnesses to view the prisoner in the Vancouver City Jail, contrary to Justice Orr's prohibition against placing Clifford Dawley "on exhibition." Initially the FBI would neither confirm nor deny this report, however, upon subsequent inquiry, it was learned the Agent's transfer was not connected to this case.

[8] Eugene F. Ivey, Op. Cit., September 3, 1974.

[9] Frank Lynch, Seattle Scene: "A still Unsolved Murder And Bank Robbery," The Seattle Times, March 11, 1955.

[10] Eugene F. Ivey, S.P.D. Case No. 288527, Investigator's Report, Op. Cit., Interrogation of David R. Auld, September 15, 1954, p. 1.

[11] The British Columbia Penitentiary was located just above the Fraser River on the outskirts of New Westminster, British Columbia, approximately 40 miles from Vancouver. This facility, built before the turn of the century, and housing some of Canada's most notorious criminals, was closed in the late 1980's.

[12] Bruce Larsen, "Dawley Loose, After Six Attempts," The Vancouver Province, August 24, 1954, p. 1. After his arrest in Montreal, Quebec and his return to custody in Vancouver by RCMP Sergeant Ernest Nuttall, within a month Clifford Dawley was free again. As The Province reported:

"Thwarted on six bids for freedom in the past week, elusive Clifford Eugene Dawley, 44, outfoxed two guards at Oakalla Prison Farm at 4:05 p.m. Monday and sprinted to freedom.

The man known to have been chosen by convicted drug kingpin George Mallock to engineer his escape tries, Dawley fled from a walled-in exercise yard after crouching out of sight as a guard counted prisoners back into Oakalla's overcrowded south wing. It was Dawley's second escape from custody in six months and one every officer at Oakalla knew Dawley was planning. He was to face an habitual criminal charge in Nanaimo Sept. 7.

Prisoners being released from the south wing at Oakalla today said Dawley's determination to escape was common knowledge throughout the prison. In the past week fellow prisoners had watched as guards foiled his efforts to dig through his cell wall, cut through bars and they saw guards take hacksaw blades and a metal digger from him."

Although The Province reporter went on to discuss the fact that the Oakalla Prison Farm was overcrowded, and although repeated escape attempts were discovered, no mention was made of the prison authorities' decision to keep this vicious escape artist in a minimum security facility rather than in a maximum security prison located just a few miles away. Nor was there any discussion on how Dawley could escape detection in his flight over the prison wall in broad daylight, with an armed guard present. Clifford Dawley would remain on the loose for 18 months.

[13] Ivey, Op. Cit., September 3, 1974.

[14] Ibid.

[15] Vancouver Police Department Annual Report - 1955, Vancouver, British Columbia, 1956, pp. 22-24. An average of 15,053 Part I or serious/felony crimes were reported each year to the Vancouver Police 1950-1954, and 16312 were reported in 1955, up over 8 per cent from the previous year. Two hundred and nine robberies were recorded in 1954 and this figure jumped nearly 16 per cent, to 241, in 1955.

Bank Worker Identifies Defendant as Robber

By CONSTANTINE ANGELOS

GREENWOOD BANK ROBBERY:

Government Rests; Recess Declared

Policeman's Slaying Nine Years Ago Still Unsolved

By DICK SALTONSTALL

ground, ...ed play

'Prison pal tells of Wasylenchuk alibi bribe idea

A Look Into the Past . . . The Greenwood Bank Job

telligencer

SUNRISE EDITION

42 PAGES   PRICE 10 CENTS

Greenwood Bank Holdup Slaying Suspect Arrested

Extradition Hearing Nears Climax in B. C.

By CONSTANTINE ANGELOS   Times

Arrest Confirms Faith Of Policeman's Widow

SGT. SLESSMAN

U. S. Jury Indicts 2nd B. C. Man In Greenwood Bank Robbery

By CONSTANTINE ANGELOS

Report Of Mayor's Special Committee To Inquire Into Alleged Police Payoffs

Judge Grants Delay In Arraignment Of Suspect In Greenwood Robbery

Ex-Mountie Claims Plot

'Criminals Out to Break Wasylenchuk Alibi'

Tolerance Policy Faces Delay Here

By DAN COUGHLIN

Fear of leak keeps probe under wraps

Haircut Price Up to $1.75

Official in B.C. Orders Review Of Extradition In Bank Case

Greenwood Suspect Whisked From B.C.

By CHARLES DUNSIRE

Chapter

4

Corruption Within

By the spring of 1955, it was common knowledge throughout the City of Vancouver and the British Columbia lower mainland that something was terribly amiss within the political framework of the Vancouver City Government, and by June, the word had spread throughout the country. A series of articles alleging corruption within the police department first began appearing in a Toronto, Ontario

Ray Munro at The Royal Commission hearing in Vancouver. A series of articles alleging corruption within the Police Department first began appearing in a Toronto, Ontario newspaper tabloid, "The Flash", under the by-line of Ray Munro. Munro was a former crime reporter for The Vancouver Province newspaper. (Photo courtesy of Vancouver Public Library)

newspaper tabloid, The Flash, under the by-line of Ray Munro, a former crime reporter for The Vancouver Province.[1]

Soon after the first story hit the street, the Vancouver City Council reacted by passing a resolution censuring The Police Commission, Chief Walter Mulligan, and the Vancouver police force for a lack of action in "setting their house in order." Shortly thereafter, stung by this attack, the Vancouver Police Commission petitioned Lieutenant-Governor Frank MacKenzie Ross for a judicial investigation into the alleged corruption within the Vancouver force.[2]

As each edition of The Flash was received at police headquarters, a flurry of activity followed as officers clustered in small groups to discuss the latest allegations. In the June 18th edition, allegations of corruption by several members of the force were printed, but the story zeroed in on Detective Sergeant Leonard W. Cuthbert, alleging that Cuthbert, the former head of the Vice Division's Gambling Squad, was involved in a bookmaking pay-off scheme which col-

Vancouver Detective Sergeant Leonard Cuthbert (released from hospital after shooting himself in an unsuccessful attempt to take his own life) appearing before The Royal Commission in 1955. The former head of the Vice Division's Gambling Squad, was involved with other officers within the Vancouver Police Department in a bookmaking pay-off and criminal protection scheme which collected thousands of dollars in bribes and protection money from members of the Vancouver underworld. (Photo courtesy of Vancouver Public Library)

lected thousands of dollars from members of the Vancouver under-world. This was not news to the command staff of the Department, nor to several past and present members of the vice squad. Just four days earlier, on June 14, at 8:00 A.M., shortly after arriving at work, Patrol Superintendent Harry Whelan approached Sergeant Cuthbert in the detective division offices and ordered him to come to his office before going off shift. At 12:25 P.M., when Cuthbert arrived at the superintendent's office, he was pale and appeared to be agitated. As Cuthbert sat down, the superintendent advised him that he was aware that the Sergeant was the "bag man" for the Department and for the chief constable, and that he had been collecting large sums of money from local gamblers and business men for illegal purposes. Whelan alleged that Cuthbert had split the take with the chief and other high-ranking members of the force and with members of his own squad. Whelan told Cuthbert that his sources were a newspaper reporter and his own brother, former Detective Jack Whelan, and he was aware that Whelan had implicated himself in this activity.

The superintendent laid the whole story of corruption within the vice squad before Cuthbert, advising him that he had sufficient evidence to put both him and Chief Mulligan "away," with or without Cuthbert's cooperation.

Cuthbert, who had been living in fear for five years that he would be found out, finally accepted the inevitable and acquiesced to the superintendent's demands. He admitted to participating in a gambling and bribery payoff and illegal collection system within the Department, dating back to 1949. The irony of it was he was first introduced to several racetrack book makers and gamblers by the superintendent's younger brother, then a detective with the Vancouver force. Cuthbert named not only the chief constable as a recipient of half of all that he collected, but also alleged that he was forced to split his half with Deputy Chief Gordon Ambrose, Criminal Investigation's Bureau Chief Jack Horton[3] and members of his own staff. The sergeant said his tasks as chief of the gambling squad were rather simple. All he had to do was follow the chief constable's direction and "take care of their friends." This, as he understood it, was to allow those gamblers who "contributed monthly payments" to

operate their bookmaking and gambling enterprises in the city without interference from the vice squad. He was also to assist these
"enterprising business men" as the chief constable called them, in
obtaining business licenses in downtown Vancouver at the most
"promising locations." For this, beginning in 1949, Cuthbert would
collect payments ranging from $300.00 to $500.00 at unspecified
time intervals and it was his understanding that upon acquiring "a
proper business license" located in the most lucrative downtown
area, each license would be worth $5,000.00 to the "right people."
The Sergeant said he assumed at the time the "right people" meant
his superiors, both in the police department and at city hall. He
admitted making several collections, each being split with the chief
constable in the chief's office. On one or two occasions he said he
received money from the chief, not knowing how his boss had acquired it, but he assumed the chief had other "connections" as he
kept referring to the source as "from our friends," referring to the
gambling interests.[4]

Meanwhile, in Victoria, in response to the belated request from
the Board of Police Commissioners, the Lieutenant-Governor of the
province, Frank MacKenzie Ross, was making plans to appoint a
Royal Commission under the provincial Public Inquiries Act to investigate the current wave of lawlessness in the city and into allegations of corruption of its police officials.[5]

In Vancouver, Superintendent Harry Whelan was looking for
hard evidence which would convict his superior, Chief Constable
Walter H. Mulligan of illegal activities involving corruption within
the Department. Whelan had a long talk with his brother Jack, now
working in consort with Ray Munro of The Flash, in an effort to
piece together Cuthbert's story of police payoffs. The superintendent had also made elaborate notes of his interview with the vice
sergeant and had taken the story to City Prosecutor Steward
McMorran for guidance. McMorran advised the superintendent to
continue to pursue his investigation and obtain documentation from
Cuthbert of the sergeant's complicity in the payoff system with other
members of the force.[6]

On June 23rd, Whelan received a call from McMorran inquiring
as to his progress, advising the superintendent that, in all likelihood,

if Cuthbert failed to come forward with the signed confession by June 24th, there was little that he could do, as he was anticipating action being taken at the provincial level "to bring this to a head." When Whelan hung up the telephone, he called Cuthbert at his desk in the detective's office and advised him of McMorran's position. Cuthbert responded that he would talk to McMorran in person the next day. However, Whelan was not satisfied that the sergeant would repeat the story he had earlier told the superintendent, and that afternoon he reduced Cuthbert's story to a two-page typewritten confession.

At 7:00 A.M. the following morning, Cuthbert was again summoned to the superintendent's office. He was surprised, for as he entered Whelan's office, the superintendent handed him the confession and said, "Read it over Len, and sign it." [7]

Sergeant Cuthbert took the document and casually read it. He appeared to be surprised at the length of it, for he had not realized that he had given Whelan so much information during yesterday's meeting. He took exception to one sentence which said he was to have "taken care of his men out of his share of the monies collected from gambling interests within the city." He didn't want to create any problems for these men, he said. The superintendent had him cross out the incriminating words, then almost as if the document were of no importance to him, he signed it. Whelan thanked him and as Cuthbert got up to leave, he turned to the superintendent and asked, "What would have happened if I hadn't signed?" Whelan responded, "Len, you're stuck in the middle of this and it wouldn't make any difference one way or the other, for it would have all come out eventually." "I suppose you're right," Cuthbert replied. As he went out the door, he said good-bye to the superintendent and returned to his office, a small cubicle just off the detective parade room.

Detective Sergeant Leonard Cuthbert, with 29 years on the Department, entered his office and closed the door. Moments later, at 8:13 A.M., he shot himself in the chest with his service revolver while sitting at his desk.

Criminal Investigations Bureau Superintendent, Jack Horton, unaware of the Sergeant's revelations to Superintendent Whelan, was one of the first men to arrive at Cuthbert's office. Cuthbert was still sitting upright at his desk with blood flowing over the front and back of his suit coat. The bullet had entered his chest near dead center and had exited through his back, tearing a hole through the chair in which he sat, and burying itself in the back wall of the office.

Detectives Donald McDonald and Bobby Hooper arrived in Cuthbert's office a moment before the superintendent. Within seconds, Horton was on the telephone, calling for an ambulance. While waiting, they tried their best to make the sergeant as comfortable as possible and at the same time stem the flow of blood from his chest. Attracted by the commotion in the parade room near Cuthbert's office, Superintendent Harry Whelan stepped out of his office and was shocked upon hearing of the officer's attempted suicide, for only he knew what precipitated it.

As the superintendent rushed into the Parade Room, Sergeant Cuthbert was being readied for the ambulance. Bending over close to the officer, Whelan spoke softly to him asking, "Do you know who this is, Len?" The sergeant responded, "Yes, Harry, I know." Whelan, then half apologizing for the circumstances which led to the shooting, said, "No hard feelings?" "No hard feelings," replied Cuthbert, "I tried to get my heart. I'm sorry, I guess I missed."

Upon arrival at Vancouver General Hospital, Cuthbert was more dead than alive from loss of blood due to internal bleeding. The .38 caliber slug, having missed his heart, passed through his left lung, but miraculously caused relatively little damage to his internal organs. The doctors in the emergency operating room had a great deal of difficulty in halting the flow of blood; but within four hours of his admittance to the emergency room, Cuthbert, although listed as "critical", was holding his own.[8]

The Inquiry

Shortly after the suicide attempt by Sergeant Cuthbert Lieutenant Governor Ross announced the appointment of a Royal Commission charged with the responsibility of investigating the allegations of corruption within the Vancouver police force.[9]

Appointed as Commission chairman was Reginald H. Tupper, who, reporting to Attorney General F. W. Bonner in Victoria, would undertake what would turn out to be a somewhat less than exhaustive inquiry into the affairs of the Vancouver police department. Tupper would be assisted by four Royal Canadian Mounted Police Constables headed by Inspector M. J. Yves-Dube from Regina and non-commissioned officers Sergeant F. G. Saunders and Corporals B. L. Johnson and J. W. Purdy from the lower mainland RCMP detachments.

Governor Ross's directive to Commissioner Tupper was simple:[10]

1. Inquire into allegations of corruption involving Vancouver City Police officials.

2. Determine if laxity existed in the enforcement of the Criminal Code by the Vancouver city police.

3. Inquire into the truth or falsity of rumors, allegations or suspicions of corruption by members of the Vancouver city police.

With Detective Leonard Cuthbert's attempted suicide and now the announcement in Victoria of the "Special Commission" which was to investigate corruption within the police department, a quiet, but obvious change occurred within the ranks at police headquarters. It was particularly noticeable within the Criminal Investigations Bureau offices. With each publication of The Flash, additional detectives were named as recipients of payoffs from the gambling and liquor interests of the city. The local press was having a "field day" speculating on The Flash's revelations and the reasons for Sergeant Cuthbert's attempted suicide. For all practical purposes, the bureau had ceased functioning as an investigative unit. For some detectives, the revelations were a complete shock and they were bitter with the thought of what this meant to them personally and to their families. In many cases, friends and neighbors alike made it a point to inquire of many of the officers, in not too subtle a way, as to the extent of corruption within the force, implying that possibly these officers too were "caught up in the same system and really couldn't be blamed if they took just a little graft." But others had more reason to be apprehensive, for The Flash identified specific constables including the chief and several members of the Department's supervisory and command staff, pinpointing dates, times and amounts of funds alleged to have been collected by these men from members of the Vancouver underworld. It now became obvious to all members of the Department that the source or sources of this information could only have come from past or present members of the force.

At city hall, news media representatives were trying to attain statements from both Mayor Fred Hume and his fellow members of the Police Commission, which included City Prosecutor Stewart McMorran and Magistrate Oscar Orr. McMorran refused to comment on the situation and Magistrate Orr, in an interview with a reporter from The Vancouver Province, "passed the buck" to Victoria stating, "Any announcement of the Police Commission's position would be premature, for we are waiting to hear from the Attorney General". Chief Mulligan also refused to talk to newsmen, but announced through his attorney of his plans to sue reporter Ray Munro and the publishers of The Flash for libel. Nor would any member of Mulligan's command staff comment on the appointment of the special commission, the status of Chief Mulligan, nor of the Department's position on the allegations revealed by reporter Munro. This "no comment" position taken by members of the force only fueled the fires of distrust and bitterness toward the command staff by many of the Department's officers. Rumors were rampant throughout the police department, ranging from the "resignation and jailing of the Chief Constable" to the "take-over of the Department by the Mounties". These continued unabated for weeks following the appointment of Commissioner Tupper and the other members of what was now referred to as the "Commission."

Commissioner Tupper wasted no time in organizing his staff and, as the inquiry got underway, the four officers assigned to work with the Commission began interviewing some 400 potential witnesses. These included police constables, prison and city jail inmates, ex-convicts, members of the Vancouver judiciary and citizens who had either offered their testimony or who were discovered to possess certain information relative to the inquiry. Many were hostile and refused to discuss with the officers their knowledge of corrupt practices within the Vancouver city force. Some witnesses had left British Columbia and were unavailable for summons. Several allegations received by the Commission related to corrupt practices which were

In a standing room only crowd, spectators at Assize Court in Vancouver await opening of the Inquiry into Corruption Within the Vancouver City Police force. (Photo courtesy: Vancouver Public Library)

supposed to have occurred many years prior to these current events, yet that was understandable for police corruption within Vancouver city government was not new. It had been less than ten years since a similar scandal had "rocked" city hall resulting in the termination of the then chief constable, thus paving the way for the appointment of Walter Mulligan, who was described, at the time by the local press, as the man who would provide "the strongest leadership available" for the police force. But for now, many witnesses came forward with allegations of misconduct directed at several members of the current command staff and others within the Vancouver Department. Several citizens contacted the Commission's investigators individually, and nearly one hundred wrote to Commissioner Tupper directly. However during the forty days of public hearings, which got underway on July 13th in the assize courtroom in the court house, following the investigative phase of the inquiry, a large part of the testimony offered by witnesses was unsubstantiated. Very little solid evidence of corruption of Vancouver officers, other than VPD vice squad members and the chief constable were ever fully explored by the Commission. Some members of the press and more than one politician in Victoria were quick to criticize the actions of the Commission even before sworn testimony was completed during the public hearings. These individuals alleged that the Commission's efforts were focused entirely on corruption within the police force rather than within the elected offices of city government, where they alleged the real culprits were.

Tupper however did have some surprises in store for the citizens of Vancouver, for the lead off witness for the government was Detective Sergeant Robert W. Leatherdale[11], a veteran detective with nearly twenty-eight years on the force. Leatherdale was concerned not only

Detective Sergeant Robert Leatherdale (2nd from left), Inspector Archie Plummer and Constable Dan Brown appear before The Royal Commission. It was Leatherdale and Plummer who assisted U.S. authorities in identifying the suspects in the Greenwood robbery and who testified against Chief Constable Mulligan before The Royal Commission. (Photo courtesy of Vancouver Public Library)

for his own personal reputation, but also for what was happening to "his" police department. The officer began his testimony by describing a conversation he had had on May 3, 1949 with Chief Constable Walter Mulligan. He said he was summoned to the Chief's office, where he was surprised to learn that he had been appointed to Detective Sergeant and assigned to head-up the vice squad's liquor detail. But he was shocked when he learned of the strings attached to his promotion. He said that after a general discussion of "bootlegging" in the city, the Chief asked him if he had any objection to allowing a few bootleggers to "run without police interference", adding, "it would do us both some good." Leatherdale said his shock soon turned to anger. He said the Chief added, "There's Sergeant's stripes in the balance here, and I can have your promotion approved at the May 20th Police Commission meeting. You don't have to worry, you can have your choice of men and if any of them do not suit you I'll have them transferred out of the squad."[12]

Leatherdale said he responded: "That sounds fine to me," referring to the selection of the best men for the detail, but he said he was still considering the price he would have to pay for this promotion.

The detective testified that as he turned to leave Mulligan added, "Sergeant Len Cuthbert knows of the arrangements, and will be contacting you." Before departing from the Chief's Office, the officer said the Chief also told him, "If you have any friends in the bootlegging business, that's all right too," implying that it was safe for them to conduct illegal operations within the city.

On May 5th, Leatherdale said that Sergeant Leonard Cuthbert showed up at his home and, the soon-to-be-appointed Detective Sergeant, went out to the Vice Sergeant's car to talk to him. Len Cuthbert was very frank with Leatherdale and came directly to the point. He said, referring to the Chief's position on the cities gambling and liquor enforcement policies, "It's no use beating around the bush. We may as well talk plain. The chief wants money. He's been there [as chief constable] two years and he thinks these things ought to open up a little."[13]

Leatherdale said he was just as straightforward. He responded by asking Sergeant Cuthbert what he was expected to do. Responding, Cuthbert told Leatherdale of the payoff operation that he, Cuthbert, was currently involved with and that he was collecting from seven gambling, bookmaking and bootlegging operations in the city at that time for the chief and members of his command staff, including Deputy Chief Gordon Ambrose and Superintendent Jack Horton. The vice squad leader claimed his unit had doubled their income and that Joe Celona (an alleged gambler) would be worth $300.00 a month for protection and possibly more at a later date. Leatherdale, continuing his testimony said that when he asked where he fit into this scheme, the Sergeant replied, "Bob, all you have to do is put pressure on the bootleggers who are not paying, so we drive business to those who are. Then I'll make the contacts and it will be your job to collect monthly and split with the Chief and your men on the liquor detail."[14]

Leatherdale, still in the witness box, in response to a question from Commissioner Tupper said, "It was now in the open. There was no misunderstanding by me as to what price I was expected to pay for my stripes." And he said, "My course of action was just as clear. I made elaborate notes of the conversation I had with both the Chief Constable and Sergeant Cuthbert and the day following this meeting with Len Cuthbert I made arrangements to meet with City Prosecutor Gordon Scott. The date was May 7th, 1949."

The Detective Sergeant continuing in the witness box, said he sought the prosecutor's advice relative to his proposed course of action, for as he put it to Scott: "There's been a member of the Leatherdale family on the force for over fifty years without a hint of scandal, and I'm not going to bring disgrace to the family name even if it means giving up any chance for promotion."[15]

Throughout the afternoon of May 7 (and again the following day), Leatherdale said he discussed the ramifications of the case with Scott . Scott told him to continue his conversations with Chief Constable Mulligan and he would make arrangements for the officer to talk to Mayor Charles Thompson and the other members of the Police Commission regarding "a proper course of action to follow."

On May 10th, shortly after he arrived at work, Leatherdale claimed he was again summoned to the chief constable's office. When he entered, Mulligan inquired of his position relative to the Chief's earlier offer to promote the detective to Sergeant, and assign him to head up the liquor detail in the vice squad. Leatherdale said he responded, "I've talked to Cuthbert, and I want no part of it. I don't care if I'm appointed or not, but if you place me in charge of that squad, everybody who's doing business illegally will be charged."[16]

When inquiry was made by the Commission's lead counsel, J. G. Hutcheson, of the chief's response to Leatherdale's refusal to "cooperate", the Sergeant said he was surprised, for the chief responded, "That's all right, you're just the man I want for the job." With that, Mulligan dismissed him. Leatherdale left the chief's office in a quandary. He had been offered a promotion contingent upon his agreement to enter into a criminal conspiracy with Detective Sergeant Leonard Cuthbert, the chief constable and others, and now it appeared that the chief may have only been testing him; Leatherdale was afraid to hazard a guess as to what to expect next. But he didn't have to wait long, for he'd no sooner gotten back to his desk that he was notified to return to the chief constable's office. When he entered, he said the chief asked him if he had consulted anyone in reference to his refusal to go along with him and Cuthbert, or whether he had made up his own mind regarding this decision. Leatherdale said he did not admit that he had talked to the city prosecutor, and responded, "I haven't talked to anyone, I just have a good record here and I want to keep it that way." Upon hearing this, the chief answered, "That's too bad, for Sergeant Cuthbert has already made "arrangements" on the west side, arrangements that might have to be changed."

Shortly after this second visit, the sergeant, continuing his testimony said Cuthbert soon contacted him in his office. Cuthbert appeared uneasy in Leatherdale's presence and said he was sorry that he had turned the chief's proposition down, for he had already "made some arrangements" for him. Leatherdale said he took this to mean that the vice sergeant had set the wheels in motion for him to begin pressuring a few selected bootleggers into paying off the police in order to operate their businesses.

Continuing, Leatherdale stated that after this conversation with the vice sergeant he again contacted city prosecutor, Gordon Scott. Scott told him that since his first visit to the prosecutor's office, he had made arrangements for the officer to meet with Mayor Charles

E. Thompson and Police Commissioner Magistrate Oscar Orr. The sergeant, looking at his notes, stated, "I met with the Mayor, Mr. Scott and Magistrate Orr on May 11th, and told them everything that I have related here to the Commission about these payoffs within the Department."[17]

With Sergeant Leatherdale's last statement, several members of the audience in the assize courtroom, in which the hearing was being held, were stunned. They, for the first time, had not only heard sworn testimony of corruption within their police department, directly from a highly respected member of the force, but, also, that the information related here today before the Royal Commission, had been made available at least six years earlier to the elected officials of their city government. Yet neither Mayor Thompson, nor anyone else who was charged with the responsibility for the operation and conduct of the police force, had taken definitive action to properly investigate these allegations.

Police Chief Constable Walter Mulligan Vancouver, B.C. Police Department (far right) appears before The Royal Commission convened to investigate corruption within the Vancouver Force. Note newspaper headline. (Photo courtesy of Vancouver Public Library)

Following this direct testimony from Police Sergeant Robert Leatherdale, T. G. Harris, counsel for Chief Walter Mulligan was first to his feet, followed by Lyle Jestly, attorney for C.I.B. Superintendent Jack Horton and also Neil Fleishman, representing John Blunt Publications, publishers of the The Flash. Blunt also represented reporter Ray Munro and former detective Jack Whelan, now working with Munro. Norris accused Commission Counsel Hutcheson of withholding evidence and failing to disclose to his client before the hearing, the full extent of Leatherdale's allegations, thus denying his client the opportunity to defend himself. But Commissioner Tupper reminded those present that this was not a trial and no one's rights were being jeopardized, contrary to Mr. Norris' charge.

During questioning of the detective sergeant by Superintendent Jack Horton's attorney Lyle Jestly, the barrister was quick to bring out the fact that the sergeant's testimony relative to the superintendent's participation was purely hearsay. This Leatherdale readily admitted. Then Jestly, pursuing the sergeant's conversations with former mayor Charles Thompson, City Prosecutor Gordon Scott and Magistrate Oscar Orr, brought out the fact that the then prosecutor Gordon Scott had advised Leatherdale to decline the chief's offer to participate in the conspiracy involving Chief Constable Mulligan and Sergeant Cuthbert. And in a sharp exchange between the two men, Jestly implied that the Police Commission apparently didn't take too much stock in the officer's story, for did not Magistrate Orr "terminate the matter?" The detective sergeant retorted, "It wasn't terminated as far as I was concerned, even though Mr. Orr later said he investigated the matter and found no direct evidence of wrongdoing."[18]

Jestly also brought out that, although the detective's notebooks contained detailed notes of his conversations with Sergeant Cuthbert and Chief Mulligan, nowhere in this notebook was there any mention of his client, Superintendent Jack Horton, nor any reference to Horton having received illegal payments from Sergeant Cuthbert, the chief constable, or anyone else. Jestly went on to ask if Leatherdale had discussed this information with anyone else. The sergeant replied, "Yes, in 1951 when Detective Sergeant Archie Plummer took over the vice squad's gambling detail I told him the entire story[19]."

"What about more recently?" asked Jestly. Leatherdale responded, "I attended a meeting this week with City Prosecutor Steward McMorran, Superintendent Harry Whelan, Inspector John Dunn, Detective George Kitson, Sergeant Plummer, Jack Whelan and an attorney from Mr. Hutcheson's office and we discussed the case."But when pressed further, the sergeant denied that anyone had told him specifically what he was to testify to at the hearing today.

Changing his line of questioning, Jestly then asked why Leatherdale had not pursued an investigation into corruption within the Department after learning of the vice sergeant's activities. Leatherdale's response was curt. "I took the evidence I had to the Mayor, to Mr. Scott and to the Police Commission. I feel I did my duty, and I expected them to do theirs. When they didn't, I lost interest."[20]

Jestly did not pursue the matter further. However, before Sergeant Leatherdale left the witness stand, Attorney Neil Fleishman rose and asked Commissioner Tupper to subpoena former Vancouver mayor Charles Thompson.[21]

As Leatherdale left the courtroom, he looked directly at the chief constable and C.I.B. Superintendent Jack Horton, for both men had been subpoenaed to appear before the Commission and were now sitting at the head counsel table with Mulligan's attorney, Mr. Norris. Neither man, however, gave any sign of recognition of their subordinate.

The second man to take the stand was Detective Sergeant Archie Plummer. Plummer, a twenty-three year veteran Canadian police officer, began his career in 1932. He served for two years as an RCMP Constable, after one year with the Alberta Provincial Police. Now, with twenty years on the Vancouver force, assigned for the last several years with the Criminal Investigations Bureau, Plummer was an experienced and capable officer. He served in the Bunco, Fraud and Intelligence units until 1951, when he was assigned to head-up the vice squad's gambling detail, where he served until 1953. For the past two years, he had been in charge of the narcotics unit.

Plummer began by telling of his conversations regarding police payoffs with Sergeant Leatherdale, and of subsequent meetings with Sergeant Leonard Cuthbert, where he said he confronted the sergeant with Leatherdale's story. Cuthbert confirmed what the newly appointed detective sergeant had told Plummer, then dejectedly responded, "Leatherdale turned down the chief's offer to share in the gambling and bootlegging shake-down venture. He had guts enough to stand up to the chief. I only wish I'd done the same thing."

During these conversations, Cuthbert advised Plummer to "Watch for the guy in the corner." "Who are you talking about?" Plummer responded. "The chief", answered Cuthbert. "If he gets you in a corner he'll maneuver you like he did one of my men in the Chinese case." The Sergeant was referring to a Chinese bribery case investigation which went awry. "And," Cuthbert continued, "The 'Old Man' says he has everything fixed in Victoria. Lamont could give you the details if he would," referring to Detective Peter Lamont. Commission Counsel Hutcheson interrupted Plummer at this point by asking, "Sergeant, what did you finally do after you learned that this conspiracy existed within the police force?" Plummer responded, "I began my own investigation to determine the facts of the case." "Did you consult with anyone Sergeant?" asked Hutcheson. "Yes," replied Plummer, "I discussed this with City Prosecutor Gordon Scott. I gave him all the facts. Mr. Scott said that he had received the same information from another source, but it was given in confidence and he was not at liberty to act. I told him he had it from me and there were no strings attached. Mr. Scott said he would study the case and make a decision whether to charge the chief constable, Sergeant Cuthbert or anyone else."[22]

Under Hutcheson's questioning, Plummer continued his story, referring frequently to his notebook, which contained a second statement allegedly from Sergeant Cuthbert, which Plummer said he obtained in April 1953 at the time Superintendent Jack Horton was appointed as commander of the Criminal Investigations Bureau. Referring to his notes, he said the sergeant told him, "I divide with the Chief on a 50-50 percent bases and (Deputy Chief Gordon) Ambrose and (C.I.B. Superintendent) Horton each get $100.00 a month out of my 50 percent."[23]

With this testimony before the Commission, both Jestly and Norris vigorously objected on the grounds of "Hearsay Twice Removed."

However, upon cross examination by defense counsel Jestly and Norris, Sergeant Plummer stuck to his story. A heated exchange between him and Norris erupted when the Attorney again inquired why the sergeant had undertaken this investigation which, "should have been of no concern to him". The officer responded, "I was involved in a gambling and bookmaking conspiracy investigation and I believed Cuthbert and the chief's involvement was relevant to this investigation."

As Sergeant Plummer was excused, former detective Jack Whelan, brother of Uniformed Division Commander Superintendent Harry Whelan, was called to the stand. Whelan told of his background, including the years he had spent as a detective on the Vancouver force. He said he was not acting as a body guard for reporter Ray Munro or anyone else as was implied earlier by the press, but was collaborating with The Flash reporter in an investigation into corruption within the Vancouver city government. He was of particular value to Munro and the editors of The Flash due to his intimate knowledge of the inner workings of the police force. He began by accusing Chief Constable Walter Mulligan (who by now had requested and been granted a leave of absence by the Police Commission and who was again present in the courtroom) of participating in the theft of property in 1945, while the chief and Whelan were working together as detectives. He also accused the chief of having everything "fixed" for payoffs from gambling interests and said the chief constable was "on the take" and "everything was go" referring to illegal gambling and bootlegging activities within the city. Nor did he stop there. He accused city alderman Roland K. Gervin of running the largest illegal gambling operation in the city.[24]

He testified that he was also present in 1949 when Sergeant Cuthbert made arrangements to pick up money from a downtown gambling joint; and that he personally took other gamblers to the chief's office to make similar arrangements with the chief constable. He said he was later told that everything was "fixed" with the chief and "they could proceed." But the chief constable was not the only target of Jack Whelan. He described how attempts to close down Alderman Gervin's games were thwarted by "city hall" and complained that the Police Commission was totally incompetent. This latter statement was not news to many of the officers of the police department, who had on more than one occasion sought the Commission's help in eliminating corruption within the force.

The former detective said he left the force six years before and since then had been investigating corruption within Vancouver's city hall. In 1954, he said he was approached by City Prosecutor Stewart McMorran to tell all he knew of corrupt practices within the Department. McMorran told him he could "blow this thing wide open," referring to the police payoff system, if he was willing to testify in court. He claimed that in February, 1955 he was also approached by reporters from The Flash, who were conducting their own investigation of the Vancouver force, and since then he had been collaborating with reporter Ray Munro in gathering information for the articles which began appearing in the paper in May. He claimed he and Munro wrote a letter to the Attorney General describing conditions in Vancouver, and naming individuals on the Vancouver force who were participating in illegal payoffs in the city, with several gambling figures. However, before sending the letter, he gave it to his brother, Superintendent Harry Whelan. His brother told him it was very libelous and deleted one paragraph of the letter. Then the three men, he, the superintendent and Ray Munro, instead of sending the letter, arranged to meet with Bill Forst, Managing Editor of the The Province, Vancouver's largest daily newspaper. At this meeting there was a general discussion of alleged illegal activities which were occurring within the city, and both he and the reporter from Montreal outlined to Forst the results of their investigation.[25] At this point the former Vancouver officer was interrupted by Commissioner Tupper who asked, "Were you paid for this?" "Oh, no sir," replied Whelan.

As the hearing continued through July 14th and 15th, 1955, Jack Whelan was followed to the stand by a series of police officials including Records Superintendent John Fisk, Detective George Kitson, Inspector John Dunn of the Uniformed Division and finally Superintendent Harry Whelan. Fisk described to the commission the status of reported crime in the city, which was prompted by a series of questions by counsel, relative to allegations that the criminal laws of the province were not being enforced by the police department under the direction of the chief constable. The records superintendent traced the history of serious crime in the city from 1936 to 1954, without mention of prostitution, gambling or narcotic activities. He explained that even though the population during this 18 year period rose over 60 percent, from 252,000 to 395,000, there was no such corresponding increase in major crime. However before Fisk left the witness stand, Commissioner Tupper advised the superintendent to be prepared to return with information relative to the enforcement activities of the gambling, prostitution and vagrancy laws. The commissioner wanted figures on the number of arrests which had been made by the Department in recent years in these traditional vice offenses.

Detective Kitson, following Fisk, described a conversation which took place in 1949, when he was asked by his superior, Sergeant Leonard Cuthbert, to meet with him and Jack Whelan at the York Hotel. When he arrived, Kitson said he was introduced by his sergeant to Pete Wallace, a known gambler, and was advised that "arrangements had been made" to allow selected gambling operations to run without interference from the Department and that the "fix was in" with the chief. Kitson said he refused to go along with any such arrangements which would compromise his job and told his sergeant he wanted out of the gambling detail. Three weeks later, Kitson said he was transferred out of the vice unit, at which time he claimed he advised the then City Prosecutor Gordon Scott of the circumstances surrounding the offer made to him by his sergeant to participate in the payoff scheme.[26]

Police Inspector John Dunn, following Kitson to the stand, told the Commission of a conversation he had had in May 1952 with Sergeant Cuthbert relative to the elevation of Gordon Ambrose to Superintendent. Dunn said Cuthbert felt Ambrose should not have been given the promotion for he was "involved in a payoff scheme" with Cuthbert and the chief constable. Dunn said he was stunned by the vice sergeant's allegations and further by the fact that Cuthbert requested Inspector Dunn to pass that information on to Mr. Scott. Asked by counsel if he complied with Cuthbert's request, Dunn said he did and that Stewart McMorran was also present at that meeting. When queried further about Cuthbert's allegations, Dunn said he did not pursue the matter. He said he passed the information on as requested and neither Scott nor McMorran commented on it.

Changing his line of questioning, Commissioner Tupper then asked Dunn a series of rapid-fire questions ranging from morale within the force to other allegations of Vancouver officers being involved in allowing criminal activity to go unchecked within the city. He was particularly interested in prostitution and drug violations, and of the commander's thoughts on the Senate committee on drugs report, that, "The criminal code in Vancouver was not being fully enforced by the Vancouver Police Department?" Dunn responded that he could only speak for the uniformed force. He emphatically denied that there was any dereliction of duty by his men. He said, "The uniformed divisions are enforcing the prostitution and vagrancy laws to the best of our abilities, even though we are faced with some severe handicaps." Finally Tupper asked about morale. Dunn replied, that he had no complaints about morale, although he acknowledged that some of his people weren't too happy. When asked about his own morale, he replied "I can't complain."

Late in the afternoon of the fourteenth of July, the highest ranking officer yet to testify before the Commission, Superintendent Harry Whelan, head of the uniformed forces, took the stand. Whelan, 51, was a highly respected, intelligent and capable officer with over 28 years on the force, having joined the Department in 1927. He served seventeen years in the detective division after seven years with the uniformed forces. He was appointed Detective Inspector in 1946 and later in the same year returned to patrol as a watch commander. In February 1951, he was promoted by Chief Mulligan to Superintendent and headed the Criminal Investigations Bureau. He was later promoted to Deputy chief constable that same year. However, two years later, he was demoted to Superintendent and assigned to the uniformed branch, the position which he now held.

Superintendent Whelan was asked to explain his relationship with Sergeant Cuthbert and recount the details of his meeting with the sergeant the day that the officer attempted to take his own life. Whelan said he first became aware of the vice sergeant's involvement with the gambling interests through his brother, Jack and reporter Ray Munro and upon hearing the story, pressed Cuthbert for the details. On June 14th, 1955 he said he called Cuthbert into his office at noontime and told the former vice sergeant of the information he had of the chief constable's involvement with Cuthbert in a criminal conspiracy with the city's gambling interests. Whelan said the sergeant was extremely agitated and nervous and, when queried of his activities, admitted to the superintendent his involvement, naming the chief and Gordon Ambrose as fellow conspirators in collecting illegal payoffs from several gambling and bookmaking interests.[27]

The superintendent said that upon completion of the interview with Cuthbert, he made elaborate notes of the officer's admission and took a copy to City Prosecutor Steward McMorran. Ten days later, on June 23rd, at McMorran's request, Whelan again approached Sergeant Cuthbert, giving him a one-day deadline to either come forward and sign a confession relative to his involvement in the gambling-payoff conspiracy or the case, he said, would be turned over to the Attorney General and taken out of McMorran's hands. The superintendent added that, were this to happen, there was little that local authorities could do for Cuthbert.

The following day, he testified, he summoned the Sergeant back to his office at 8 A.M., at which time Cuthbert signed a confession the superintendent had prepared the evening before and a few minutes later, after returning to his own office, Sergeant Cuthbert shot himself.[28]

As the former vice sergeant's confession was about to be presented to the Commission as evidence, a barrage of objections was raised by Lyle Jestly, counsel for Superintendent Horton, Tom Norris, counsel for Chief Mulligan, and H.A.D. Oliver, representing the wounded Cuthbert who was still in Vancouver General Hospital. All three men objected to acceptance of the confession by the Commission, for Cuthbert was still alive and, they argued, he should be given the opportunity to face his accusers in open court. Besides, argued Norris, "Any such evidence is totally inadmissible for it was obtained by intimidation, threats and promises. It was purely hearsay, hearsay of the type that may do incalculable harm if admitted before the Commission." The defense counsel for the three accused men convinced Commissioner Tupper that it would be in the best interests of justice to hear from the former vice squad sergeant first hand.

It was late Thursday afternoon, now only two days into the hearings, when the Commissioner adjourned the hearing for two weeks, or until they could hear directly from the wounded officer. But before adjourning, Tupper agreed to counsel's request to subpoena several witnesses for the defense, including former mayor Charles Thompson, former alderman R. K. Gervin, City Prosecutor Steward McMorran, all members of the Police Commission, Detective Inspector Peter Lamont, eight present and four former members of the vice squad, and seven alleged local gamblers including Pete Wallace, Al Nugent and Joe Celona. As these later names were mentioned, it was quite evident that RCMP Inspector Yves-Dube and his staff, assigned to assist the Commission, would have their work cut out for them in attempting to locate some of those named and alleged to have been involved in this police gambling conspiracy.

As the Commission adjourned, news media personnel attempted, unsuccessfully, to interview the three ranking officers of the force who had been accused by their fellow constables of accepting payoffs. Tom Norris, speaking for his client, Chief Walter Mulligan, said that upon reconvening the Commission, the Chief would take the stand and would refute each and every allegation leveled at him by Superintendent Whelan and the two detective sergeants. Deputy Chief Gordon Ambrose refused comment, but Lyle Jestly, speaking for Superintendent Horton, said his client denies the accusations totally and would so testify before the Commission.[29]

On Wednesday, July 27, doctors attending the injured officer at Vancouver General Hospital agreed that the former vice squad sergeant was now fit to testify before the Commission and late on the morning of the 28th, Commissioner Tupper reconvened the Royal Commission in assize courtroom.

The wounded officer was the first and only witness summoned to testify this day. Under the careful guidance of his counsel, H.A.D. Oliver, Cuthbert began by telling of his introduction by Detective Jack Whelan to several professional gamblers and "bookmaking artists" in 1949, in downtown Vancouver. The object of the meetings between him, Whelan, Pete Wallace and other alleged gamblers was to make arrangements to allow professional gambling and bookmaking activities to operate in the downtown area without interference from the vice squad. He said he personally made arrangements between several gamblers and the chief constable to allow gambling and bookmaking activity to continue uninterrupted in several locations in the city. He also claimed some members of the vice squad's gambling detail, including Detective George Kitson, refused to go along with the plans and were transferred out of the detail. When questioned whether, as a result of these arrangements, any money changed hands, the sergeant replied that he had collected, on several occasions, sums of money ranging from $300.00 to $500.00, and had split it 50-50 with the chief constable. In addition, as a result of his agreement with the chief, on an equal number of occasions the chief gave him varying amounts of money, up to $350.00 at a time, which the chief claimed he had collected from "his friends," as he described them, but the sergeant said he was not privy to the exact source of these funds. However, he assumed that Pete Wallace and a man named Sutherland were the chief's "benefactors." When pressed for names of other Department members who were recipients of funds from these illegal sources, Cuthbert readily admitted that he split his share equally with other members of the force, but said he "could not remember their names." When queried as to whether or not he had shared these funds with Superintendent Horton or Deputy Chief Ambrose, he said, "Never". He did state, however, that Superintendent Horton had approached him requesting a cut of Cuthbert's "profits."[30]

Continuing his testimony, Cuthbert said that some weeks after be began collecting the illegal payments and making deliveries directly to the chief, Mulligan asked who Cuthbert considered trustworthy enough to head up the vice squad's liquor detail. The sergeant replied that Bob Leatherdale, a man he personally respected, should be considered. However, after Leatherdale's meeting with the chief, he later came to the Cuthbert's house to find out "just what price he would have to pay to take the promotion offered." Cuthbert said he advised Leatherdale of the chief's proposition to "shake down" bootleggers as he was doing with those involved in illegal gambling within the city. But Leatherdale was astounded by what he heard and would have nothing to do with it, declaring that if he were assigned to the vice squad, he would enforce the laws impartially in all areas of the city.

Cuthbert, continuing his testimony, claimed that in 1949, some weeks after this meeting with Bob Leatherdale, he received a call from City Prosecutor Gordon Scott, now Magistrate Scott. Judge Scott told him, that both he and the mayor were fully aware of the sergeant's involvement in the police corruption conspiracy currently under way within the police department, having been fully informed of the conspiracy by Sergeant Leatherdale. Shortly after this telephone call, at Scott's insistence, Cuthbert met with the prosecutor and Mayor Charles Thompson. After assurance from them that everything he was to tell them would be kept confidential, he told the full story of his involvement with the chief constable in a gambling-bootlegging payoff conspiracy involving several members of the force and a half dozen professional gamblers. All of these gamblers were operating out of licensed business establishments in the downtown Vancouver area.

By early afternoon, the Commission was now fully aware of the strain the injured officer was under, for the sergeant was quite pale and began to show considerable signs of tension. His testimony came in disjointed and halting sentences and he stumbled over his words, frequently repeating earlier testimony. Finally, after nearly two hours of continuous questioning, at the request of counsel, he was excused and the Commission adjourned for the day. However, he was back on the witness chair by 11A.M. the next day. He appeared much more relaxed than the day before and again, under the careful guidance of his attorney, Mr. Oliver, took up his story from the day before.

He began his testimony by telling of a visit to his house in 1951 by Detective Sergeant Archie Plummer of the gambling detail. Plummer said he was investigating a gambling-bookmaking conspiracy and it involved payoffs to members of the force. He told Cuthbert that he had been briefed by Sergeant Bob Leatherdale about the payoff problems within the Department and he wanted to confirm his predecessor's story.

After hearing Plummer out, Cuthbert confirmed Sergeant Leatherdale's account of the chief constable's involvement with other members of the Department in the illegal activity, adding, that, "Leatherdale was strong enough to stand up to the Chief; I wish I had done the same thing when I had the opportunity."

In response to a series of questions from Counsel pertaining to his recent contact with the reporter from the Montreal tabloid The Flash, Mr. Oliver guided his client through a bizarre story of fear and intimidation, unprecedented in the history of police reporting in the Vancouver area.

In the early spring of 1955, while working in the C.I.B. administrative offices, Cuthbert was approached by Ray Munro and Jack Whelan. Munro told him, "You're in serious trouble, Len." Because he had been transferred out of vice almost five years ago, Cuthbert did not immediately realize that Munro, who insisted upon meeting in private with him, was referring to his earlier problems in the gambling squad. Cuthbert gave him his home telephone number, advising the reporter to call him there after he got off work.

That evening Munro unexpectedly arrived at the sergeant's small home. Jack Whelan was with him. Cuthbert invited the two men in and asked what business they had with him. Munro, beginning the conversation, repeated the same statement he had made to the former vice squad officer at police headquarters earlier in the day, "You're in real trouble, Len, it's that 1949 business. Jack and I are fully aware that you're in a bind. We've been investigating the activities of the police force, including corruption within the city government and you're the key to making a criminal case against those involved in a gambling payoff scheme with other city officers. Those guys are collecting thousands of dollars every month in bribes from several of the city's gambling and bookmaking business locations. And you're part of it."[31]

The Officer said Munro then displayed a bundle of "official looking" papers, holding them sufficiently far enough away so the sergeant could only read the large headings at the top of the pages. The reporter said, "These are depositions, Len, which means trouble for you. These will be taken this evening to the Attorney General in Victoria unless you cooperate with me here and now."[32]

Cuthbert was worried. He was also frightened that his wife and child, who were in the next room, might overhear part of the conversation, or worse, enter the room. In order to end the conversation, he asked what his choices were. "Munro told me I had three: I could go to jail, talk to his attorney, or blow my brains out. The reporter then reached into his brief case and produced a 38 caliber automatic pistol and held it in the palm of his hand, just out of my reach."[33]

Cuthbert admitted he was by that time very distraught. He said he told Munro that he would let him know before the week was out what his choice would be. But the reporter warned him, "He said, that I had to make my decision one way or the other that night, for if I didn't, the briefcase and all its documents would be delivered to Victoria before the evening was over."

At this point, Cuthbert's counsel asked, "Sergeant, did Mr. Munro say who his attorney was?" "Yes, Neil Fleishman", responded Cuthbert. "Did Mr. Munro indicate who Mr. Fleishman was working for?", asked Oliver. "Yes", he responded, "The Attorney General."[34] With this "big lie" now before the Commission, it was obvious that a member of the press had attempted to pass himself off as conducting an official investigation on behalf of the government and was using tactics which smacked of coercion of the worst kind. Munro had encouraged an obvious emotionally distraught man to confess to his wrongdoing or take his own life.

After the journalist and Jack Whelan, the former Vancouver city detective, left his home, Cuthbert advised his wife of his current problems within the police department and of the alternatives offered to him by Ray Munro. In discussing Munro's threats at some length, they agreed that, as Magistrate Gordon Scott was fully aware of the sergeant's involvement in the vice payoff scheme, they would seek his advice.

In a phone call that evening to Scott, Cuthbert told him that what they had discussed with the Mayor in 1949, about corruption within the force, was no longer a secret and he was worried that The Flash reporter Ray Munro was a threat to him and his family. He said Scott told him to "Sit tight." Cuthbert said Scott claimed he was not aware that the Attorney General's Office was involved in an investigation of the Vancouver Police Department or with any member of the force.

The next day he went to work as usual, but was uneasy and felt sure something was very wrong. About noon, his fears were confirmed when he was called to Superintendent Harry Whelan's office and was told by him that it was, "time to bring things out in the open."

Cuthbert said he had at one time worked for Whelan and that now the superintendent said if they worked together the two of them could put this business to an end and, "put the chief constable in jail." But, warned Whelan, the sergeant would have to declare himself. He was either in or out, but if he chose not to cooperate, there would be little that he could do for him. It was at this point Cuthbert told Superintendent Whelan the full story of his involvement with the chief constable in the gambling payoff conspiracy.[35]

A day or two after this first visit with the superintendent he was again called to Whelan's office, at which time his former boss told him he wanted to pick him up that evening at his home and take him to City Prosecutor Stewart McMorran's office. Whelan said the Attorney General was coming to Vancouver the next day and once the case was taken over by the provincial authorities, Cuthbert would be on his own.

Interrupting the officer's story, Mr. Oliver asked, "Do you remember the date of this second visit to Superintendent Whelan's office?" The Detective answered, "That date will never be forgotten so far as I'm concerned. It was June 23rd, the day I decided to kill myself." Oliver, now speaking quietly, asked the sergeant to explain what happened after he left Whelan's office. He said he returned home that evening and as the events of the past week had been very upsetting to his wife, decided it would be best if the two of them went out for the evening. They attended a theater in the neighborhood, but his mind was not on the picture. He did a lot of thinking, trying to decide what alternatives were left to him. However, whatever he did, he thought ultimately, the results would be, at best, the loss of his job, and beyond that, jail.

Before leaving the theater, he said he had made up his mind what he would do, and the next morning he reported for work at 6:45 A.M. as usual. At this point Oliver interjected, "What had you decided to do?" "I had decided to shoot myself," he replied. Oliver:

"Where were you going to do this?" Cuthbert responded, "Right there in my office next to the detective parade room. But I had just barely got my hat and coat off when the superintendent entered the room and said he wanted to see me right away. I was surprised to see him at headquarters so early in the morning, but I followed him to his office."

"What happened there?" asked Oliver. At this point, Sergeant Cuthbert repeated the story heard earlier by the Commission from Superintendent Harry Whelan.[36]

Cuthbert, now in tears and testifying before a packed court room, which included many police officials and friends, said that after signing the confession presented to him by the superintendent, he returned to the detective administrative office. Once there, he requested the detective covering his desk to get him a cup of coffee; when the officer left, he took his service revolver out and shot himself.

After a short recess, which allowed the wounded man some relief, defense counsel Oliver led him through a series of questions which disclosed that Sergeant Leonard Cuthbert paid a high price for the relatively small amount of money he realized out of his illegal relationships with the chief constable and others within the police department who were connected with the professional gambling interests of the city. But the detective refused to disclose the names of those within the force, other than the chief constable, who had shared in "these profits." When asked whether or not he had distributed part of the payoff money to Superintendent Jack Horton or Deputy Chief Gordon Ambrose, as was alleged earlier by Superintendent Whelan, he denied that either had received any money from him. However, upon further questioning, he admitted that Horton had demanded a share of "the take" and had told the sergeant that "Ambrose should be included for a share." When he discussed this with Chief Mulligan, he said the chief told him he thought it was probably a good idea, but any further distribution of moneys collected would have to come out of the sergeant's share.

As on the previous day, the strain of nearly six hours on the stand was beginning to take its toll. Cuthbert looked pale and drawn and although his responses were clear, his voice was barely audible in the court room. It was now late Friday afternoon and his counsel requested that he be excused. Commissioner Tupper agreed, but advised counsel to have his client back in court on Monday morning.

Cuthbert returned to the sanctuary of Vancouver General Hospital for the weekend, but on Monday he was back to face an even more severe challenge, cross-examination.

During this examination, from outward appearances, he held up surprisingly well. There was some indication, however, that in earlier testimony he had either overlooked or forgotten a point or two which could have been considered important to the defense, but for the most part, it was evident to all that the story of corruption[37] within the Vancouver force, as told by Sergeant Leonard Cuthbert, would stand without fear of contradiction.

Notes

[1] The Vancouver Province, June 24, 1955, p. 1.
[2] Ibid. Also see Province of British Columbia, "In the Matter of the Public Inquiries Act," *Final Report of the Vancouver City Police Force Inquiry.* Victoria, B.C., February 17th, 1956, Appendix One.
[3] Inspector John C "Jack" Horton, appointed to the Vancouver Police Department in 1926, would remain supportive of the American officers in the Greenwood case throughout their investigation activities in Canada. He was born in 1904 and was respected and considered "the elder statesman" of the force by many members of the Department. At this writing, Horton, age 88, still resides in Vancouver.
[4] The Province, July 13, 1955, July 14, 1955, July 16, 1955, p. 1. Also see Testimony of Vancouver Police Detective Sergeant Leonard W. Cuthbert, pp. 60-63 in *The Final Report*, above. And testimony of Superintendent of Police Harry Whelan in *The Interim Report* of "The Royal Commission", December 31, 1955. This testimony is summarized in *The Final Report* of "The Commission," pp. 67-68.
[5] The Province, June 24, 1955, p. 1.
[6] The Royal Commission, *The Final Report*, Op. Cit., testimony of Superintendent Harry Whelan, pp. 67-68.
[7] Ibid.
[8] The Province, June 24, 1955 p. 1.
[9] Ibid.

[10] The Royal Commission Report, Op. Cit., February 17, 1956, p. 1.

[11] Robert W. Leatherdale, born in 1905, was appointed to the Vancouver Police Department in 1929 and to the rank of Detective Sergeant in 1949. Leatherdale would play a significant role in the Greenwood Bank robbery probe throughout the investigation, both in Canada and in the U.S.

[12] Ibid. See Testimony of Sergeant Leatherdale, The Royal Commission Report pp. 12-15, and p. 63.

[13] Ibid.

[14] Ibid.

[15] Ibid.

[16] Ibid.

[17] Ibid., pp. 12-15, and p. 63. Also see The Province, July 13, 1955, pp. 1, 3, 40.

[18] Ibid., The Royal Commission, *Final Report*, Op. Cit., pp. 12-15.

[19] Detective Sergeant Archibald F. Plummer, who was appointed as a Vancouver Police Officer on February 13, 1935, would later play a significant role in Canada in the Seattle Police Department investigation of the Greenwood Bank robbery.

[20] Ibid.

[21] Ibid.

[22] Ibid., testimony of Police Detective Sergeant Archie Plummer, pp. 64-65.

[23] Ibid.

[24] The Province, Op. Cit., July 13, 1955, pp. 1, 3, 40.

[25] Ibid.

[26] The Province, Op. Cit., July 14, 1955, pp. 1, 39.

[27] The Province, July 15, 1955, pp. 1, 16, 17.

[28] Ibid.

[29] The Province, Op. Cit., July 16, 1955, pp. 1, 2.

[30] The Province, July 29, 1955, pp. 1, 12, 16, 29.

[31] The Royal Commission Report, see Sergeant Leonard Cuthbert's testimony.

[32] Ibid.

[33] Ibid.

[34] Ibid.

[35] Ibid.

[36] The Royal Commission, *Final Report*, Op. Cit., testimony of Police Superintendent Harry Whelan, December 31, 1954, pp. 67-68.

[37] Unfortunately for the officers of the Vancouver police force, as in so many American cities, charges of corruption once raised are difficult to live down and few royal commissions or grand juries empaneled to investigate corruption within "city hall" are ever entirely successful in rooting out all the "bad apples" in a large public organization. As in the 1940's and 1950's, Vancouver officers were again stung by the allegation of corruption within the ranks in 1965. In the Murray Investigative Report issued in 1965, which was initiated by allega-

tions of: "Possible police involvement in a number of crimes, including the $1.2 million robbery of perforated money from Canadian Pacific Merchandising Services, two bank holdups, breaking and entering and protection payoffs." See "Fear of Leak Keeps Probe Under Wraps," The Vancouver Province July 14, 1965, p. 23.

Chapter

5

Political Response

Throughout that first week of August, 1955, following Leonard Cuthbert's testimony, Commission counsel J.G.A. Hutcheson called a series of witnesses before the royal commission, including several past and present members of the vice squad, members of the Police Commission, and he recalled John Fisk. But their testimony, some supportive, others in direct contradiction, was anti-climatic after listening to Sergeant Leonard Cuthbert's testimony over the preceding three days of the hearing. On Friday, it appeared that the testimony which was about to be offered by other witnesses to the events described by the former vice sergeant may well strengthen that which was heard earlier by the Commission from both Leatherdale and Plummer, but particularly from Leonard Cuthbert; for Superintendent Harry Whelan was scheduled to be the leadoff witness. He was to be followed by Edwin P. "Pete" Wallace, the alleged gambler. Former Mayor Charles Thompson, was also scheduled to be heard from later in the day. But as the hearing convened, Commissioner Tupper's staff were startled to learn that their first witness, Superintendent Harry Whelan, had taken his own life shortly before he was scheduled to arrive at the court house.[1]

The superintendent arose early that morning, but after getting dressed and eating breakfast, had gone into the living room and laid down on the davenport. Shortly thereafter he took his service revolver out and shot himself through the heart. At 8 A.M. he was pronounced dead at Vancouver General Hospital.

The uniformed services chief had testified before the Commission for only a few minutes on July 14th, at which time he described the events which preceded Leonard Cuthbert's attempted suicide on June 12. Due to objections by defense counsel however, he was precluded from continuing with his testimony on that date. The Commission concurring with defense counsel that Sergeant Cuthbert should be heard from in person if and when he recovered.

But even with the death of this highly respected police command officer, Commissioner Tupper wasted no time in continuing the business at hand; "Call your next witness, Mr. Hutcheson", he said. One of the principals in this alleged gambling and police payoff conspiracy, Pete Wallace, was called to the stand. But Mr. Wallace, like several others before him, had declined to accept an invitation to appear. With this, Tupper ordered the staff to locate Wallace and personally serve him with a subpoena.

Charles Thompson then took the stand. Thompson had been Mayor in 1949 when Leonard Cuthbert came to him with Magistrate Gordon Scott, at which time the story of the vice sergeant's illegal activities were discussed, including the alleged involvement by the chief constable and several other members of the force. Thompson said he had also been advised of the situation by Detective Sergeant Leatherdale. When asked by Hutcheson what action his office had taken on the matter, the former mayor said he took the story to the other Police Commission members, Magistrate Oscar Orr and Judge Ray Sargent. The three men agreed, "that something should be done," which was somewhat of an understatement for the leading elected officials in the city to make under the circumstances. However, they agreed, after discussing the case with the Attorney General, to seek the help of the Royal Canadian Mounted Police, hoping to initiate "a quiet investigation" into the allegations of corruption leveled against Department members by two experienced detective sergeants, both of whom were held responsible for overseeing the police department's investigative and enforcement role in vice related crimes in their city. Thompson said Judge Sargent went to the RCMP with a request for investigative assistance, and the Commission's request was refused outright. Later, Mayor Thompson proceeded to Ottawa and sought out RCMP Commissioner Wood and the Minister of

Justice; both, however, rejected Thompson's request on the grounds it was purely a local matter and they felt the Mounties could not get involved, for if they did, they would be faced with similar requests for assistance from local authorities all across Canada.

Mayor Thompson reported back to the Police Commission that he was not successful in obtaining help from Ottawa. The Commission members then agreed that they had little choice but to hire a professional private investigator, as suggested by the Attorney General, and thus sought the services of former RCMP sergeant Terry Parsloe. Not surprisingly, however, the Parsloe investigation turned out to be about as deficient and incomplete in uncovering corruption within the Vancouver force as the many prior investigations into corruption within city government had been. In reading Parsloe's investigative report from the witness stand, Mayor Thompson quoted: "There is not the slightest semblance of truth in the assertion that Chief Mulligan is engaged in anything illegal," and "Any suggestion that Superintendent Jack Horton, Deputy Chief Ambrose, or any Criminal Investigation Bureau inspectors could be approached is a monstrous lie." That, said the Mayor, is what was reported to him in 1950. In effect, the former RCMP officer's report completely cleared the accused members of the Department.

As the days and weeks wore on, allegations of bribery, extortion and corruption within the Department continued to be heard by the Commission. Many of these allegations were never fully explored by the Commission and some were very obviously without any foundation of fact. There were also allegations which involved several officers known to have been consorting with convicted felons. Had these allegations been believed, for example, under an internal departmental code of conduct hearing or criminal investigation, these charges could have cost several officers their jobs and may well have resulted in the filing of felony charges for either bribery, grafting, or theft against more than a dozen officers. Unfortunately the management of the police department was at this time in complete disarray and little thought was given to the internal integrity of the organization. Nor was the Prosecutor's Office inclined to pursue these matters.

Charges of using their office for private gain were leveled against Staff Superintendent, (now acting chief constable) Alan H. Rossiter and Detective Superintendent Ben J. Jelley. The list seemed endless, but finally after nearly five months of investigation into corruption within the Vancouver Department and hundreds of hours of direct testimony, Commissioner Tupper brought the first phase of the public hearing to a close.

At police headquarters, most members of the force were relieved that the pressure from the news media had slackened with the ending of the public sessions, but not everyone was satisfied. Chief Mulligan hadn't been heard from yet, and the allegations of criminal misconduct on the part of several officers not connected with the gambling interest, was of great concern to many members of the force. For testimony had been heard to the effect that some constables supplied information to those engaged in criminal activity, information on proposed police actions, which frequently abrogated weeks of police investigative effort. Allegations of "fixing cases" in the courts and outright theft of public property by some officers were also leveled against members of the Department. Inspector Peter Lamont, the present vice section commander, was singled out for allegedly having accepted money from Joe Celona and others, for corrupt purposes. But for now, it looked like there was little chance that these allegations would receive much attention from the RCMP investigative task force assigned to assist the Royal Commission, for there were "bigger fish" to worry about.

Chief Constable Walter H. Mulligan, now on voluntary leave of absence, asked the Board of Police Commissioners to fire him; he claimed the Royal Commission had destroyed his usefulness as Chief of Police. In a written statement to the Board, he preferred to be fired rather than submit a voluntary resignation, as he would then qualify for an extra fifty dollars a month on his pension. On October 25th, 1955, the three-member board, Mayor Fred Hume, Judge Ray Sargent and City Magistrate Oscar Orr, complied with the chief's request and issued a statement that, "The usefulness of the chief constable to the City of Vancouver was at an end." Mulligan was dismissed effective October 31, 1955. Superintendent Rossiter, who had been appointed Acting Chief during Mulligan's voluntary leave, would continue in this capacity.[2]

So, eight and one-half years after he was appointed as the chief constable of the largest police force in Western Canada, Walter Mulligan, following in the footsteps of several of his predecessors, was removed from office. His immediate predecessor had not been nearly as durable as Mulligan, for he survived only eighteen months, being suspended by Mayor Jerry McGeer along with the deputy chief constable and six other officers in 1947, pending an investigation of alleged improper activities involving corruption within the gambling and morality details of the vice squad. But Mulligan was no novice to police operations; prior to his appointment as chief constable, he was superintendent of the Department's Criminal Investigation Bureau and had earned a reputation as an outstanding police officer. When he was first appointed, Mayor McGeer praised his past performance and said that he was, "capable, courageous, honest and thoroughly devoted to the citizens of Vancouver." Even the news media hailed the new chief constable at the time as a "proven criminal catcher."[3] The Vancouver Province, one of the leading daily newspapers in Western Canada, in an editorial, four months after Mulligan's appointment, stated, "His youth and energy in selling his department is infectious and it may not be long before we will be regarding Vancouver's finest with pride and cooperative benevolence."[4] This, just one year before, as Sergeant Cuthbert later testified, the chief constable approached him with a proposal which would be "mutually beneficial to both," if the vice sergeant would allow certain bookmakers to operate illegally without police interference.[5] What the chief constable hadn't taken into account was the inherent honesty and integrity of the vast majority of Vancouver's officers and their reaction to offers to join his vice sergeant in "shaking down" bookmakers and bootleggers who were operating illegally within the city. Nowhere was this better demonstrated than by Sergeant Robert Leatherdale's response to the chief's proposal when he said, "Under no circumstances would he jeopardize his family's name and reputation by operating outside the law."

During this time, the American officers, assigned to the Greenwood bank robbery and murder case, followed closely the events which were occurring within the Vancouver Department and which were being reported daily in the press. During the preceding year,

FBI agents and Detective Eugene Ivey had become well acquainted with several members of the Vancouver force who were now the subject of investigation by the Royal Commission, and it was disheartening to see those officers whom they knew were trying to carry out the responsibilities of their office being smeared publicly because of the reprehensible conduct of a few of their fellow workers. But beyond this, the investigators remained noncommittal for they had no authority in British Columbia, but were in effect guests of the RCMP and the Vancouver police department, each and every time they undertook a phase of the Greenwood robbery investigation in Canada.

On December 1, 1955, in response to public and news media pressure, Commissioner Tupper issued an interim report on the, "Inquiry into Corruption Within the Vancouver Department." The Commission's published document, however, did little to remove the cloud of suspicion which hung over the officers of the Vancouver force, for it divulged little that was not common knowledge at city hall and to a majority of the news reporters who had been assigned by the local media to cover the Royal Commission's progress. The chairman, however, used this document to explain the direction in which the Commission was proceeding in its attempt to uncover the truth or falsity of the allegations leveled against members of the force and to make recommendations for change in the administrative structure of the Department. But the star witness, chief constable Mulligan, had not yet been heard from and the Commission failed to express an opinion in the interim report relative to the chief's alleged involvement in corrupt practices within the department. Mulligan, although apparently eager at first to defend himself, was seen less and less in the courtroom as the hearing progressed. Finally, when his opportunity came, the chief was nowhere to be found. He avoided service of a summons to appear and shortly after release of the interim report, he fled the country.[6] As news of Mulligan's flight reached the public, both Chairman Tupper and Attorney General Robert Bonner came under attack by several public officials and by the news media.

In Victoria, Leo Nimsick, a C.C.F.[7] member of the provincial legislature, from Cranbrook, British Columbia, was quoted as saying

Police Chief Constable Walter Mulligan, Vancouver, B.C. Police Department fled Canada to avoid prosecution and sought sanctuary in the U.S. (Photo courtesy of Vancouver Public Library)

that the inquiry into corruption within the Vancouver police department had turned into a farce, because, "The Star Witness," referring
to chief constable Mulligan, "had been allowed to fly the coop."
Nimsick criticized the Attorney General for the manner in which the
Commission conducted the inquiry, for "its indecisiveness," and for
allowing the chief constable to get away without appearing before
the Commission.[8] However, Walter Mulligan, who had by this time
quietly slipped across the border to the United States, taking up
temporary residence in Seattle (later moving on to Los Angeles), was
not talking, nor would he accept a belated invitation to return and
appear before the Commission when it resumed hearings later in the
year.

As the second public session of the Royal Commission got
underway in December 1955, defense counsel for the accused gamblers, several of the police constables and former public officials,
were quite successful in contradicting much of the earlier testimony
received by the Commission during its first session. However, it
appeared, with the former chief constable "out of town," that
Leatherdale, Plummer and Cuthbert's testimony against their former
boss would stand.

After nearly forty continuous days of public hearings in which
the Commission heard testimony from witnesses and argument from
several of their attorneys, on February 17, 1956, Commissioner
Tupper closed the inquiry into corruption within the Vancouver
police department and submitted a final report to Attorney General
Bonner in Victoria. Twelve days later, on February 29th, Bonner
released the report to the public. Of sixteen separate allegations that
were heard of alleged corrupt practices within the Vancouver police
department the Commission found all but two to be untrue and
exonerated all but two of the accused officers. But as the evidence
against Detective Sergeant Leonard W. Cuthbert and chief constable Walter H. Mulligan went, "uncontroverted," the Chairman of the
Commission reported, in his opinion, "The Sergeant had accepted
monies as bribes to dissuade him from his duty as a police officer."[9]
In reference to the chief constable, Tupper reported, "In my opinion,
W. H. Mulligan, in the year 1949, corruptly accepted monies as
bribes given for the purpose of dissuading him from pursuing his

duty as chief constable in the Vancouver police department and accepted by him with that understanding."[10]

Nor did Tupper take lightly the fact that the chief constable refused to face his accusers, as he reported, "While recommendations following opinions relating to the enforcement of the Criminal Code in the City of Vancouver and the administration of the Vancouver Department were included in the interim report dated December 31, 1955, in accordance with the directions in my commission, I take it to be improper to make any recommendations upon the opinion I have expressed upon allegations of corruption in the Vancouver police department. In one sense the enforcement of the law is the duty and is within the power of every subject who may on his own information and complaint bring before the courts any person he charges with the commission of a crime. Wisely I think, we usually leave it to the law officers of the Crown where a serious crime is suspected, which by its nature or by its consequences might be a crime against us all, to determine the course to be pursued upon the evidence before them. Therefore, I say no more than would be said by any person sharing my opinion that two police officers have engaged in corrupt practices, one, and the junior of them, stood to face and admit the allegations against him; the other did not."[11]

In referring to the other eight members of the gambling squad, Tupper although not accepting the premise that no complicity existed between Sergeant Cuthbert and these men, stated that, "As adequate evidence of proof of conspiracy was not forthcoming, (during these hearings) therefore we must find, "that these allegations are untrue."

And so the inquiry ended; the findings of the Royal Commission remained front page news for a few days, but soon the press turned its attention to other matters which would catch the eye of the public. After all, from the Commission's report, the press had given the public an insight into the "dirty linen" of the police department and had wrung from it all that they could in order to sell their wares; surely that would satisfy most of those who were demanding that the government "do something," referring to the alleged corruption within the Vancouver city government. Even though Tupper had briefly mentioned in the interim report and again in the final report, specific problems which plagued the administration of the police department and the Department's failure to respond to the ever-increasing crime problem, little mention was made of this in the press. In 1954, over 30,000 separate criminal complaints were recorded by the Department. Fifteen thousand of these were reported as Class I or serious crimes; yet criminal suspects were arrested and the cases "cleared," in less than eight percent of the cases. Ninety-two percent of the felony cases of murder, rape, robbery, larceny, burglary, aggravated assault and auto theft, which were reported to the Vancouver police department, went unsolved.[12]

Although these figures were little noticed by the general public, many Vancouver officers were stung by this obvious public disclosure of their own inefficiencies, for even the most poorly administered police departments in Canada were able to solve at least a quarter of the major crimes reported to them. Beyond this, most Vancouver police department officers were proud that they wore the police uniform, but many were disappointed that the Royal Commission had not been more forceful in uncovering the truth of allegations of corruption in areas other than just within the police department's vice squad. It was not their wish that police officers would be charged based upon unsubstantiated evidence; but they knew that evidence existed of other corrupt police and public officials, evidence which was never aired during the public hearings of the Commission, and evidence which was completely ignored in the final report to Lieutenant-Governor Ross.

Vancouver officers knew that corruption within the police department could not have existed without the tacit, if not active, support of their elected officials, both judicial and legislative, in the highest levels of government. The officers had good reason for this belief as the pattern of corruption of civil officials in British Columbia was well known. But, as in the investigation into police corruption in Vancouver in the mid-thirties and again in 1947 and now in 1956, those who were to pay the price for their misconduct would be police officers, not the elected official.

Nor did the officers accept the fact any more than did Commissioner Tupper that Sergeant Leonard Cuthbert and the chief constable were the only officers involved in "shaking down" members of the

Vancouver underworld for financial favors. For the Department had lost too many criminal cases in court because of "misplaced subpoenas" or "missing evidence" from the property room; or through the appointment of pro tem judges who frequently, yet surreptitiously, dismissed cases for "lack of evidence." And it didn't end there, for it was a well-known fact that besides "fronting" for known felons, a practice common with some of their local RCMP colleagues, corruption was common if not pervasive through out upper management of the Department and within both city and provincial governments. Gratuities were commonly accepted by the cop on the street and by their supervisors. However less visible, the widespread practice of police "favoritism" shown to selected police clients had a much more insidious effect on the administration of justice in the city of Vancouver than the indiscretions of the lower ranking beat cop. For at the street level, several officers had become little more than "ambulance chasers" for attorneys and bail bondsmen, channeling business to their favorite barrister or bond agent for a fee. All of this was condoned by the Department's management staff with little thought of what these gratuities were costing the Vancouver taxpayer.

Even though the officers knew that their department must bear the brunt of any allegation of a breakdown in the law enforcement system, it was difficult for them to accept this, when others outside their profession, but just as culpable, escaped unscathed. For this reason alone, several members of the Department escaped detection; for as much as the majority wanted to be rid of those who brought discredit upon all of them, few would be willing to risk their careers without assurance that those management personnel responsible, both inside and outside the Department, would be required to answer for their involvement in "this payoff system."

And so it was over. Some called the Royal Commission's findings a complete whitewash of the Vancouver Department; others said the Royal Commission was a "red herring" and accomplished little other than to further the political career of those connected with the Commission. This criticism was neither complimentary nor descriptive of the problems encountered by the Commission. Although there was little direct evidence of wholesale corruption within the Department that was aired in public hearings, enough light was shed

George Archer, the former RCMP Vancouver Detachment Commander selected as the new Chief Constable to replace Walter Mulligan who fled to the U.S. Archer took office in January 1956. (Photo courtesy of Vancouver Public Library)

upon the police department's problems through the hearings, to awaken the city fathers to the fact that corrective action was necessary. Some city council members recognized that greater attention to the Department's ever-increasing and often perplexing role in the enforcement of the Criminal Code was necessary. This need was most evident in the area of gambling enforcement, where the enforcement policy changed almost with the wind, dependent upon which group was most successful in exerting its influence on city hall.

Nor had the city fathers met their obligation as public employers to look after the training and welfare of their officers. Training for the new officer was minimal and funds to support ongoing or refresher courses for older officers were nonexistent. Thus, although sound policy decisions were frequently conceived, had they been understood and implemented by police department management, the breakdown in the administration of the force could have been prevented. Few denied the fact that the city fathers failed in their responsibilities to the Department. This was most notable when one looked at the salaries earned by the city constables. This was also brought home to the police commissioners and the public, when the chief constable asked the commissioners that he be fired, rather than resign, in order to collect fifty dollars a month more on his retirement.[13] The constable on the street made less than the day laborer and were almost on par with the garbage men; yet they were required to work odd shifts and most weekends, holidays and overtime without extra compensation. Nor was there any great reason to seek advancement through the ranks, as there existed little differential in pay from rank to rank. Tupper took little note of these deficiencies in the Department in the Royal Commission's final report. There was, however, little doubt, not only that corruption existed at all levels of the Department, but also that it permeated the entire political structure of the city and even tarnished the enviable reputation of Canada's finest in the RCMP. It was equally clear that the Vancouver "city fathers" who escaped their responsibilities thus far were as culpable as their chief constable.

During the difficult months of the Commission's inquiry into corruption within the Department, former Staff Superintendent Alan Rossiter, sitting in as Acting chief constable, held the Department together only because he was supported by several able commanders of his choice, all of whom were anxious to put this history of crooked cops and venal city politicians behind them. The police commissioners continued their search for a replacement for the chief constable, with George Archer, the former RCMP Vancouver detachment commander, eventually being selected as the new chief constable, taking office in January, 1956.[14]

Vancouver Citizens turn out to honor two of "Vancouver's finest," Constables Charles Boyes and Oliver Ledingham killed in the line of duty by bank robbers. (Photo courtesy of Vancouver Public Library)

The Royal Commission cut a deep swath through the Department; Mulligan was gone and Archer, within weeks, appointed a few new members to his command staff and these in turn selected new staff personnel and reassigned many mid-management and lower staff officers throughout the Department. Although Paddy Sherman, publisher of the influential daily newspaper The Vancouver Province, was later to describe the Royal Commission hearings as a "travesty," the hearings brought a much needed change in the operation of the force.

In Seattle, Homicide Captain Charlie Rouse, following closely the stories of corruption within the Vancouver Department, knew that the adverse publicity directed at the Canadian officers could seriously hinder the progress of the combined S.P.D.- F.B.I. investigation in Canada of the Greenwood bank robbery, the murder of Officer Frank Hardy, and the shooting of Sergeant Howard Slessman and Officer Vernon Chase. Yet Rouse who, before his career ended, would also be charged with corruption in a yet-to-be-uncovered gambling and police payoff scandal that would rock the very foundation of the Seattle Police Department, a pattern of corruption and political intrigue not dissimilar to that which the citizens of Vancouver British Columbia had just witnessed.

Notes

[1] The Province, August 5, 1955, pp. 1, 3, 13, 44.
[2] The Province, October 25, 1955, p. 1.
[3] The Province, January 1, 1947, p. 1.
[4] The Province, April 30, 1947, p. 13.
[5] The Royal Commission, *Final Report*, Op. Cit., testimony of Detective Sergeant Leonard W. Cuthbert, February 17, 1956, pp. 60-63.
[6] The Province, February 8, 1956, p. 1.
[7] Co-operative Commonwealth Federation Party.
[8] Ibid.
[9] The Royal Commission, *Final Report*, Op. Cit., p. 207.
[10] Ibid., pp. 207-208.
[11] Ibid.

[12] Ibid., p. 211. Also see City of Vancouver Police Department Annual (statistical) Crime Report, 1954.

[13] The Province, April 30, 1955, p. 1.

[14] G. M. "Joe" Swan, "A Century of Service - The Vancouver Police 1886 - 1986, Vancouver Historical Society and Centennial Museum, Vancouver, British Columbia, Canada, 1986, pp. 82, 93. George Archer did much over the next several years to professionalize the Vancouver police; he remained in office until 1962.

Cook, 7 Other Policemen Named in Testimony

Officer Says He Tried to Halt Payoffs

By DEE NORTON
and LOU CORSALETTI

3 Admit Taking Police Payoffs, Name Others

Assistant Chief Fuller on Stand

Councilman Carroll Linked to Payoffs

By DEE NORTON
and LOU CORSALETTI

Wall Street Final

Today's Dow Jones close: up 0.62. | Complete Markets

The Seattl

Former Chief Lawrence Implicated

Two Admit Taking Payoffs as Policemen

By DEE NORTON
and LOU CORSALETTI

Mystery Money Left Mayor's Office: A Trap

Cook Perjury Trial

Testimony Linking Chief To Payoffs Inadmissible

By DEE NORTON
LOU CORSALETTI

No Action Taken to Stop Shakedowns, Says Officer

By DEE NORTON
and LOU CORSALETTI

Grand Jury May Resume Crime Probe

M'Cullough Dismissal Is Opposed

P.I. 4/14/70

Chapter

6

The Informant

With the change in the administration of the Vancouver police department, the American investigators, both in Seattle and in Canada, hoped to establish improved working relationships with their colleagues in the Canadian city. To date, they had experienced not only indifference, but in some cases open hostility from the Vancouver city officers. They knew they needed to obtain some solid evidence in Canada from the Canadians that Clifford Dawley, John Wasylenchuk and possibly Bobby Talbot were the men they wanted for the murder of Officer Frank Hardy and the wounding of Sergeant Howard Slessman and Officer Vernon Chase. Thus far, however, in British Columbia, the investigators believed they had been deliberately thwarted by the Canadians at nearly ever step of the investigation. But despite that, the Americans had still been able to make some headway in this investigation; they disproved Clifford Dawley's alibi and discredited RCMP Corporal Ernest Nuttall's report that "John Wasylenchuk could not have been a participant in the robbery."[1] Furthermore,their investigation disclosed that Corporal Nuttall's criminal "friend," The Farmer planned to make a "big score in the States" and had in his possession prior to the Seattle robbery, false plastic noses and horn-rimmed glasses, similar to the ones used by the three robbers in the U.S. The investigators also found that the coat "George" left behind at the scene of the robbery was made in Canada and they traced it to a cleaning shop in Vancouver, although they could not as yet tie it to any of their three robbery suspects.

In addition, the officers, with the identification of Dawley, were quick to note that the disability of his left hand matched that of the number one robbery suspect as observed and described by the bank manager. The affliction was such that they believed it would be very difficult for a person to put on a pair of gloves. Yet this, too, was best described as circumstantial. The officers also determined that shortly before the stickup in Washington, John Wasylenchuk had fallen and injured himself and was seen to have had an abrasion on his left cheek, prior and subsequent to the March 12, 1954 robbery. The abrasion was similar to the one and one-half inch scar seen by several witnesses on the number three man's face. Seattle Detective Eugene Ivey and the FBI agents also identified two Canadian law enforcement officers, who had assisted on more than one occasion, in setting up bank robberies in Western Canada in the past and, for a price, also had provided false alibis for the criminals involved. Now the two officers, one a Mountie and the other a Vancouver city detective, were providing alibis for two of their suspects for the day that three Seattle officers were gunned down in that city. Still there was no direct physical evidence linking any of the three principal suspects to the Greenwood case nor was there any direct evidence which the Americans could use to tie the two Canadian Officers to the Seattle crime.[2]

Agent Dean Rolston was considered, by most Seattle police detectives who knew him, to be one of the most skilled investigators in the Seattle FBI office. He regularly taught classes on interrogation and criminal investigation for local law enforcement agencies and was an occasional instructor in the Seattle Police Academy. He had a razor sharp mind and a tongue to match, which may have been part of the problem in Canada in obtaining the full cooperation of the Canadian authorities. For when he learned that two Canadian officers were "fronting" for two of the chief suspects in this case he made his suspicions known both to the Vancouver authorities and to the RCMP. First, he informed RCMP Sergeant Edward Murton, then talked directly to Murton's boss, RCMP Regional Commander George Archer. But the more Rolston insisted that Corporal Ernest Nuttall was "covering" for Wasylenchuk, the more defensive the Canadians became. He could see that no matter what evidence was laid before the Canadian police they were not about to admit that "one of their own" would act illegally, particularly an RCMP officer. Finally, one day after several hours of haggling, one of the Mounties told FBI agents that, had the Seattle police not been made aware of "this situation," referring to the allegation of collusion by the Canadian officers, the Mounties could have reached a "mutually agreeable decision" with the FBI, which would have given the Americans what they wanted and still protected the reputation of the RCMP and the Vancouver police department. But as things stood today, there was no way the Canadians would "turn on one of their own" without being forced to do so.[3]

By February, 1956, it appeared little else was to be gained by the American officers in Canada, as solid evidence against the holdup trio was not forthcoming in the Greenwood case, the officers returned to Seattle. What leads were to come in from Canada would be checked out by the resident FBI agent, stationed at Bellingham, Washington, just a short distance from the Canadian border.

With the return of the agents to the U.S., Richard D. Auerbach, Special agent in charge of the Seattle FBI office, again appealed to the public for information which may have been overlooked or forgotten by witnesses to the events surrounding the 1954 robbery and murder at the Seattle First National Bank. No response came forth from the community. Meanwhile in Canada, shortly after the departure of the American officers, John Wasylenchuk was captured after robbing a bank in Burnaby, a Vancouver suburb. He subsequently received a life sentence for this crime, only to escape from custody shortly thereafter. His escape was short-lived; he was recaptured on March 14, 1956. After repeated court appearances, he received a two year sentence for the escape, with the sentence to run consecutively with the life term previously imposed.[4]

On January 30, 1956, Clifford Dawley had been recaptured, this time in Toronto, Ontario after his earlier escape[5]. He was soon to be sentenced in British Columbia to a seven year term on the multiple charges of escape, auto theft and possession of burglary tools. (Earlier, Wasylenchuk's colleague, Maurice "Bobby" Talbot's luck also ran out, for on November 15th, 1955 he was sentenced to seven years in the penitentiary for the illegal sale of narcotics, resulting from his arrest in New Westminster, British Columbia that same year.)[6]

With the three principal suspects in custody in Canada and both FBI and Seattle officers having exhausted all known leads, the case appeared to be destined for the "losers file" in Captain Charlie Rouse's office—the name given to those cases which ended up in the unsolved homicide case files. During the next several months, nothing of substance was added to the case by Seattle detectives. Although every officer on the street continued to carry the three suspects' "mug shots" in their patrol cars and the details of the 1954 robbery were frequently discussed, for all practical purposes the investigation was at an end. The investigation by Rolston and other agents of the FBI had met with a similar fate. Fridays continued to be the day when most bank robberies occurred in the city, and the unsolved Greenwood case convinced bank robbers that Seattle was a likely target.[7] Detective Gene Ivey was assigned other cases, but he couldn't forget the Greenwood assignment; he believed that someday the pieces of that case would come together, if only the officers were allowed enough time and money to continue the investigation in Canada.[8] But current cases in the city now took precedence, and little time was available to contemplate the possible outcome of a case, which no longer could claim a high priority for investigative man hours.

Although Captain Rouse retained the highest respect for the FBI, he was disappointed that the Bureau had not been able to build a case against the three Canadian suspects.[9] He also was well aware that, without a continuing investigative effort in Canada by the FBI, there was little hope that this crime would be solved. Through 1956 and on into 1957, little worthwhile information on the case was uncovered, but in August, 1957, a faint hope of a solution was offered when, in California, the Los Angeles Police uncovered a narcotics ring, which had connections with the Vancouver underworld. Their main suspect had formerly lived in Vancouver and, it was rumored, he was the principal figure in the trafficking of narcotics in that city prior to 1955. This was the same man who had reportedly provided John Wasylenchuk with weapons for a job whenever needed. The man had left Vancouver in August, 1954, after being pistol-whipped by the opposition in the narcotics wars. It was believed that one of the Talbot brothers was the principal participant in this assault; a crime which was not reported to the police by the victim. The Los Angeles police were not successful in obtaining additional information which would be of help in solving the Greenwood case and this lead was eventually written off.[10]

It was not until early November, 1958 that the first real break came in the case. U.S. Postal Inspector Fred Worthington in Seattle notified Captain Rouse that a Canadian criminal, Irvin Terrance Lester Teague, claimed to have information on the Greenwood case and was willing to talk to Seattle Police about it for a price. Teague's home was in Vancouver, and he was well acquainted with many Canadian criminals, having served time in both Oakalla Prison and the British Columbia Penitentiary for burglary, robbery and theft. He was being held in the King County Jail in Seattle, charged with cashing stolen Canadian postal money orders in Washington, Oregon and California. In order to save his own skin, Teague "fingered" several Canadians who were passing the stolen postal money orders in the three western states, and he furnished detailed information on the subjects involved in the theft of the stolen documents. The information was determined to be extremely accurate and resulted in criminal indictments of several of the suspects. Teague pleaded guilty on the charges of possession of stolen documents and forgery for his part in cashing the money orders; as a result he was sentenced to eight years in the federal penitentiary at McNeil Island.

On November 10, he was interviewed in the King County Jail in Seattle by Rouse, and agents Rolston and Chet Crisman. Teague was a medium-sized man, 31 years old with a muscular build, and had hazel-gray eyes which matched the pallor of his skin. Immediately after the interview began, he told the officers that his price for information was not money; but he would talk, on the condition the officers promised to notify the U.S. probation officer assigned to his case that he had been cooperative with the police and the Bureau in their investigation. He further insisted that his identity be kept confidential, for he feared for his life if it became known that he had supplied information on the identity of the killers in the Greenwood case.

Teague at first tried to be evasive in answering the officer's questions, in an apparent attempt to see if he could furnish incomplete or misleading information without specifically naming a participant in the Seattle robbery. The officers, however, were quick to point out to him that what he had told them thus far did not jibe with the facts of the investigation as they knew them to be, and unless he got down to business and told a straight story, they would have nothing further to do with him. Upon seeing that the officers meant business, the prisoner admitted that he had not been straightforward with them because he said if it became known that he was the one who "fingered" the participants in this case, he believed he would be killed.

After being reassured that the source of the information would be kept confidential, Teague told a story that the officers had waited four and one-half long years to hear. Teague said that his story came directly from John Wasylenchuk, while the two of them were cellmates in 1956 in the British Columbia penitentiary. During that time, he, Wasylenchuk, Clifford Dawley, Charles Talbot and Bobby Lewis were all housed in the same cell block and The Farmer's cell was on the same tier right next to his. Wasylenchuk and he became very close during this time, as prisoners who are confined together frequently do, and one night shortly before Teague was released, his friends smuggled a bottle of whiskey into the prison for him. Because Wasylenchuk had given him some leads on who to contact when he got out the following month, he claimed he decided to share the whiskey with the stickup artist.

Teague said that the two of them drank the entire bottle that night and, as the evening wore on, they began to reminisce of past jobs in which they had participated. The Canadian stated that his drinking partner admitted to being involved in two bank robberies in Edmonton, Alberta and after their discussion of these incidents, The Farmer becoming quite talkative, admitted to having been involved in at least eight or ten other bank robberies, either as an actual participant, or he planned the jobs, which were then carried out by his associates. Wasylenchuk admitted, according to Teague, that he had "capered" with the Talbot brothers and Bobby Lewis. Teague, in recalling this part of the conversation, said he told The Farmer that he thought Bobby Talbot had a lot of guts, because he knew he had robbed the Treasury Bank in Edmonton, Alberta. Hearing this, he said his cell-mate responded: "I set up that robbery and went in on it with Talbot and Bobby Lewis. We got $28,000.00 on the job".

Teague said the holdup man went on to discuss other western Canadian bank robberies in which he had participated, and that Clifford Dawley's name came up frequently in the conversation. Teague told Wasylenchuk that, from what he had heard about Cliff Dawley, he wouldn't want to tangle with him because of the man's reputation of being too quick to use a gun, and that in Seattle in 1954, a cop had been killed in a bank robbery. Teague recalled that, upon hearing this, Wasylenchuk at first appeared to be surprised that his fellow prisoner knew of Cliff Dawley's involvement in the Seattle crime, yet he continued to confide in him, responding, "The Seattle job was mine and there was no need for the killing, Cliff got excited and began shooting when the cops arrived. I fired a couple of rounds myself, but only to scare them away. I didn't think they'd be so brave after being shot at."[11]

Wasylenchuk claimed that he had planned the Seattle robbery as he "owed his partner a favor." Dawley was facing a life sentence on a habitual criminal charge, if caught, and he needed the money to hide out in eastern Canada. Teague said his cell-mate claimed that they had made plans to "hit" two banks in a row, the first in Seattle and then a bank in Eugene, Oregon. For in addition to Dawley's needs, Wasylenchuk's expenses were such that, unless they "scored" heavily in Seattle, they would not have sufficient funds to take care of both of them.

The robber also claimed that he was instrumental in both of Cliff Dawley's escapes from Oakalla prison and that, "It cost me over a grand each time to get the 'right people' at the penitentiary to 'look the other way' during the escapes."[12] He recounted that after Dawley's first escape in March, 1954, just a few days before the Seattle robbery, the man hid out with the Talbot brothers. Wasylenchuk also professed, according to Teague, referring to Seattle that, "In addition to the necessary bribes, I took care of all the expenses involved. I planned and financed both the Seattle and our proposed Eugene robberies. But I scrapped the Oregon job because of the heat generated by the killing of the Seattle cop.[13] According to Teague, Wasylenchuk did not elaborate on who were the recipients of the monies allegedly paid out in bribes.

He said that Bobby Talbot was the third man on the job, and that when the cops showed up outside the bank during the robbery, Talbot dived through a bank window, right through the glass. According to Teague, The Farmer stated that, two or three days before the Seattle robbery, Bobby Talbot and his common-law wife, Jackie, went to Seattle and stayed in the Blue Bird Motel, which was just a few miles south of the city. Talbot stole a set of license plates and the 1952 Oldsmobile which was used in the robbery. Teague mentioned that his cell-mate bragged that he always insisted upon using a high-powered Oldsmobile for a getaway car in robberies, as there wasn't a better automobile suited for that type of activity, "I've used an Oldsmobile in every bank we've hit, and I'm usually the 'wheel man,' but in the Seattle job, Talbot drove, as he was more familiar with the city and had planned the getaway route."[14]

Continuing his recollection of the prison conversation, he said The Farmer had selected Seattle for the robbery because Dawley was so "hot" in western Canada that he couldn't show his face on the street in any Canadian city. Because of this, before they crossed the border Wasylenchuk had to drop Dawley off at a farmhouse some distance from the Blaine, Washington port of entry; his partner then made his way on foot through an open field, crossing into the United States. Wasylenchuk crossed the Washington border at Blaine, then picked up his accomplice and the two of them drove to the motel in Seattle, arriving the night before the robbery. There they quietly slipped into the Talbots room unnoticed by the management. Teague again quoting the stickup man, said, "Upon our arrival at the motel, Bobby Talbot and his wife had already obtained the getaway car and license plates and laid out the escape route from the bank, which was to be followed the next day. Each of us had our own gun. I was driving the third car, I had borrowed it from a friend of mine in Vancouver for the return trip to Canada. After the stickup, Dawley was to proceed to Detroit alone and I was to meet him there later."[15]

Teague couldn't remember what The Farmer, or "J.W.," as he frequently referred to his former cell-mate, said about his accomplice's travels to Detroit, other than that he recalled him saying that his partner caught a train out of a nearby town immediately after the robbery. But, regarding this event, Teague was not sure of the exact details of the conversation, reminding the officers that the conversation between him and John Wasylenchuk had occurred over two years ago.[16]

During the next few weeks, Rolston accompanied by either Crisman or Special agent William J. Drescher and Captain Rouse, returned several times to the county jail to re-interview the federal prisoner. Each interview provided the officers with a better picture of the events surrounding this case, both preceding and following the actual robbery. Their informant had great difficulty in recalling either the name of the motel or that of the motel manager where the three robbers had stayed in Seattle. However, he remembered Wasylenchuk stating that after the robbery it had cost him an extra thousand dollars for the motel because of the killing of the officer, indicating that the motel people were either in on the concealment of the subjects, or were aware that at least the Talbots had participated in the crime.

In early January, 1959, the federal prisoner was transferred from the county jail to McNeil Island Federal Penitentiary in lower Puget Sound, and on January 8th, Rouse, Rolston and Crisman visited him there. The prisoner, after arriving at McNeil Island, had been able to be by himself for a long period of time and had plenty of opportunity to reflect back on his conversations with his former cell-mate in Canada. He mentioned to the officers that this facility, with its spacious housing conditions, was a great improvement over the continual hubbub and confusion which existed in the "tank", where he was housed while confined in the King County Jail. As a result, he said he now remembered the name of the owner of the motel which Wasylenchuk had mentioned. He had thought about a woman, an acquaintance of a bootlegger by the name of Ed Werner, and recalled that the owner of the motel had the same name. The "bootleg joint" was just outside the city limits of Edmonton, and the owner's friend was a good looking, sexy gal. That's why he went there.

He also recalled his former colleague mentioning that, during the robbery at the Greenwood Bank, Talbot had dropped a large amount of money on the floor of the bank. He said his young partner was shocked that the police had arrived, before they made their getaway; but "J.W." did not appear to be upset by the loss of the money stating, "That's the breaks of the game."

After obtaining as much information as the prisoner could or would relate to the officers of his conversation with John Wasylenchuk about the 1954 robbery, the officers informed Teague they wanted to know everything that the prisoner knew of the alleged involvement of Canadian officers or other public officials in Canada, who were fronting for criminals in the Vancouver area.

The Americans were unsure of where this question was going to lead, but they wanted to know who was providing alibis for criminals in the lower British Columbia mainland area, and who was setting up business places to be burglarized or robbed, as ostensibly Canadian police were involved. Teague's response, was not entirely unexpected. He said, "I was told by more than one con that at least two cops, one a Vancouver City Police Inspector and the other an RCMP Constable, would 'set up a score' for selected friends, and provide alibis for these same people when needed. I discussed this at length with Wasylenchuk and he told me of the activities of both of these officers while we were in the pen and that a B.C. cop had prior knowledge of his plans to hit a bank in Seattle. This same officer was described to me by Wasylenchuk as the 'fixer.' He said he was a central figure in the PD as he believed the man held a key position in the Vancouver police department. He claimed the reason this officer was so successful was that he was in a position to divert police units from a given area any time a crime was being committed; the diversion arranged by the officer, working in collusion with the police radio dispatchers."[17]

The prisoner told the investigators that he too had become personally aware of the Vancouver officer's activities long before meeting John Wasylenchuk in prison, alleging that, in 1952, two city police detectives tried to talk him into burglarizing the Vancouver Sun Building. During that conversation, the officers mentioned that they would have to "take care of the fixer," again referring, he assumed, to their fellow officer. Teague said it was this same "fixer" who allegedly provided Bobby Talbot with an alibi in the Greenwood Bank case; and the man took a 25 percent cut of the monies obtained in these illegal ventures.[18]

When queried about the suggested burglary of the Sun Building, Teague claimed that even though there was supposed to be over $100,000.00 available in the building, he told the detectives, "I can't do it, the risks are too great and besides it would take more than one guy and I usually work alone." (Although Teague frequently worked alone, he was often involved with others in criminal activity, as was the case which lead to his most recent arrest and conviction on forgery charges in Seattle).

Returning to the investigator's primary objective, in response to a question from Rouse, Teague recalled that the bank robber, in addition to the motel people, had to, "take care of a Mountie by the name of Nuttall," who provided the holdup man with an alibi for the time of the Seattle robbery. He couldn't remember the exact figure mentioned by his former cell-mate, but thought it was either $2,500.00 or $3,000.00. Wasylenchuk alleged that this was worked out with the officer through a Vancouver police detective, noting that the Mountie felt better about dealing with the detective, rather than directly with Wasylenchuk, particularly since he was aware that Wasylenchuk planned to rob a bank in Seattle.

After Lester Teague's release in Canada in December, 1956, he said he made contact with Corporal Nuttall and became fairly well acquainted with his activities. Teague was a neophyte stickup man, but a professional when it came to breaking into buildings, specializing in the burglary of post offices and the forging of postal money orders.[19] He claimed he had been solicited by the Mountie to burglarize a post office substation on East Hastings Street in Burnaby; and that the Mountie told him that he could furnish Teague with a list of the RCMP patrol schedules for that part of the municipality, thus assuring that he would have ample time to enter through the roof, "punch" the safe and get out before the next patrol.[20] He said that this same Mountie had set up the burglary of Gripps Pharmacy on Granville Street, across from the Belmont Hotel. It was this burglary that lead to Teague's undoing, as the postal money orders he was passing in Washington came from this pharmacy.

On June 7, 1958, 534 postal money orders and $5,600.00 in cash was taken from the post office substation at that location. On July 31, Teague cashed several of these in Seattle en route down the west coast of the U.S. and his confederates cashed others in cities from Vancouver to Los Angeles and as far east as Salt Lake City. He "fingered" all of his colleagues on this venture for the postal authorities in order to win his own freedom, or at least to shorten the time he would have to spend in prison.[21]

In continuing his conversation with the officers, the prisoner reported that The Farmer felt confident that he and his partners were safe from the U.S. authorities, in that in addition to their alibis, no one could identify any of them, as they all wore horn-rimmed glasses and false plastic noses and, "The Fraser had the guns." Here, indicating with a wave of his hand, which Teague understood to mean that the stickup men had thrown the guns into a body of water, possibly the Fraser River, which flowed through lower British Columbia near the penitentiary.

Teague recalled that his fellow prisoner told him that, after the robbery, he was to meet Cliff Dawley in Detroit and both would then cross over into Canada from there. But Teague couldn't remember the name or location of the hotel where the two criminals were to meet in the Michigan city.

At the conclusion of the interview with this burglar and forgery artist, the officers were elated. For the first time in four years, they felt they now possessed enough information, that if it could be substantiated to a considerable degree, they would be in a position to present it to the U. S. Attorney for Western Washington, with a request for indictment of John Wasylenchuk, Clifford Dawley and Bobby Talbot by the Federal Grand Jury. But having worked with hardened criminals for several years, Rouse, as well as the FBI agents, was well aware that this prisoner may well be inclined to tell a story which would reflect favorably upon himself, in the hope that the officers would pass this information on to his parole officer. They knew there were bound to be several loopholes in the story. And they had heard a dozen stories before this one about crooked cops, not only from ex-cons, but from citizens in all walks of life. They were well aware that honest and aggressive police officers were frequently maligned publicly in an attempt to discredit an officer's testimony or to render him less effective within his own organization. But Teague's story appeared to be good; Rouse and the agents had questioned the convict several different times over a period of weeks and basically he told the same story each time. As Captain Rouse was very familiar with the 1955 investigation into the corruption of the Vancouver police department and of the Royal Commission's findings relative to the subject of police corruption within that city, he was inclined to believe that Lester Teague was telling the truth. But he knew corroborating the story would be difficult.

Before leaving the island prison, Rouse showed the convict photographs of several Canadian criminals, including those of the three principal suspects in the Seattle case. The prisoner, without hesitating, correctly identified all of these men.[22]

Upon their return to Seattle from the federal penitentiary at McNeil Island, the officers began a two pronged approach to uncover additional evidence which could lead to a verification of the prisoner's statements. Detective Andrew Zuarri and Donald Waters, who had been assigned earlier to check locally on the ownership of the Blue Bird Motel, had their report available for Rouse upon his return to the city. The FBI agents, now armed with Teague's story, returned to Vancouver where they contacted Wasylenchuk's former associates, again confronting them at the British Columbia Penitentiary in an attempt to obtain an admission from them, something they had failed to obtain in previous interrogation sessions.

In Seattle, Rouse got off a letter to the chief constable at Edmonton, Alberta regarding Ed Werner, and on January 31, 1959, he received the following police report which tended to support Teague's story:

27 Jan. '59
Seattle police department H. J. Lawrence, Chief Const.
Attn: Captain C. A. Rouse

1.On 27 Jan. '59, correspondence was received by this department from Chief Constable H. J. LAWRENCE, SEATTLE police department, Washington, U.S.A, with regards to information concerning one Edward WERNER, Ed. Photo. #L2965, FPS # 665269.

2.Information is requested concerning whether or not WERNER was engaged in the unlawful sale of liquor in this city some time prior to 1955.

3.It can be definitely established that WERNER was engaged in such operations prior to 1953, while residing in a residence on the Calgary Highway - such residence being outside the city limits and under the jurisdiction of the Royal Canadian Mounted Police.

4.Sometime during 1953, WERNER moved from the residence into a house situated inside the city, and there have been recent reports that WERNER is again becoming active in the unlawful sale of liquor. No prosecutions have been made to date.

5.Prior to the year 1953 all of WERNER'S activities were outside the City with regards to liquor offenses, although he was charged in the city with several indictable offenses which include Theft and Taking a vehicle without consent of the owner.

6.WERNER presently resides at 9603 - 81 Avenue in this city and is employed as a laborer with the City of Edmonton.

7.It is requested that this information be forwarded to chief Constable H. J. Lawrence, Seattle police department, Washington, U.S.A.

Fw'd 29 Jan 1959
   J. Cookson
   Insp. Dets I/C C.I.D.
Detective A. E. Smith, Edmonton police department
29 Jan 59, 11:30 A.M.

Upon receipt of the memo from Edmonton, Rouse began to feel more comfortable with Teague, particularly since Zuarri and Waters had traced ownership of the Blue Bird Motel, on Pacific Highway, to

Junita Warren. Zuarri and Waters also discovered that the County Sheriff's office had an extensive case file on the activities occurring in and around the Blue Bird Motel. Prior to 1958, sheriffs had been called to the motel several times to settle disturbances arising out of domestic problems between Junita and her husband, Peter Warren. These eventually culminated in his arrest for the destruction of property on a complaint signed by his wife. The Warrens were divorced in November 1953 and, in the division of property, Mrs. Warren acquired ownership of the motel. Mrs. Warren had since moved to Spokane, Washington, where she was located and interviewed. In this interview, she denied any knowledge of the facts of the case as they were presented to her by the officers. Mrs. Warren was questioned extensively about the events surrounding activities at the motel on March 12, 1954, but she said she had no recollection of what occurred at the motel on that date and little was gained in this entire interview. She did tell the officers, however, that the motel registration cards for that period had long since been destroyed.[23]

Rouse solicited the help of Seattle Police Captain Jack Porter, Commander of the Burglary, Larceny, Intelligence and Narcotics squads. Forged Canadian money orders were being scattered throughout the western states like confetti, with a large number being cashed in western Washington. The Vancouver area was still suffering from a series of post office burglaries, and throughout the summer and fall of 1958, stolen postal money orders taken in these burglaries were passed in most of the western United States. Of the 177 money orders taken in the burglary of the post office substation in the Neale Pharmacy in Vancouver on April 16, 1958, over forty were cashed in Vancouver, Washington, or in and around Portland, Oregon, each for $100. And of the 534 documents taken in the June 7, 1958 burglary of Gripps Pharmacy, several were cashed in Seattle.[24]

As a result of the information furnished earlier by Teague to Postal Inspector Worthington, Rouse had obtained the names of all the Canadian participants who, Teague claimed, were passing the stolen money orders in Washington and Oregon. All of these people were being sought by the postal authorities. Most were burglars or "narcotic hypes," who nearly always used Hertz rental cars, acquired locally after flying into one of the larger west coast cities. The Sea-

Tac Airport police detail was alerted, and a team of detectives contacted the Hertz agency at the airport in an attempt to locate cars which were rented by Teague's associates. Teague claimed nearly all of his associates, who were now involved in the stolen money order racket, had formerly been with him in the British Columbia Penitentiary, and several were well aware of the story of Dawley and Wasylenchuk's involvement in the Greenwood case. Captain Rouse's hope was to apprehend just one other Canadian criminal who could confirm Teague's statements, or who may have had first-hand information on the two suspects' involvement in the Greenwood robbery and murder. This, he was sure, would assist in their efforts to obtain an indictment against the pair. This was a long shot, but Canadian criminals frequently visited Seattle and were usually not too difficult to locate. Teague claimed this group always registered in hotels using their own names and only used assumed names when passing the stolen money orders. Rouse hoped if they were caught passing the postal money orders in the United States and were knowledgeable about the suspects' activities, the local prosecutor would be in a position to trade their freedom for the information Rouse needed.

Whether Rouse would be successful in this investigation or not, it was now obvious that the corruption and ineptness of the Canadian authorities in dealing both with bank robbers, burglars and forgers, was creating an inexcusable crime problem in Seattle and other American cities, problems whose very roots could be traced directly to the doorstep of the Royal Canadian Mounted Police and Vancouver police department.

As a result of Rouse's meeting with Captain Porter, orders were issued to all detectives, to the effect that every Canadian criminal who was arrested by Seattle officers was to be interrogated relative to their involvement with Teague as to whether or not they had any knowledge of John Wasylenchuk or Clifford Dawley's activities while in the U.S. Over the next few months, several Canadians were arrested and S.P.D. detectives were careful not to identify Teague as their source of information during interrogation, but unfortunately none were found who would or could substantiate Teague's story.

In the meantime, the FBI was having some success on their end of the investigation in Canada. They were looking for fellow inmates and friends of Lester Teague who could verify his story, plus friends of the two principal suspects in the case, who would now be re-interviewed, in the hope of corroborating the prisoner's story. Dean Rolston interviewed Bobby Talbot in the penitentiary without success; Talbot was completely uncooperative and refused to even discuss the Greenwood case. Talbot's release date from the penitentiary was set for June, 1959.

Mrs. John Wasylenchuk was also interviewed and here again the agents failed to elicit a favorable response; it was obvious she would not cooperate with American authorities in any investigation involving her husband. Having interviewed both suspects earlier without success a few months after the bank stickup in Seattle, Rolston returned again to the British Columbia Penitentiary to re-interview the two stickup men, with the hope that one would slip or drop a word that may incriminate one or both of the suspects.

John Wasylenchuk was unusually agreeable during the initial interview with agent Rolston, in a session which lasted for over two hours; as the agent persisted in his interrogation, the bank robber became uneasy and began to exhibit extreme signs of nervousness. Finally Rolston met with some success; Wasylenchuk became careless and gave conflicting stories relative to his whereabouts at the time of the Greenwood robbery and the agent was able to contradict Wasylenchuk several times. When confronted with these discrepancies in his story, he was first startled and immediately became excited and nervous, but he was "con-wise" and soon quit talking altogether. Upon subsequent visits to the penitentiary by the agent, Wasylenchuk refused to be interviewed. But the agent's investigation had refuted the story given by the robber about his whereabouts and activities in Vancouver at the time of the Greenwood robbery.

The Mountie who had provided the alibi for Wasylenchuk, Corporal Ernest Nuttall, was also interviewed again, this time in the presence of his superiors and the question arose whether the entry in the officer's notebook, which placed the criminal in Vancouver, between 12:00 and 12:30 P.M. on the day of the robbery, was accurate. RCMP Sergeant J. E. Murton, Nuttall's supervisor, stated that he believed that the notebook entry relative to the check on Wasylenchuk was inaccurate. During this interview, it was also learned that Nuttall had provided another alibi for the convict in the robbery of a New Westminster bank on April 29, 1954. The Mountie had made a similar entry in his notebook, in that upon hearing of the robbery, he claimed he again "checked" the man and found him to be home. RCMP investigators, however, disputed this and reached the conclusion that the New Westminster bank robbery was in fact engineered by Wasylenchuk.[25]

FBI agents again returned to the British Columbia penitentiary, this time to re-interview Dawley who was now serving seven years, after being convicted in Nanaimo, British Columbia in 1956 for auto theft and possession of house breaking tools. He had received an additional one year sentence for his prison escapes of March 7, and August 23, 1954.

Clifford Dawley was a model prisoner now, working towards parole, one year away. In prior interviews with the American officers, he was uncooperative, evasive and denied any knowledge of the Greenwood robbery, but on this visit he "dropped a bomb shell" on Rolston. He stated, after much preliminary hedging, in the early part of the interrogation, that "Wasylenchuk 'pulled' the Greenwood bank robbery," and that he, Dawley, had no part in the job. But he would add little else other than to say that he had got his information from Mary Peters , who was a friend of both him and The Farmer. When pressed for further information about the details of the crime, or where Mary Peters could be located, Dawley became evasive and finally broke off the interview and refused to answer any further questions.[26]

FBI agents and Seattle detectives had spent weeks in Vancouver and had been hopeful that they could have substantiated Teague's story and returned with corroborating evidence, evidence which would have lead to the indictment of the two suspects. They often believed during the preceding years that the solution to this crime was within their grasp; but after five years of almost continuous investigation, even with Clifford Dawley's latest revelations, they felt they had failed and the solution that they were sure would come was slipping through their fingertips. The fact that the alibis for Talbot and

Wasylenchuk came from two fellow law enforcement officers sickened the American officers. If it weren't for these two Canadian officers' stories, they were sure the U.S. Attorney would have asked for an indictment on at least John Wasylenchuk and perhaps even Dawley, based upon both the eye witness testimony and the circumstantial evidence which was evident at every turn. But before the United States government would ask for the extradition of a foreign national, the Americans knew additional evidence would have to be secured, evidence that they now felt they may never be able to obtain.

Upon returning to Seattle, the agents again met with Captain Rouse and his staff and discussed the case, each bringing the other up-to-date on their search for Canadian criminals who could corroborate Teague's story. In the investigation of Mrs. Warren, with regard to the Blue Bird Motel allegation, the agents were advised that Mrs. Warren could not or would not place Clifford Dawley or John Wasylenchuk in Seattle on March 12, 1954. At this meeting, the Seattle officers expressed their revulsion with the Canadian cops who were fronting for the bank robbery and murder suspects in the case. Rouse was most upset with this aspect of the investigation and very disheartened about the outcome of the Bureau's recent investigation in Canada; but he was now more than ever convinced that the solution to this crime would come only from Canada and that a new approach would have to be undertaken. Just how this could be done he wasn't quite sure, but whatever happened, he knew that either he or one of his top investigators would have to be reassigned to the Canadian end of the investigation. Further, if they were to be successful, a competent and dedicated investigator familiar with the Vancouver underworld would have to become involved in the investigation.

Rouse was fully aware that quite frequently there was a visible lack of cooperation between many local police agencies in the United States and the FBI. This was particularly evident in the hierarchy of several agencies. Perhaps, he thought, this could be the case in Canada. It was common knowledge locally that when it came to the FBI supplying information on criminal activities, quite frequently it became a one-way street and it was not unusual that local departments would not be given criminal information which was available to the FBI. This was particularly noticeable in bank robbery cases which were the Bureau's "bread and butter." He knew full well that this relationship existed and it was no small problem to keep his own personnel from responding in kind. He began to speculate that Dean Rolston's hard-nosed approach in trying to discredit the Canadian officers, who had provided the alibis for Talbot and Wasylenchuk, had resulted in the Bureau being "frozen out" by the Canadian authorities. However, it was also possible that there was just a lack of interest by the Vancouver authorities in the Seattle case. But, thinking that either of these theories may be true, he decided it was time for his people to move back in on the Canadian end of this case.

On May 21, 1959, shortly after a meeting with agent Rolston, Rouse sat down, and in a written report to the chief of detectives summarized the current status of the Greenwood case, elaborating on Teague's story and the problems that the FBI agents were experiencing in Canada. His report clearly expressed his strong personal feelings toward the investigation, yet he tried to remain as objective as possible in his request for personal involvement in the case by Seattle police detectives in Canada.

May 21, 1959
To: Deputy Chief V. L. Kramer, Detective Division
From: Captain C. A. Rouse, Detective Division
Subject: Greenwood Bank Robbery-Case No. 288-527

I have been talking to an informant over the past several months and believe he has accurately reported the information he heard. He has good contacts in the underworld in Vancouver, B.C., and he is convinced the story he is telling is the truth. This informant gets his information from several sources and the main source cannot be doubted. He insists that, due to the personal dangers involved for him, that no further disclosure of this source be made. I have promised him I would not disclose the source.

The informant says that the Greenwood Bank was robbed in 1954 by CLIFFORD DAWLEY, JOHN WASYLENCHUK, and MAURICE (BOBBY) TALBOT.

He identified DAWLEY by photograph as being Vancouver, B.C. Police [Identification] No. 10263, TALBOT by photograph as being B. C. Penitentiary No. 7233, and identified a photograph of JOHN WASYLENCHUK that was furnished us by the FBI but does not have a police or penitentiary number.

He said WASYLENCHUK had already cased the bank and was the brains of the job, and that the robbery was pulled mainly because DAWLEY, who had just escaped from prison in Vancouver, needed money to hide out in eastern Canada. They had planned to go on from Seattle and rob another bank near Eugene, Oregon. JOHN WASYLENCHUK owed CLIFFORD DAWLEY something for leaving him alone on Vancouver Island in December, 1953 when DAWLEY was arrested. JOHN WASYLENCHUK had been instrumental in CLIFFORD DAWLEY'S escape and had put up $1,000.00 for someone to "look the other way."

The informant states JOHN WASYLENCHUK arranged to borrow a car to be used by MAURICE TALBOT and TALBOT'S female companion in connection with the bank robbery. He was unable to identify Talbot's friend, except to say that her name was JACKIE and that her maiden name was BROWN. He has never seen her. He does not know whether they were really married, although she bore TALBOT'S child. She later lived with CHUCK BAILEY in 1956 in Vancouver and then went to jail. He said the car came from a car lot operated by a man whose first name was DANNY, last name unknown. A friend, name unknown, suggested to WASYLENCHUK that he get the car at DANNY'S. He said DANNY is now dead and the car lot was probably on Commercial Street between 5th and 9th in Vancouver. He said that KRIS MCRAY and a PAUL MCRAY assisted WASYLENCHUK in getting the car from DANNY'S lot and he turned it over to the TALBOT's to use. He said KRIS MCRAY worked at DANNY'S and had a police record as a firebug in Edmonton, Alberta. PAUL MCRAY also has a police record in Vancouver, B.C. as a thief. DANNY had been a big fence before his death.

The actual robbery was as follows:

MAURICE TALBOT and JACKIE TALBOT came to Seattle in the borrowed car 2 or 3 days before the bank robbery. They stole an Oldsmobile in an area in Seattle where WASYLENCHUK had told them to look and in the way WASYLENCHUK had taught them. They also stole an automobile license in another part of town where WASYLENCHUK had told them to steal it and planned the getaway route and picked the places for the second car to be placed for the bank robbery. When they came to Seattle, they registered at the Blue Bird Motel south of Boeing on the highway because WASYLENCHUK had told them to register there.

On the night before the bank robbery, PETE NOVIS of Vancouver, B. C. brought WASYLENCHUK and DAWLEY to Seattle in his car. DAWLEY walked across the border at Brown's Road near Blaine, Washington. He identified a photograph of NOVIS as Vancouver, B. C. police department No. 13790. Informant said that at that time NOVIS was a big-time narcotics distributor in Vancouver. He said NOVIS was at that time living in Vancouver with a girl known as PAT. She is a narcotic user, well acquainted in criminal circles and a friend of RED HENDERSON. He identified her by photograph as Vancouver, B. C. Police No. L 16979. NOVIS was on his way to eastern Canada by way of the United States to pick up narcotics, and agreed to bring DAWLEY and WASYLENCHUK to Seattle the night before the bank robbery in conjunction with his trip. He may have taken WASYLENCHUK to Detroit, Michigan.

This informant says that MAURICE and JACKIE TALBOT had checked into the Blue Bird Motel after prior arrangements had been made by WASYLENCHUK, and DAWLEY did not check into the motel. He identified the motel owner as Mrs. WARREN. Informant advised that WASYLENCHUK had made a contact with an unknown person in Seattle to furnish a second cool car. Each of the bank robbers had their own gun and on the morning of the bank robbery MAURICE TALBOT drove the getaway car because he was familiar with the get-away route, having cased it beforehand. Informant stated that DAWLEY, TALBOT and WASYLENCHUK went into the Greenwood bank with disguises and were surprised by the Seattle police while they were in the process of robbing the bank, following which CLIFF DAWLEY got scared and did some shooting which resulted in the killing of an officer and the wounding of two other officers. This caused them to give up the Oregon bank robbery. According to this informant, MAURICE TALBOT was reported to have jumped out the bank window and CLIFF DAWLEY was left behind during the trouble which resulted from the shooting. Informant stated that all of the bank robbers went back to the Blue Bird Motel, following which CLIFF DAWLEY made his way to Detroit by train from a nearby town. DAWLEY and WASYLENCHUK are believed to have met in a big hotel in Detroit several days following the bank robbery. Neither of them were registered at this hotel.

Informant stated that MAURICE and JACKIE TALBOT went directly back to Vancouver, B. C. with the guns and money, driving the borrowed car. The money taken in the robbery was fenced by WASYLENCHUK through an acquaintance of DANNY BRENT, for a 10% cut. Informant stated that BLONDIE MARTIN, 30-35 years, 6' 2", 190 pounds, dark hair and eyes, and A FRIEND, no description, who runs BRENT's car wash in Vancouver on Burrard Street, were involved in assisting in the fencing of the money. The guns were thrown into the Fraser River in B.C.

Following the bank robbery, the owner of the Blue Bird Motel in Seattle was paid $1,000.00 for her assistance through money brought to her from Vancouver to Seattle by DONNA CLEARIDGE. She was suggested as a messenger by a friend of WASYLENCHUK, name unknown. Informant described CLEARIDGE as the madam of a house of prostitution at 816 Burrard Street in Vancouver, B. C. She is white, 170-180 pounds, tall, in her 40's and changes the color of her hair. She did not know why she was delivering the money.

According to the informant, other people, besides the participants, who may know this story and who could verify portions of it are GEORGE McKNIGHT, CHARLES TALBOT, Mrs. JOHN WASYLENCHUK, FRANK DOUHAM, WILLIAM ALLEN BABCOCK, BOBBY LEWIS, and JOE HALL.

As you know, our file shows that Sgt. ERNEST NUTTAL, RCMP (now retired), made an alibi for WASYLENCHUK by reporting he checked WASYLENCHUK in Vancouver, B. C. within an hour or so of the bank robbery. Our file also shows that investigation conducted in Vancouver, B. C. by Inspector PETE LAMONT of the Vancouver Police Department on March 12 and 13, 1954 located MAURICE and CHARLES TALBOT in Vancouver about 2:00 A. M., March 13, 1954. They claimed to have been in Vancouver all day and his inquiry tended to verify it. With all of this in mind, I told the informant that two of the men mentioned as robbers had what appeared to be good alibis.

I feel certain all of the above is factual and does not vary from my confirmed belief that DAWLEY and WASYLEN-CHUK perpetrated this robbery-murder. The presence of TALBOT on the job is possible, to me. I would like very much to check this story in Vancouver and suggest that the chief of the Vancouver police department be contacted. I would like to work this out personally and with the assistance of Sergeant C. K. Waitt.

Respectfully,
C. A. Rouse, Captain
Homicide and
Robbery Squad
Detective Division

Seattle Police Detective Sergeant Charles Waitt
(Seattle Police Records Archives)

Chief of Detectives Victor L. Kramer agreed to the captain's request as did the chief of police, and within a week, Chief Lawrence, at Kramer's behest, was en route to Vancouver to meet with Chief Constable George Archer of the Vancouver Police Department. Rouse persuaded both Kramer and Chief Lawrence that there was no doubt that, without the intervention of the chief, the Vancouver authorities would continue to stonewall American officers as they had done in the past. Rouse was now convinced more than ever of the culpability of several Canadian officers in either the planning, or at least of providing false alibis and safe haven refuges for both Clifford Dawley and John Wasylenchuk after the Seattle robbery. Although, in his memoradum, he wisely did not mention his concerns regarding the suspected culpability of the Canadian officers in this case, he made sure the chief of police and Kramer were fully aware of facts which led the Americans to be highly suspicious of the actions of more than a half dozen RCMP and Vancouver police officers.

Two days later, upon Lawrence's return to Seattle, in a report to Kramer and Rouse, he outlined in detail the events that occurred in his meetings with Chief Archer, and of Archer's subsequent commitment to begin again with a full and cooperative investigation with both Seattle police department and FBI investigators. Lawrence had also by now received concurrence from the FBI command staff in this new approach suggested by Rouse, which would hopefully lead to the solution of this most difficult investigation. Lawrence noted in his report that the Vancouver officers were critical of the Bureau in that they believed the FBI's agents, while in Canada, failed to fully provide the Vancouver Department with complete details of the case.

Seattle Police Department
May 28, 1959
From: H. J. Lawrence
        Chief of Police
To: All Concerned
Subject: Trip to Vancouver, British Columbia Regarding
         Greenwood Bank Robbery and Murder
I went to Vancouver and met Chief Constable George Archer by himself first. We reviewed some of the things that have taken place in the past in the Greenwood Bank job and arrived at the following agreements:
1. This would become a full-time project of the Vancouver police department and that they would do everything they could to further this investigation. Up to now the chief feels this has not been an investigative thing of the Vancouver police, that they just had individually acted at the request of someone, for instance interrogating a person or thing of that nature.

2. We agreed that one man would be from the Seattle police department; one man from the Vancouver police department and one man from the FBI.

Also it was agreed that if any news was released from this investigation, it would be released from the Vancouver police department. If this case comes to a successful conclusion and the news is released in Seattle, they would like the privilege of releasing it at the same time in Vancouver.

Besides making a man available for this investigation, Chief Archer also stated they would have a car available for use in Vancouver.

In preliminary discussion with Chief Archer, I was told that Clifford Dawley is in the penitentiary and is at the present time "stooling" to the RCMP, also that he is having his face altered or lifted, which will change his appearance. He is also such a natural leader that he has become a leader of a section of the convicts who help keep order in the penitentiary.

After this preliminary discussion with Chief Archer by himself, [at a downtown hotel] we went to the Vancouver police department. A conference was held which included Archer, Deputy Chief Constable Gordon Ambrose, Detective Superintendent Ben Jelley and Inspector Archie Plummer. We reviewed the entire situation to determine the best way to operate. On instructions from Don Hostetter [Acting Special agent in Charge of Seattle FBI Office], it was suggested that if Dean Rolston or [agent] Crisman were not acceptable, a new man would be chosen, who was not disclosed to them as being Alf Gunn. After this was talked about for some time, it was decided it would be best if [agent] Dean Rolston did not come to Vancouver himself, but Crisman would be an acceptable man. Also Archer himself thought maybe a brand new man would be better, but Plummer made the point that Crisman had the knowledge and background of the case and should be the man. We tried to steer their selection to some of the men who were suggested by Alf Gunn. They indicated that Sergeant Bill Morphett of the Homicide and Robbery Squad would be detached from duty and would work with two men from the United States as long as necessary.

It was felt that it would be better to have this operation away from the Vancouver police headquarters, and they could work from a hotel or a motel. Inspector Plummer will reserve a room at the Georgian Hotel for next Monday. Then if a new place is selected, they can move to wherever they would like.

Due to the fact that all of the people in the reports taken to Vancouver are known to the Vancouver police and have been talked to several times before, they feel that the crux will be in skilled interrogation.

The new man in charge of the RCMP Detachment in Vancouver was a protege of Archer when he was the commanding officer in the RCMP. Today they will try to get the complete RCMP file for review. They feel that their file is not complete and they do not have too much information about this case. They asked me if I knew anything about a resumé that had been turned out by the FBI and I had to say I did not.

Next Monday, Inspector Plummer will meet the Great Northern train, which arrives in Vancouver at 12:59 PM, daylight time, their time. He will have a long conference with Captain Charlie Rouse regarding this case. It was worked out that Captain Rouse would go up for one day and get this project on the road. He would return to Seattle and our selected detective sergeant will remain in Vancouver to work with the other two men.

We have agreed that this phase of the investigation will be a matter between the Seattle police department and the Vancouver police department. Any contacts to be made with the RCMP will be made by the FBI.

After this meeting broke up and Inspector Archie Plummer was driving me back to the depot, he said probably the two best men acceptable from the Bureau would be [agent Chet] Crisman or Alf Gunn, that Alf Gunn has worked with the Vancouver police and has been very acceptable by the decision of the group of commanding officers. Probably for the best job, Crisman should be the man because he has the greatest knowledge. Plummer said Rolston should not be too far away in the background due to his great knowledge of this case, but should not be in Vancouver as there are some personal feelings that have been ruffled from a previous investigation.

In the discussion with the group I was told that Red Henderson and [Robert] Stewart, known safe crackers whom we have been attempting to get in jail in the United States for purposes of establishing more information about the Dawley group, are both in the penitentiary.

During the staff meeting with the top people of the Vancouver Police Department, they felt that the complete knowledge of this case had not been passed on to them and they feel that better liaison should take place in the future for all operating agencies. They also promised that they would do everything in their power to bring this case to a successful conclusion.

I feel this trip was completely successful and that everything will be done to move forward to a solution.

H.J.L.am

So FBI agent Dean Rolston, who had spent the majority of his investigative effort during the last five years trying to solve the Greenwood case, and who was more knowledgeable about this investigation than anyone else, was "out of the picture" and Special agent Chet Crisman would now be assigned to the investigation nearly full-time. Crisman had spent many weeks in Canada with Rolston in the months following the shooting of the three Seattle police officers in 1954, and had kept up-to-date on the progress of the investigation by frequently assisting Rolston both in Canada and in the United States whenever investigative help was needed. As for the Seattle police department, Rouse would continue to manage the investigation, but he would assign Detective Sergeant Charles K. Waitt to represent the Department in Canada and to work with Crisman and Vancouver police Sergeant William Morphett on the investigation. Waitt had been working on several bombing cases involving the punch-board and pinball gambling interests in Seattle; the bombings which began occurring in the city in late 1957 were still continuing. He was highly respected within the police department. As a twenty-year police officer having spent the bulk of his career assigned to the Detective Division, he was well-qualified to undertake the responsibility now handed to him.

Notes

[1] Eugene F. Ivey, interview with the author, September 3, 1974.

[2] Eugene F. Ivey, S.P.D. Case 288527, Op. Cit., Investigator's Report, November 1, 1954, p. 2.

[3] Ivey, Op. Cit., September 3, 1974.

[4] City of Vancouver police department, Criminal Identification Bureau Record No. 12515. John Wasylenchuk's criminal career, for all practical purposes, came to an end with his arrest and conviction for the robbery of the bank in Burnaby, British Columbia (a Vancouver suburb), in 1955. He, like Clifford Dawley, was convicted as a habitual criminal after this bank robbery and was sentenced to life in prison.

[5] The Vancouver Province, January 30, 1956 "B. C. Convict Cliff Dawley Captured By Toronto Police," Metropolitan Edition, p. 1. "Jail-escape expert Clifford Dawley, 47, who fled from Oakalla Prison Farm in August, 1954, was recaptured at gunpoint in Toronto today.

Detectives Walter Heaslip and Norman Smith greeted him with drawn guns when he entered the locker room of a coal company to begin work. He had been delivering coal bags for the past six months under the name of James Pearce."

[6] The criminal career of RCMP Identification Services F.P.S. No. 596488, Maurice "Bobby" Talbot, alias Bob Dionne, spanned three decades in western Canada. Although somewhat younger than John Wasylenchuk (he was born in 1921 in Saint Boniface, Manitoba) and Clifford Dawley, his first arrest occurred in 1942 at the age of twenty-one in Jasper, Alberta for violation of the Canadian Railway Act, while "riding on trains." But Talbot, like his mentors, Wasylenchuk and Dawley, soon turned to bank robbery. In 1943, he was convicted of robbing a bank in Victoria, British Columbia. He was sentenced to seven years in the B.C. Penitentiary for this crime. Subsequent arrests and convictions for drug trafficking soon followed.

[7] There were 481 armed robberies reported to the Seattle police department in 1954 (By 1990 this figure had increased to 2695), and as separate crime statistics for bank robberies were not maintained at the time by law enforcement, officers of that era who were interviewed estimated that 10 percent of these crimes were bank robberies. Police reports indicate that bank robbery is a western phenomenon in the U.S. More specifically bank robberies occur with greater frequency per population group in the Pacific coast states of Washington, Oregon and California than in any other geographic area of the United States. (They also occur more frequently on Friday than on any other day of the week).

Bank robbery is a violent crime as can be seen in the following data:

U.S.- TOTAL ROBBERIES		*BANK ROBBERIES	INJURIES	DEATHS
1954	67,420	307	NA	NA
1962	100,156	1000	NA	NA
1974	328,782	3517	174	20
1990	639,270	7837	96	18

The pattern of bank robberies in Canada since the World War II era is not dissimilar from that of the U.S. in that it is also primarily a western phenomena. In the ten year period 1982 - 1991, eighteen per cent of all bank robberies in Canada, occurred in British Columbia, yet this province accounts for less than 12 per cent of the total population of the country. During this period, 90 per cent of the bank robberies reported in Canada occurred in the three most populous provinces of British Columbia, Ontario and Quebec and "in terms of absolute numbers (of bank robberies in 1991), Montreal (population - 1,783,700) with 423 robberies, - - - retains its dubious title of bank robbery capital of the country. Expressed in ratio of holdups to (bank) branches, however, Vancouver is number one with almost every bank, on average, held up in 1991."** Toronto, with a population of 2,248,000, experienced 258 bank robberies in 1990 and Vancouver, with a population of 457,100, had a total of 204 bank holdups in 1990. The true picture of the enormity of the bank robbery problem in Vancouver becomes evident when these numbers are converted to rate, or number of robberies, per 100,000 population. Here we find that the rate of bank robberies in Vancouver is twice that of the City of Montreal and four times that of Toronto - the largest city in Canada.

Of the 1609 bank robberies in Canada in 1991, as in the U.S., more occurred on Friday than on any other day of the week. See Michael Ballard, "On The Safe Side - Bank Robbery 1991," *Canadian Banker*, Vol. 99, No. 3 - May-June 1992.

*There were 75 reported bank robberies in the State of Washington in 1974, this figure had increased to 218 by 1990 and to 311 in 1991, with 112 of these occurring in Seattle. (See Darrell Glover and Michael A Barber, "Masked Men Seize Bank in Lynnwood," Seattle Post Intelligencer, November 21, 1991 Section C, p. 1-2).

**See Michael Ballard, "On The Safe Side - Bank Robbery 1991," *Canadian Banker*, Ottawa, Ontario, May - June 1992, pp.28-30.

[8] Ivey, Op. Cit., September 3, 1974.

[9] Captain Charles A. Rouse, conversations with the author, 1972.

[10] Captain Charles A. Rouse, S.P.D. Case No. 288527 Investigative Report- Case Summary, April 24, 1959. Also see S.P.D. Captain Frank C. Ramon's letter to Los Angeles Police Intelligence Division Commander James Hamilton, September 10, 1957.

[11]   Captain Charles A. Rouse, S. P. D. Case No. 288527 Case Summary, November 10, 1958.

[12]   Ibid.

[13]   Ibid.

[14]   Ibid.

[15]   Ibid.

[16]   Ibid.

[17]   agent Dean C. Rolston, FBI Interview Report, December 5, 1958. pp. 1-2.

[18]   Ibid.

[19]   RCMP Identification Services Report F.P.S. No. 568976 on Irvin Lester Teague. Lester Teague's first arrest occurred in 1942 in Calgary, Alberta when he was still a juvenile, but he, unlike Clifford Dawley and John Wasylenchuk, with one or two exceptions, avoided the use of weapons in his criminal forays and specialized in "passing" stolen money orders and travelers checks which he acquired by burglarizing post offices throughout the western United States and Canada. He did try his luck in the armed robbery business in Edmonton, Alberta in June 1949, but unfortunately for him, he was apprehended at the scene by the police. He was sentenced to six years in the penitentiary for this crime. In 1953, he was again arrested for robbery in Victoria, B. C. and received a two-year sentence. He would serve an additional ten years in four different Canadian and U.S. prisons for burglary, theft and forgery; he was in fact confined in either the U.S. or in Canada during most of the decade which the Greenwood Bank Robbery and Murder investigation covered.

[20]   Rolston, Op. Cit., December 8, 1958, pp. 1-2.

[21]   Rouse, Op. Cit., April 29, 1959.

[22]   Ibid.

[23]   Detectives Andrew Zuarri and Donald B. Waters S.P.D. Case No.288527 Op. Cit., Investigator's Report December 4, 1958.

[24]   Rolston, Op. Cit., December 19, 1958, p. 7.

[25]   Rolston, FBI Investigative Report, May 25, 1959, p. 18.

[26]   Rouse, Op. Cit., Conversations with the author, 1972.

Moore Reassigned

Californian Named Acting Police Chief

By DAVID RUFFIA

SUNRISE

THE WEATHER — Cloudy early today, clearing this afternoon. High about 70. Low tonight 55 to 60. Chance of rain 10 per cent. YESTERDAY'S High, 69; Low, 55. Table on Page 27.

June 22, 1970

10¢; 15¢ in Canada

Closing Markets

Dow Jones

Seattle Post-Intelligencer
THE VOICE OF THE NORTHWEST... SINCE 1863

Wednesday, June 24, 1970

Six Say They Made Payoffs
To 19 Seattle Policemen

Bircher Criticizes
Corruption Probe

Sunday, February 1, 1970   The Seattle Times

OF THE P-I

Honest Police
Should Speak

(The views of the writer are not necessarily those of the P-I Editorial Board.)

By LOU GUZZO
Managing Editor, The P-I

Police Search for Pattern in Seattle Bombings

BY LOU CORSALETTI

The Times' Opinion and Comment:

The Crackdown on Vice

California
Man To
Be Chief

BY RICK ANDERSON

Wednesday, February 4, 1970

Subpoenaed Law Officers
Mum About Testimony

POLICE

Prostitution to Be Stopped—Gain

BY RICK ANDERSON

P-I JULY 17 '70

Wednesday, July 29, 1970

Post-Intelligencer

JUVENILE

Police Manpower

Lie Tests
On Police
Blocked
By Court

BY CRAIG SMITH

Retired Police Captain Charged

Black Silent Majority
Denounces Militants

WASHINGTON (AP) —

Chapter

7

A Return to Canada

On Monday, June 1, 1959, four days after receiving the go ahead signal from Chief Lawrence, Captain Rouse, Sergeant Charles Waitt and Special Agent Chet Crisman departed from Seattle on the morning train for Vancouver. They were met in Vancouver that afternoon at the train depot by Sergeant Bill Morphett who took them to the Georgia Hotel in downtown Vancouver, where Waitt and Crisman would establish their headquarters. En route, the four men got acquainted, and in general terms, discussed the scope of the investigation which Rouse hoped to carry out in the Vancouver area. Morphett had been with the Vancouver Department for twenty-five years, and having been assigned as a detective for many years, was well acquainted with not only the three principal suspects in the Greenwood case, but also with most of the "heavy criminals" in western Canada. As a young officer, he worked as a beat cop and in patrol car assignments during the gang wars which erupted in 1934 and 1935 in Vancouver. Most recently, he had been investigating a series of robberies and shootings in the city which were touched off by illicit drug peddlers.

Soon after their arrival at the hotel, the officers met with Morphett's superior, Inspector Archie Plummer,[1] and reviewed the results of the investigation thus far, with particular emphasis on the information Crisman furnished from reports of the case previously prepared by FBI Agent Dean Rolston. Plummer expressed to Rouse his displeasure with the fact that the Vancouver officers had not been kept abreast of the progress of the FBI's investigation in Canada, and it was soon evident to Rouse that some of the information that took the FBI weeks or months to learn had been common knowledge to many Vancouver officers, due to their prior investigations involving Clifford Dawley, John Wasylenchuk, the Talbot brothers and their associates over the past several years. However, the FBI had secured some valuable information on the activities of the three principal suspects, which was previously unknown to the Canadian officers. By the time the conference had ended, Rouse was now more than ever convinced that if a solution to this case was to be found in Canada, it would only be brought about through a cooperative investigative effort by the Seattle and Vancouver police departments in conjunction with the FBI and possibly the RCMP. He was aware that there was a noticeable reluctance on the part of both the FBI agents and the Vancouver officers to fully confide in one another. This was understandable in that the Canadian officers were well aware of the allegations of complicity in criminal activity leveled against some members of their department by some American officers who had been involved in the earlier investigations. These allegations had been discussed with Rouse and Chief Lawrence and were in the summary of this case which Rolston had prepared for his superiors some weeks earlier. It was this summary which was referred to by Chief George Archer and his personnel in their meeting with Chief Lawrence, in which they expressed their displeasure with the FBI for not keeping them abreast of the investigation. It was at this same meeting that the Canadians made known their displeasure with FBI Agent Dean Rolston.

It was obvious to Rouse that the Vancouver officer's relationship with the FBI was following a pattern that had occurred so many times before in American cities, wherein cooperation between FBI representatives and local police departments often left much to be desired. For this very reason, Rouse was glad that he had selected Waitt for the assignment in Canada; Waitt was not only a competent investigator, but a very personable and outgoing individual. He had a reputation for being able to charm a confession out of the most hardened criminal. Rouse thought that, with his ability, Waitt could act as a catalyst in developing a more cooperative working relationship between the Vancouver officers and the FBI.[2] As the meeting progressed, complete agreement was reached between all the parties relative to the direction the investigation should take and what each department's investigative responsibilities would be. Inspector Plummer relieved Sergeant Morphett of all duties relating to his past assignments and directed the Vancouver officer to work fulltime on the Seattle case with Sergeant Waitt and Agent Crisman. Plummer agreed that the Vancouver Department would, as was promised earlier by Chief Constable Archer, take this investigation on as if the bank robbery and murder had occurred in their own city.

The three men began to outline their plans, plans which would be undertaken immediately. Morphett cautioned Waitt and Crisman that they were dealing with the toughest criminals in the whole of Canada and that Dawley and Wasylenchuk's influence on several associates was such that they were not likely to talk to the officers, even though some were currently awaiting trial. Presumably they could have obtained information from some of these people by recommending reduced sentences for those convicted of a criminal offense, had the circumstances been right. However, the Vancouver sergeant suggested that they use a slow, cautious, well planned and well coordinated attack in their efforts to develop the information which would lead them to the three criminals. The Americans, although concurring in principle with the Canadians, were not anxious to go too slow; they did agree that they would begin by re-interviewing Dawley and Wasylenchuk's associates, particularly those that Agent Rolston and Detective Ivey had spoken to shortly after the robbery occurred. It was assumed that these individuals could have supplied worthwhile information to the Americans had they been so inclined. Morphett concurred and said they could possibly plant a seed of mistrust among these people and at the same time Vancouver police could place several telephone taps on their phones to see what could be learned.

All parties were ready to move, and the next day, June 2, 1959, after a lapse of over 5 years from the date of the crime in Seattle, for all practical purposes the investigation began anew. After dropping Rouse off at the train depot for his return to Seattle, the three officers began their hunt for associates of the three principal suspects who Agent Rolston and Detective Ivey had either identified or interviewed in 1954 and 1955.

The first man to be interviewed was Steve Polanski. This was the man that David Robert Auld, the bank robber and drug trafficker, had bragged about to Detective Eugene Ivey in 1955, that he knew Dawley and Wasylenchuk pulled the Greenwood Job and that Steve Polanski was involved.

Steve Polanski was well known to Morphett, and the drug pusher greeted the three men at his home in Vancouver with "Hello, Bill, who are these people? I hope not those damned FBI agents again." Upon hearing this, Waitt thought to himself, Rolston must have given this man quite a going over when he interviewed him earlier.

The man spoke broken English, and it was hard for Waitt to understand him as he rambled on with the officers about his personal troubles. Earlier in the day, he had been bound-over in superior court for trial, for trafficking in narcotics, and now made the statement that if he got ten years on this "beef," which he expected, it would probably kill him. Waitt was glad to hear of the man's problems with the Canadian courts as the FBI hadn't had this kind of leverage over this criminal when they interviewed him earlier. But Polanski had little to add to what he had told the FBI earlier. Although he recalled telling Detective Ivey that Dawley and Wasylenchuk committed the robbery, he now said he just couldn't believe that these two men could have committed the crime. However, he said that about a month ago, he and Frank Douham, Cliff Dawley's brother-in-law, had again discussed the Greenwood robbery, admitting that at the time neither could place Dawley in Vancouver on the day of the robbery. He claimed that he and Rose Dawley set up her husband's first escape from Oakalla Penitentiary on March 7, 1954, when the prisoner was in Vancouver General Hospital having been admitted there from Oakalla Penitentiary after faking an injury. He also participated in the bank robber's second escape in August of 1954, although he claimed he only drove the escapee to a "Honkie" friend's house to hide him out, then picked up Rose just ahead of the police and took her to her husband. Polanski also tried to help in The Farmer's escape from the penitentiary in 1955, where the stickup man was held after he got caught robbing a bank in Burnaby, British Columbia. Polanski said he had clothes and money ready for the prisoner, but was intercepted by the police before he could make his delivery.

As the interview continued, Polanski's personal demeanor appeared to change, almost as if he now felt comfortable in the presence of the officers. He became very talkative; he admitted that within the past few months, he had got word from "J.W." that he was to put $250.00 in a pipe and throw it over the wall so Wasylenchuk could buy materials for the workshop in the penitentiary. Polanski grinned when he mentioned this, but then added, "At least the man did not ask for a gun."[3]

Waitt was beginning to feel even more confident now, and thought that if they could be fortunate enough to find other "friends" of the principal suspects in this case that were in a similar bind to Polanski, they may very well solve this crime. Meanwhile, Morphett kept the suspect's hopes up for a light sentence on the drug trafficking charge by frequently reminding him that the Vancouver police would help him in the courts if he were to tell the officers all he knew of the three bank robbery suspects' criminal activities and, in particular, of any knowledge he may have of their involvement in the Seattle robbery. The officer went on to explain that this investigation was a big thing now, and that both the Canadian and American authorities were deeply interested in bringing it to a satisfactory conclusion. If he cooperated said Morphett, it would go a long way towards mitigating Polanski's problems on the drug charge. Upon hearing this, the ex-convict contradicted himself by readily replying, "Cliff and 'J.W.' could very well have pulled the Seattle job, as it was The Farmer's method of operation, and both of these guys have worked before as a team in similar operations such as in the Seattle job."

During the conversation, he brought up the subject of the reward, stating that Inspector Plummer had questioned him some years ago and had mentioned that $50,000.00 was available for the right information on this case. Waitt confirmed that the reward was still available to the "right man," giving no indication that the figure mentioned was several thousand dollars over that which was being offered by the City of Seattle and the Washington State Banking Association and others who had contributed to the reward fund. The man then asked if anyone had ever found Wasylenchuk's money; he stated that the two bank robbers made a practice of burying their "hot money" after they pulled a job. Waitt immediately recalled that, in one of Rolston's reports, there was some mention from an inform-ant that Wasylenchuk had money buried in the States. He made a note to check on this when he got back to the hotel. Their host, continuing, said several years ago he learned where Cliff Dawley had buried loot from a bank robbery and he went out and dug it up; he was having a ball spending the stolen money when word got back to Dawley. Learning of this, the bank robber went to where he had hidden the money and, finding it gone, came to Polanski's house. He was armed and carrying a blanket and a blow torch, and he gave Polanski twenty minutes to come up with the money or he would take him out in the woods, shoot him, roll him in the blanket and burn his body. Polanski said he handed over what was left of the money and that was the last time he double-crossed his colleague. It was late now and the officers returned to their hotel with Morphett reminding Polanski that they would return.[4]

The following day, the Vancouver sergeant met Polanski as he left the courthouse in downtown Vancouver; the man was quite shaken. He had just come from his preliminary hearing and the prosecutor threatened to ask for the maximum sentence on the drug charge. Polanski said he couldn't "take a ten year sentence," but said he just couldn't remember any additional information that would be of help to the officers on the Seattle case. He asked for the sergeant's home telephone number indicating that he would call the officer later with information if he thought of something else that was pertinent to the detectives' case.

Late that same day the three officers located Kris McRay, a produce truck driver who used to work in a used car lot owned by one Danny Danahur at 2010 Commercial Street in downtown Van-couver. The officers had learned earlier in the investigation that there was a possibility the car The Farmer drove to Seattle before the robbery, had been loaned to him by Danahur and that the vehicle, a 1953 Chevrolet, was picked up by Bobby Talbot. McRay denied any knowledge of the vehicle transaction, nor could he identify any of the suspects except Clifford Dawley when shown their mug pictures. He readily identified Dawley, but stated this was because the criminal had frequently "made the papers" in Vancouver. Danahur, whom McRay worked for part-time, was injured in an accident on his car lot on March 1st, 1954, and died the day before the Greenwood robbery. The truck driver claimed that after Danahur's death, he and a friend of the car dealer, Bob Jarvis, inventoried the vehicles on Danahur's used car lot and turned the inventory over to Attorney John Milne who was handling the estate for Danahur's wife. Milne was contacted later that same day but he could not find a 1953 Chevrolet listed on the vehicle inventory, nor the title for such a car.

Shortly after returning to the Georgia Hotel that night, Waitt received a call from Sergeant Morphett who said that Detective Sheppard of the Vancouver Police Morality Squad had located Donna Clearidge, a woman Irvin Teague had mentioned as being the person who allegedly took $1,000.00 to the owner of the Blue Bird Motel in Seattle for John Wasylenchuk, shortly after the Greenwood robbery. Sheppard had talked to Donna and the detective said he would set up an interview whenever the American officers were ready.

The next day, June 4th, the three officers again met with Inspector Plummer to bring him abreast of the developments of the investigation during the preceding three days. Plummer was glad to hear that the officers were making headway on the case and again stated it was Chief Archer's desire that the Vancouver Department cooperate fully in the investigation. During this conversation, it was suggested by Morphett that they could possibly be of more help if he were aware of the complete details of the entire case. He realized that it was impossible for the American officers to be totally aware of all of the details of this case, as the investigative reports now ran into hundreds of pages, but suggested the Canadians needed more complete knowledge of this investigation to do their job properly. Waitt agreed and suggested that the two Canadians come to Seattle and go over the case files of both the FBI and those in the Seattle Police Department. Plummer contacted Chief Archer and he immediately concurred; arrangements were made for both men to come to Seattle the following Monday, June 8, 1959.[5]

The day following the meeting with Inspector Plummer in Vancouver, Waitt and Crisman returned to Seattle to spend the weekend with their families. On Monday, the two Canadian officers arrived in the city and spent the next two days going over the investigative reports on the case. They also discussed with the American officers the various aspects of the investigation, particularly in respect to the statements previously reported by Detective Ivey and FBI agents regarding both the involvement of the two principal suspects and the Canadian police officers' alleged collusion with them as reported by several informants. After review of the case files in Seattle, the Vancouver officers returned to Canada with a much better understanding of the events of the case that occurred outside their own jurisdiction, as earlier reported by the agents and Seattle detectives. Before leaving police headquarters, the Canadians expressed their regret to Waitt that the FBI had spent so much time in gathering data about the activities of these criminals in Canada when much of the information collected was common knowledge to the Vancouver officers. What wasn't known could have been discovered sooner had their department been kept fully informed by the FBI of the status of the case in the early stages of the investigation.

Upon Sergeant Morphett's return to Canada, he re-contacted Steve Polanski, for now he had a much better understanding of the case than on his previous visits with the narcotics trafficker and he had some questions of his own to ask. But Polanski was not nearly as interested in helping the officer now as before, for he had retained another attorney who had assured him that he would not receive a prison sentence exceeding two years on the pending drug charges. His response to Detective Morphett was, "I can do the two years easy and with good time be out in sixteen months." However, he still wanted to keep his options open; he knew there was no guarantee of a short sentence. And before the officer left his house, Polanski reiterated that it was quite possible that the two principal suspects they discussed earlier, were the ones responsible for the robbery in Seattle, and that the detective should try to locate Mary Peters, for she knew who "pulled that job," alleging Peters was a close friend of The Farmer. He volunteered that he could "accidentally" drop in on her, get her drunk and try to con the woman into admitting to him her personal knowledge of the actual robbery and of the suspects involvement. Sergeant Morphett was acquainted with Mary Peters, a young attractive girl, who was believed to be associated with John Wasylenchuk and he knew that she frequented the Astor Bar and the Canadian Legion Building on Kingsway in the city.

On June 14th, Crisman and Waitt returned to Vancouver and were met by the Vancouver police sergeant at the Georgian Hotel; he brought the two Americans up-to-date on his investigation during the past three days, and told them that Steve Polanski was still reluctant to talk. The following day he took the two officers to meet RCMP Sergeant Jack Purdy. Purdy had worked on the post office burglary cases in which Irvin Teague was involved. He was aware of Mary Peters activities also and stated that the young woman hung out with a group the Mounties were interested in and they were about to pick up a friend of hers for questioning in connection with a murder case in a Vancouver suburb. During the meeting, the RCMP officer was told of Peters' possible involvement in the Seattle case and the Mountie agreed to see what he could develop from her acquaintances now that he was informed of her potential value as a witness.

During the next several days, Waitt and Crisman spent some time going over the information gathered by Morphett since their last visit. They also expended a great deal of time and effort trying to locate witnesses on their own, but were not very successful. And to further complicate the matter, Sergeant Morphett had been temporarily pulled off this assignment to assist in the investigation of a homicide and was not relieved of that duty until June 24th.

The sergeant had just come from assize court that morning where he had learned that Steve Polanski had been sentenced to five years in the penitentiary for trafficking in drugs; he had not received the lenient sentence promised by his attorney.[6] The officers felt that with their witness now in the penitentiary with the two principal suspects, there was little hope he would provide any further information to them on the two holdup men.

Sergeant Morphett brought other news which was disappointing to the Americans. George McKnight, another associate of Clifford Dawley's, who had earlier been considered as a potential source of information by the FBI, was sentenced to ten years in the penitentiary the same day as Polanski. He was convicted of arson and, because of his extensive criminal record, was sentenced as a habitual criminal.[7] The officers were hoping to be able to convince both Polanski and McKnight that if they would produce some worthwhile information on the Seattle case, it would go a long way toward their efforts to obtain lighter sentences. That hope had now vanished, for they could do nothing to shorten the prisoners' confinement.

The following day, June 25th, the three officers met with Sergeant Robert W. Leatherdale, the star witness before the 1955 Royal Commission; he was still with the Vancouver vice squad. Leatherdale brought to the investigators several "trick books" seized from Donna Clearidge in a vice raid earlier in the year. Clearidge was operating a call-girl racket in West Vancouver at the time and the records of over 3,000 customers and "senders" in both Vancouver and Seattle were listed, along with the names of the girls who were being rotated through Clearidge's houses. Waitt copied the names of both customers and girls from the Seattle area, and Crisman obtained those listed to addresses in other American cities. It was hoped that, through one or two of these girls, Clearidge could be traced to Seattle shortly after the time of the Greenwood robbery, and thus the officers would be able to corroborate Lester Teague's story, that Clearidge had, in fact, delivered money for John Wasylenchuk to the manager of the Blue Bird Motel. The Americans knew that this would be an almost impossible task, but their case against the Canadian bank robbers rested almost entirely on an accumulation of circumstantial evidence which they hoped would eventually lead to an indictment and ultimately to the conviction of one or more of the stickup trio.

The two Americans spent their final day in Vancouver going over the case with Sergeant Morphett. They would not return to Canada again until the first week in August and it was intended that, during the intervening time, each officer operating independently would check out various leads in their own jurisdictions. Waitt and Crisman had more than enough to keep them busy and Morphett was to locate and interview the Talbot brothers. Norman Talbot had been released from the British Columbia Penitentiary in March and Bobby Talbot was released on June 23, 1959, the day Steve Polanski and George McKnight were sentenced to serve time in the same institution. The Vancouver sergeant would also go to the provincial automobile license bureau at Victoria to check for the ownership by Danny Danahur of a 1953 Chevrolet vehicle, which John Wasylenchuk reportedly borrowed for his trip to Seattle in March, 1954.

On August 4, 1959, Agent Crisman and Sergeant Waitt returned to Canada. The Seattle sergeant had run into a dead-end on his investigation of prostitutes or their customers who could place Donna Clearidge in Seattle shortly after the March, 1954 robbery. He was all the more disheartened, because he had wasted almost a week unraveling a story given to Captain Charlie Rouse by a Canadian criminal taken into custody in Portland, Oregon after being apprehended passing stolen postal money orders there. The man had learned of the reward being offered in the Greenwood case and, being acquainted with the Canadian bank robbery suspect's reputations, tried not only to cash in on the reward money, but he also hoped to receive favorable consideration for his "good deed" from his parole officer. Waitt hoped that the information would be of value, but after checking the whereabouts and past history of the man, he concluded that the entire story of "first hand knowledge of the Greenwood case" was completely fabricated.

FBI agents, in the meantime, had located and interviewed Robert John Jarvis, formerly a close friend of Danny Danahur. Jarvis was living in Edmonds, Washington, a Seattle suburb. He had been identified in 1954 by the FBI as a friend of Danahur who would possibly have knowledge of the auto dealer loaning a car to John Wasylenchuk. The man had been close to Danahur when Danahur was alive, he had been to his home on several occasions, and was the auto dealer's frequent fishing partner in the early fifties. He worked for the Great Northern Railroad for eighteen years and, in 1954, was living and working for the same company in Vancouver. When shown pictures of Clifford Dawley, the Talbot brothers, and three or four other Canadian bank robbers, Jarvis told the agents that some looked familiar, but he could not identify any of them. He was then shown a picture of John Wasylenchuk and the railroad man reacted more noticeably. Jarvis said he didn't think that Wasylenchuk was the name he had remembered this man by. When the name Wesley was mentioned, Jarvis responded that that was the name he recalled and he was sure John Wesley had rented cars from his friend at the used car lot. Upon inquiring as to the type of vehicles the lot owner handled, Jarvis responded that most were vintage models with the exception of a very few late-model automobiles. When asked if one of these could have been a 1953 blue and white Chevrolet, the man said he thought that he remembered seeing the auto dealer driving this type of vehicle, but it was such a long time ago he could not be sure. Little else was learned from this witness.

The two officers again met Sergeant Morphett in Vancouver at the Devonshire Hotel where they had now set up their base of operations. The Canadian had successfully located not only the Talbot brothers, but also Jackie Brown, Bobby Talbot's wife, and had made arrangements for interviewing the subjects when Waitt and Crisman were ready. He had also arranged for interviews with Donna Clearidge on August 11th at her home in West Vancouver.

From F. W. Cummings, warden of the British Columbia Penitentiary in New Westminster, the sergeant had learned of the current status of the two principal suspects in the American's case. The Warden advised him that Clifford Dawley's release date from the penitentiary was set for September 16, 1960, just one year away, and that the convict was now acting the part of a model prisoner. He was doing "easy time," and was assigned to paint murals on the walls of the main dining room in the penitentiary. Cliff Dawley was an excellent artist and had painted portraits of his wife and daughter and several of his fellow convicts. But the Warden had had misgivings about his prisoner. The man was a natural leader and commanded respect from his fellow prisoners principally through fear, but respect nevertheless which, if misdirected, said Cummings, could very well lead to unrest within the prison. However, the bank robber gave every indication that he would not jeopardize his chance for parole by challenging prison authority. Waitt and Crisman were again startled when Morphett said the warden promised to forward a new mug shot taken of Dawley, as the prisoner had undergone his second facelift operation, the first in May of 1958, the second within the past month. The Canadian officer had not questioned the warden relative to how a vicious criminal such as Clifford Dawley, who both Canadian and American authorities had been trying to connect to several serious crimes on both sides of the border, could manage to obtain such an operation while held in a government institution. The detectives had experienced many strange things in their careers as police officers, but facial surgery which would very likely change the appearance of a known murder suspect while he was held in custody, was hard to accept. Although Waitt was shocked by this turn of events, the tone of Chief Lawrence's earlier memorandum had forewarned him that some officials at the highest levels within the Vancouver city government had, in effect, attempted to forestall their investigation at every turn. Waitt was thankful, however, that the Seattle case did not hinge solely upon eyewitness identification of the perpetrators of the robbery and murder in Seattle.

The Canadian officer had also learned that Rose Dawley, now at the family home on Beach Drive in Vancouver, was seeking a divorce from her husband, a separation which was being contested by her husband.[8]

On August 11, Waitt, Crisman and Leatherdale drove to Donna Clearidge's home in West Vancouver. Sergeant Charles Campbell of the Vancouver police Morality (Vice) Squad had arranged for their visit. Upon arrival, Clearidge said she would be glad to talk to the three men. The Vancouver sergeant was quick to point out that he was not interested in her current prostitution operation nor were the two Americans, but only in what light she could shed on Irvin Teague's story about her delivery of $1,000.00 to the manager of the Blue Bird Motel in Seattle in 1954 for John Wasylenchuk. After extensive questioning of Miss Clearidge, the officers were reasonably certain that Teague's story would not hold up. Donna readily admitted that she exchanged both girls and customers with call-girl operators in Seattle, Portland and San Francisco, and had made several visits to Seattle in the early 1950's, but none in 1954 or 1955. Although not given Teague's name, she said whoever told them the story about her acquaintances with the three Canadian bank robbery suspects, was certainly talking about her. She knew the three suspects well, and she had in fact sent $1,000.00 across the border. But the money was sent to a friend after she sold the man's car and he had left town before the sale was finalized. Clearidge said she could remember three incidents, however, that occurred in 1954 which would tend to discredit the story of her delivering money for anyone across the line; first she visited her husband George almost daily in March and April of 1954, when he was a patient in the Willow Street T. B. Hospital. Secondly, she was involved in an accident in downtown Vancouver and her car was impounded by the police about this same time. She claimed she was so broke that she couldn't pay the impound fee, so she left the car in storage for several weeks. She also claimed that, during the spring of 1954, she was living with her husband's parents and she not only had the care for her four-year-old son, but also looked after the elderly Mrs. Clearidge.

During the next several days, the officers checked out Donna's story. At police headquarters, they found an accident report which verified the story about the auto accident and subsequent impound. The accident occurred on April 16, 1954 and the car was not released until August 10, over five months later. This indicated that Donna had possession of her car for approximately thirty-four days after the March 12 robbery date, but the report did confirm her story about the vehicle being in storage during much of 1954. The officers next went to the Canadian Imperial Bank of Commerce on Granville, and learned that Donna had, in fact, deposited $2,000.00 on March 21st and withdrawn $1,000.00 the same month, which again tended to confirm her story of the sale of the friend's automobile. However, the possibility still existed that the money in question could very well have come from Wasylenchuk. But Sergeant Waitt was now convinced that this part of Teague's story about the delivery of the $1,000.00 by Donna to the owner of the Blue Bird Motel in March or April of 1954 was not true. He knew that, before he could discount the story altogether, some additional evidence would have to be uncovered to substantiate her story; but for now he was ready to write off this part of the investigation and concentrate on other leads. Her version of the circumstances surrounding the transfer of the money was later further supported when Sergeant Morphett verified, through hospital records, that Donna's husband was in fact in the Willow Street T. B. Hospital in Vancouver during the spring and summer of 1954, and the nursing station patient personal laundry records indicated that she visited her husband nearly every week during that period.

In discussing the outcome of their investigation, Waitt and Crisman decided that it was time to move on to other areas where there appeared to be greater hope in unraveling the true story of this case. They agreed that it was time to contact the Talbots directly, as Sergeant Morphett had collected some information on the activities of the three brothers and their families during the preceding month. In checking the Bureau of Vital Statistics in Vancouver, it was learned that a baby girl was born to Jackie Brown-Talbot and Maurice Talbot on January 24, 1954, approximately six weeks before the date of the March robbery in Seattle; this would still have made it possible for Jackie Talbot to have been at the Blue Bird Motel at the time of the robbery. Saint Paul's Hospital records indicated Mrs. Talbot's baby, Sharon, was born premature and was not released from the hospital in Vancouver until February 22, 1954. However, the mother had been discharged from the hospital a few days after delivery of the baby.

But the Vancouver officer had gained little else and he was having a difficult time setting up a telephone tap on the brothers. Both Norman and Bobby were frequently on the move. Because of the large number of people going in and out of the houses where the Talbots had been seen, Sergeant Morphett said it was difficult to zero in on one location which would be most productive. Waitt had little hope that a telephone tap would be of much value to their case because of the elapsed time since the Seattle crime, but it could prove worthwhile if the Canadians could intercept the brothers in the act of committing another crime. However, this was nothing more than a long shot and Waitt knew such investigative tactics usually proved fruitless. Sergeant Morphett thought there was still a possibility of success in using a "wire" for he located Jackie Brown-Talbot's residence in an apartment on Caribou Street in Burnaby, British Columbia. She left Bobby Talbot and was now married to Charles Bailey, a commercial fisherman. The Vancouver officer thought if they could apply some pressure on Mrs. Bailey, a "recorded" warning phone call from her to one of her ex-husband's associates may not be too much to expect. The officers made arrangements to interview the ex-Mrs. Talbot at her home on August 24th.

It was 7:30 in the evening when the three officers arrived at Jackie and Charles Bailey's apartment in Burnaby. Sergeant Waitt and Agent Crisman waited in their car as the Vancouver officer went into the apartment house. The sergeant wanted the two men to wait until he had a chance to talk to the woman alone as he thought he might be able to convince her to see them. Upon identifying himself at the door of the apartment, Mrs. Bailey immediately became hostile and, at first, even refused to talk to him; but the officer persisted and eventually she invited him into her apartment. When advised of the reason for his visit, she refused to meet with Crisman and Waitt. After considerable coaxing and a promise from the sergeant that he would not disclose to the Talbots anything she told him, she agreed to answer Morphett's questions regarding the activities of the Talbot brothers; but she said she would not talk to the two Americans unless her husband, who was at sea, was present, nor would she talk about any criminal activity Bobby Talbot may have been involved in.

The woman said she married Charles Bailey after her former husband, Bobby Talbot, was sentenced to seven years in the penitentiary on a drug charge in November, 1954. She gave birth to her first baby on January 24, 1954 and Talbot was the father. She claimed the baby was in an incubator for six weeks (although this time period was not supported by hospital records), and during that time she said she visited the baby every day and never once left the Vancouver area. She claimed that the only person who could support this was Norman Talbot's girlfriend, Peggy Teller, and Bobby Talbot himself. The detective asked if she knew Clifford Dawley. She responded, "Who is he?" Morphett explained that the man was a bank robber and had escaped twice from the penitentiary, whereupon Jackie said, "Oh, he was The Farmer's partner." She then identified The Farmer as John Wasylenchuk. Mrs. Bailey expressed surprise that the police would consider that she would be associated with the same group as Clifford Dawley and Wasylenchuk in 1954, for at that time she was only eighteen years old. Further she denied participating in any illegal activity with either man, yet she refused to elaborate on how she knew of one of the men as "The Farmer," a nickname the stickup man had picked up in prison.

After the interview, Morphett reported what he had learned to the two Americans who had waited on the street for over an hour. The woman agreed to meet with the three officers at their hotel when her husband could be with her; but under no circumstances would she talk to the FBI, nor to any American officer, unless her husband were present. She claimed that she would contact the Vancouver sergeant's office when Bailey came in from his fishing trip.

The day following Morphett's interview with Jackie Bailey, Waitt and Crisman went to Saint Paul's Hospital to follow up on the medical records of the baby born there to Jackie (Talbot) Bailey in January, 1954. They found the attending physician to be Doctor H. E. St. Louie whose office was located on West Broadway. Later, in an interview with the doctor, he immediately recognized a picture of Mrs. Bailey and clearly recalled her case. Doctor St. Louie said that, upon a baby's release from Saint Paul's Hospital, particularly a premature infant, he always gave well-defined instructions to the mother on the proper care and feeding of the child, and it was his practice to see the mother six weeks after birth, which in this case would be near the date of the Greenwood robbery. But the doctor was unable to locate his appointment books for 1954, and thus was unable to determine if the mother had returned for her final physical examination. He had moved to his new office in 1955 from the Medical Dental Building on West Broadway and believed the appointment books for 1954 must have been misplaced in the move. Before the officers left, the physician agreed to continue to look for the records in question and told Waitt that they might be in a storage locker at his home.

The two investigators returned to their hotel and met Bill Morphett, explaining what transpired. The Vancouver detective then called Jackie Bailey from the hotel and she stated that she went back to Doctor St. Louie for the examination as directed, about six weeks after delivery of her baby, and the doctor was still located in the Medical-Dental Building, but she could not recall the exact date of this visit. After the baby was released from the hospital, she chose Doctor Schuman to care for her new daughter. Later Sergeant Morphett located this doctor at 1734 West Broadway and the physician's receptionist had no trouble finding the file on the baby. The record indicated that the doctor first saw the baby girl and her mother on May 13, 1954, a date which would be of no help to the officers.

The next day the Vancouver sergeant, picking up where the two Americans left off; called on Dr. St. Louie to determine if he had yet located his appointment books for 1954. The doctor regretted that he had located most of his old records back to 1951, but his house-call files for the first part of March, 1954 were not among them. He thought this was very strange, but agreed to keep looking for them. He suggested that the detective check with the Victorian Order of Nurses, a nursing service sponsored by the Community Chest to help young mothers who were destitute, to see if they may have cared for Mrs. Talbot and the new baby. Upon checking with the Order, their records indicated that a nurse first visited Mrs. Talbot and her newborn baby at Saint Paul's Hospital on February 17, 1954. Their next visit was at Jackie Talbot's residence on May 4, 1954, neither date being of any value to the investigating officers. The officer noted that on the Talbot Baby's record card there was a notation that Doctor St. Louie had seen the child between the February and May dates, but there was no indication that he had visited the Talbot home during the first two weeks of March, 1954.

While Waitt and Crisman had returned to Seattle during this last week of August, 1959, Sergeant Morphett continued to investigate the Talbot family movements. On August 27, he found Jackie and her husband, Charles Bailey, at home at their Burnaby address. Bailey agreed, after some discussion with his wife, to help the officer any way that he could with the investigation into the Talbot brothers' activities. Bailey knew Charlie Talbot and his wife quite well and had lived with them for a few months in 1954. It was shortly after this that Bobby Talbot was committed to the penitentiary. He didn't know whether Jackie had ever gone to the States with Bobby Talbot, nor did he ever overhear any conversation or discussion about a bank robbery in Seattle.

When Jackie was questioned regarding her visits to Dr. St. Louie and the help she received from the Victorian Order of Nurses, she emphatically denied she went to Seattle in March, 1954 with any-one. During that time, she said, she had to feed her newborn baby one ounce of milk through a tube, every two hours, and that the Victorian Order of nurses came to her apartment almost daily to help. She assumed the nurses were willing to help her because she was so young. It was a very difficult job to feed the child, and the nurses tried to assist as much as they could.

Later the sergeant sent word to Peggy Teller through Detective Simmons of the Vancouver Department that he wanted to see her. The woman agreed to meet with the Vancouver officer on September 1st in a downtown bar. During this meeting, Peggy declined to give the sergeant her home address, as she was afraid of the Talbots and said she didn't want them to find out where she was living. She had heard that Norman and Bobby were looking for her, and if they found out she was talking to the police about their past criminal activity, she said she would be in serious trouble. Peggy could fill the detective in on a few of the things that her friend and Bobby Talbot had been involved in in Canada, but she knew nothing about a robbery in Seattle. Peggy left Norman Talbot in 1952, but occasionally visited him at the penitentiary until shortly before he was released. She recalled that the FBI had visited her several years before and had used her telephone in checking with the penitentiary on the dates that she had last visited.

In discussing Jackie Talbot, Peggy Teller confirmed Jackie's story of the problems she experienced with the new baby in 1954 and assured Morphett that the woman could not have left Vancouver because of this. Peggy frequently visited Jackie Talbot during that time as she felt sorry for the girl, but didn't really care for her, as one time when Jackie was hustling on the east side, she picked up Peggy's friend, Norman, and "laid him" for ten dollars. Jackie laughed about it when she told Peggy, but she said Norman was just a street pickup and there wasn't anything between them.[9]

Peggy related a story which tended to confirm Teague's statement of the Talbot brothers' concealing Clifford Dawley after his escape in March, 1954. One day on her way back to her apartment from Jackie Talbot's, where she had been assisting with the new baby, Franky Douham, Dawley's brother-in-law and Charlie Talbot stopped her as she was about to enter her apartment, took her key and told Peggy not to return to the apartment until they notified her.

She told them she would need a few clothes, and they went in and got the things that she asked for. Peggy couldn't remember the date that this occurred, but said that about six days later, Douham called her at Jackie Talbot's and told her it was okay to return home. When she entered her apartment, she found nothing disturbed except that there was a blanket covering the front window. Peggy surmised that the Talbots had used her apartment as a hide-out for Cliff Dawley, after his escape from Vancouver General Hospital.[10]

When the Vancouver officer discussed this later with the Americans, Waitt recalled Teague's statement that, after the prison escape, two of the Talbot brothers hid Clifford Dawley for a few days until he left Vancouver to "pull" the planned robbery in Seattle. Waitt guessed Peggy's apartment must have been the hide-out used by the holdup man.

Sergeant Morphett questioned Peggy Teller closely as to whether Jackie Talbot had remained in Vancouver after Douham and Charlie Talbot moved her out of her apartment. Peggy responded that Jackie Talbot never left her house until several weeks after the new baby returned home from the hospital. But she said it was not uncommon for the Talbot brothers to disappear frequently from the city for two or three days at a time, and one time while at Jackie Talbot's, she heard Charlie, Bobby and Franky Douham discussing the Seattle robbery, but she could not say definitely whether any of them admitted to actually "pulling the job," or if they were talking about someone else. But Peggy recalled one of them saying, "It was a quick trip, down and back." She assumed they were talking about their trip to Seattle at the time of the robbery.

Morphett's next task was to trace the movement of Bonnie Murphy, Charlie Talbot's girl friend. Although the American officers could not definitely rule out Jackie Talbot as having made the trip to Seattle in the spring of 1954, they wondered if the couple at the Blue Bird Motel could not have been Charlie Talbot and his girl friend Bonny Murphy. Morphett found a medical record of Bonny Murphy at Pearson T.B. Hospital on West 57th Street, after learning from Peggy that Bonnie had tuberculosis and was confined at Pearson in 1954. The record indicated that Bonnie had been admitted to Pearson Hospital in 1953 and released in July, 1955. However, it was not uncommon for patients to be released to go home for a few days, whenever a doctor thought it may be in the best interest of the patient. But there was no record of Bonnie having been released during the first or second week of March, 1954. While at the hospital, a supervisor told Morphett that the only sure way to determine if a patient had been furloughed for a few days was to check the patient's temperature charts. These were obtained from the hospital staff, and they indicated that Bonnie Murphy had entered Pearson Hospital on November 19, 1953, and had remained there each day through February, 1955, except for two days, December 23 and 24, 1953. This record definitely eliminated Bonnie Murphy as an accomplice in the Seattle robbery.

On September 3, 1959, Sergeant Morphett again picked up Detective Waitt and Agent Crisman at the Devonshire Hotel. Waitt had called Warden F. W. Cummings at the British Columbia Penitentiary in New Westminster and the three officers had an appointment to see the warden that afternoon. Warden Cummings had obtained permission for the two American officers to talk to Bobby Talbot, Clifford Dawley and John Wasylenchuk. But before they could interview several other prisoners, whom Teague claimed had knowledge of the two suspect's involvement in the Greenwood case, as earlier requested by Waitt, the Warden said he would again have to clear this with the Bureau of Prisons in Ottawa.

Later, the two officers related to Cummings the story Teague had told of him and The Farmer splitting a bottle of whiskey in their cell and of Wasylenchuk's admission to their informant during that drinking session that he, Cliff Dawley and Bobby Talbot robbed the Greenwood Bank and that Dawley had shot three police officers. Warden Cummings confirmed the fact that several attempts, some successful, were made to smuggle whiskey into the penitentiary, for he had found several empty "mickeys" in the dining room at Christmas time in 1954, and found five bottles of whiskey buried in the flower beds outside the walls. However, to the best of his knowledge, Wasylenchuk was not involved in these incidents. Warden Cummings also told the officers that this prisoner, like his colleague, was now playing the model prisoner role, always very polite to the prison staff and no longer bragging of his exploits. He was more apt to say

"Crime doesn't pay," than to expound on his past criminal adventures.

After learning of the present status of the three convicts, Waitt and Crisman decided not to interview them at that time, but asked Warden Cummings to keep the officers advised as to who came to the penitentiary to visit the three men. Upon their return to Vancouver, the two Americans interviewed two ex-convicts who had been cell-mates of Teague and Wasylenchuk, but no worthwhile information was obtained, as both men denied knowing anything of the two suspects' involvement in any crime in the U.S.

Before this visit to Canada on August 24th, Crisman had been notified by his Seattle office that Irvin Teague, now in the federal penitentiary at Leavenworth, Kansas, sent a letter to Agent Rolston through the FBI's general delivery post office box in Seattle. In the letter, Teague indicated that he had additional information on the Greenwood case for the FBI, but would not put it in writing. As the officers had again been unsuccessful in developing any further solid leads on this trip to Canada, it was decided that upon their return to Seattle, they would proceed to Kansas to interview the federal prisoner. While they were out of Canada, Sergeant Morphett said he would continue to try to place a "phone tap" on the Talbot's telephone, provided he could pin them down to one location. He was also to check with Dr. St. Louie again to see if the doctor had yet located any further record of his visits to Jackie Talbot in March, 1954.

Notes

[1] Since the Royal Commission hearings of 1954-55, Archie Plummer had risen to his current rank of Inspector of Police and now commanded the General Investigation Section of the Detective Division. This Section included Burglary and Theft, Homicide and Robbery, General Investigations and the Special Squad units under the direction of Detective Superintendent Ben Jelley. Jack Horton, whom Plummer had testified against before the Royal Commission, was the superintendent of the Patrol Division at this time.

[2] Charles A. Rouse, conversations with the author, 1972.

[3] Sergeant Charles K. Waitt, S.P.D. Case No. 288527, Op. Cit., Investigator's Report, June 6, 1959, p. 2.

[4] Ibid., p. 3.

[5] Ibid., p. 5.

[6] Sergeant Charles K. Waitt, S.P.D. Case No. 288527, Op. Cit., Investigator's Report, June 29, 1959, p. 1.

[7] Ibid.

[8] Ibid., p. 5.

[9] Sergeant Charles K. Waitt, S.P.D. Case No. 288527, Op. Cit., Investigator's Report, September 8, 1959, p. 4.

[10] Ibid., p. 3.

Organization of the Vancouver, British Columbia
Police Department
1956

BOARD OF POLICE COMMISSIONERS

CHIEF CONSTABLE
GEORGE ARCHER

DEPUTY CHIEF CONSTABLE
GORDON AMBROSE

STAFF SUPERINTENDENT
ALAN ROSSITER

SERVICES DIV.
INSP. R. ABERCROMBIE

ACCTG. & RECORDS
DICK PICKERING

PATROL SUPT.
JACK HORTON,

TRAFFIC SUPT.
JOHN FISK

DETECTIVE SUPT.
BEN JELLEY

VICE SECTION
INSP. P. LAMONT

CRIMINAL INV. SEC.
INSP. A. PLUMMER

SPECIAL SERVICES
INSP. R. CRAY,

CRIME LAB
INSP. P. EASLER

WOMEN'S SECTION
INSP. NANCY HEWITT

MORALITY
D/SGT.R.LEATHERDALE

BURGLARY-THEFT
D/SGT TOM STOKES

STOLEN AUTO-YOUTH
D/SGT. D. RICHARDSON

NARCOTICS
D/SGT. JOHN GILLIS
D/SGT. BILL PORTEOUS

HOMICIDE-ROBBERY
D/SGT. BILL MORPHETT

CHECKS/BUNCO & FRAUD
D/SGT. BILL ANDERSON

LIQUOR
D/SGT. DON ROSS

GENERAL INVESTIGATIONS
D/SGT. DON McDONALD

2ND HAND SQUAD
D/SGT. JOHN SCHRETLAN

GAMBLING
D/SGT. LOU KELLY

SPECIAL SQUAD
D/SGT. ALEX STOBIE

WARRANT-SUMMONS
D/SGT. ROY SLATTERY

Chapter

8

Informant Revisited

Upon returning to Seattle in September 1959, Sergeant Waitt was temporarily relieved of the Greenwood Bank robbery assignment in order to again assist homicide detectives on several gambling-related bombing cases which he had worked on earlier in the year. By November he and FBI SA Chet Crisman were back together en route to the state of Kansas. On November 2nd, on a cold and miserable day, they arrived in Kansas City, Missouri. They were there to interview Irvin Teague at the Leavenworth, Kansas, federal penitentiary.

At the penitentiary the following day, they found the prisoner in good spirits; he was tanned and appeared to be in good physical condition. He said, "Doing time in Leavenworth isn't as hard as it was rumored to be; I work out regularly and in the summer I participate in several athletic activities. But I do miss being close to my friends in Vancouver."[1] He even asked the officers to look up an old girlfriend for him when they returned to the city. The last few letters Teague had sent to her had come back marked, "Address Unknown." The girl worked at a cafe on Granville Street across the street from the Dominion Theater. Waitt assured Teague that he would look her up and give her a message.

After other preliminary conversation, the two officers discussed with the informant the story he first gave to Special Agent Dean Rolston and Captain Charles Rouse in the King County jail in Seattle in November, 1958. Particular emphasis was placed on three areas of the story: the 1953 Chevrolet which Wasylenchuk was to have borrowed from the Vancouver car dealer Danny Danahur, Jackie Brown-Talbot's supposed involvement at the Blue Bird Motel, and Donna Clearidge's alleged delivery of money to Mrs. Warren at this motel for John Wasylenchuk. The officers also quizzed Teague about other prisoners in the British Columbia Penitentiary who, the prisoner said, were familiar with The Farmer's story and the part Pete Novis had in this case. He had advised Captain Rouse and Dean Rolston that Novis had driven the two suspects to Seattle the day before the March 12th bank robbery. He repeated the original story as he said he had heard it from his cell-mate without variation, except for one or two minor points which the officers accepted as normal for anyone who was repeating a story told to him years earlier. Teague added that he now recalled the name of the hotel, Sheraton Cadillac, where Dawley was to have stayed in Detroit after the robbery, before crossing back into Canada. After listening to the story again, the officers told him that his story didn't square with the facts of the case. They advised him that Jackie Talbot did not leave Vancouver at the time of the Seattle robbery because of the difficulties she was having with her newborn baby, and that Danny Danahur could not have loaned a car to Wasylenchuk during the first week of March, 1954, as Danahur was injured on March 1st and died ten days later, one day before the robbery in Seattle. Also, Donna Clearidge had not left Vancouver and could not have delivered a package for Wasylenchuk at the Blue Bird Motel in late March or early April of 1954. In addition, Waitt said Pete Novis had just been released from the penitentiary shortly before the robbery, had no car and had not left Vancouver to drive the two stickup men or anyone else to Seattle on the date of the robbery.

Hearing this, Teague was taken aback; he said the officers' investigation made him look bad and he realized that they may now be reluctant to believe anything he had to say. But Teague stuck to his story; he said the story he had told was as told to him by John Wasylenchuk in the penitentiary in 1956, and he believed it to be true. His cell-mate was no braggart and had no reason to give him a false story. There was nothing more he could do to prove the story, nor could he add to it. He expressed concern over his future relationship with the officers and made a comment relative to this affecting his parole. The officers assured him that they were not interested in prolonging his stay in the federal penitentiary, but only in gaining the facts on this case, and wished that Teague could have been more helpful. Before leaving, they advised Teague to think again about the conversation he had had with Wasylenchuk in the British Columbia Penitentiary and the officers would return the following day to discuss that conversation again in detail.

Upon leaving the penitentiary that afternoon, the officers expressed their disappointment that Teague had really added nothing new to the investigation, and they felt that this trip half way across the country was a waste of time. On the following day, November 4th, the two officers again interviewed the prisoner, but little was learned. Teague mentioned that Wasylenchuk fenced his hot money from every bank robbery through a carwash operation in downtown Vancouver and that the owner, Danny Brent, was "bumped off" in a city park in Vancouver by one of his rivals in the "narcotics wars," which were underway in Vancouver in 1954 and 1955. He added that the "hit man" was paid only $3,500.00 for the job. He also claimed that one reason his story didn't match with what the officers had learned from the suspect's associates was because Corporal Nuttall and the Vancouver detective known as "the fixer" undoubtedly warned everybody to keep their mouth shut.[2] After interviewing dozens of people in Canada, Waitt doubted that, for no one had indicated that they had been threatened.

The interview ended on a conciliatory note, with the officers assuring the prisoner that they would not interfere with his parole. Teague was scheduled for release in July of 1961, just nineteen months away.

The two discouraged officers returned to Seattle. Waitt had been on the case for six months now and had hoped by this time, to have found some solid evidence to tie the three Canadians to this robbery; but all he seemed to be accomplishing was proving that several other Canadian "hoods" had not participated in the crime.

In December, Waitt contacted Sergeant Morphett in Vancouver and advised him of the results of his and Crisman's trip to Leavenworth. The Vancouver officer agreed to continue his surveillance of the Talbots and said he was still trying to locate the permanent residence of the three brothers in order to place a phone tap on at least one of their telephones.

Although Sergeant Morphett had worked hard on this case, Waitt was not impressed with the Canadian officer's response.[3] The Seattle officer believed the general attitude of the Canadian authorities was once again one of complete indifference, thus adversely influencing the perspective of the Canadian officers assigned to the case. Waitt was more convinced of this than ever when, in a telephone conversation with Sergeant Morphett, Morphett advised Waitt that he had just been reassigned from Homicide to Narcotics investigations. Morphett was now directly under Inspector Peter Lamont, the Vice Section Commander and the same man who had reported that the Talbot brothers could not have been involved in the Seattle robbery as he, had found that the brothers were gambling in downtown Vancouver shortly after the robbery occurred in Seattle.

Later, Waitt briefed Captain Rouse on the problems that had recently developed in his investigation and the difficulties he and Crisman were encountering in Canada with both the RCMP and the Vancouver Police Department. Rouse was sympathetic to Vancouver's plight in reference to the continued assignment of one of their detective supervisors to a case which was outside their jurisdiction and as all three of the principal suspects were currently in custody and serving time for other offenses, he was sure there were other cases which were of more immediate concern to the Canadians. Granted, the robbery of a bank and murder of a police officer in the United States over five years ago now appeared to be of little interest to the Canadians; but Rouse wanted this case solved, and the only avenue left to him was through the continued assignment of Sergeant Waitt to the investigation, with the hope that between him and the FBI agents in Canada, another break in the case would develop.

Rouse requested another meeting of the participating law enforcement agencies to discuss the ramifications of the investigating officers' findings to date and also to request continued support from the newly-assigned Special Agent in Charge (SAC) of the local FBI office, J. Earl Milnes, who had replaced retiring SAC Richard Auerbach at the beginning of the year. Rouse also needed to convince his own superiors that progress was being made in the investigation in order to continue to receive funding for Waitt's expenditures in Canada.

After hearing the two investigator's report on the case, Chief Lawrence took the position that the Seattle Police Department would continue to pursue this investigation in Canada, alone if necessary. The new FBI SAC, however, agreed that the Bureau would continue in their efforts both in Canada and in the U. S. to attempt to solve this case as long as there was any reasonable expectation that a satisfactory solution could be obtained. It was decided at the meeting to keep Waitt and Crisman working as a team on the case in Canada, and it was also agreed that additional work would be undertaken by other officers to assist these two men. This decision was briefly outlined in a report from Captain Rouse to the Chief of Detectives. His report also included a statement relative to the continuing lack of cooperation on the part of the Canadian authorities, and expressed Rouse's suspicions relative to the motivation of these people. He expressed these thoughts in this memo to his boss shortly after the multiple agency meeting of the first week in January 1960:

SEATTLE POLICE DEPARTMENT
INTER-DEPARTMENTAL MEMORANDUM

From: Captain C. A. Rouse   Date: January 12, 1960
To: V. L. Kramer, Detective Division Chief
Subject: CONFERENCE-GREENWOOD BANK ROBBERY
Special Agent in Charge J. Earl Milnes, Chief of Police H. J. Lawrence, Captain C. A. Rouse, Sergeant C. K. Waitt, Chief Postal Inspector George Worthington and Special Agent C. C. Crisman discussed the subject with the following results:
1. The Vancouver, B. C. Police Department has operated at about one half speed. Detective Bill Morphett is now in Narcotics under Inspector LaMont. Chief Lawrence believes the Vancouver attitude is to "forget it."
2. The U. S. Attorney General's Office is receiving full reports on this case but there is no possibility of federal process now.

3. The FBI will contact the Federal Narcotics Bureau to stimulate their interest in Canadian narcs who might be developed under pressure as sources of information.

4. The ex motel owner (Blue Bird), now in Spokane will not be re-interviewed until more data is available.

5. Our opinion is that we will have to prove the Leavenworth inform-er's story and we must recognize we may eventually have full proof in this case and still not be able to go to trial.

6. Postal Inspector Worthington expects (to obtain) a warrant and extradition of Patsy Novis possibly by February 1st. (Wife of Pete Novis, narcotic addict and wanted in the U. S. for forgery of Cana-dian postal money orders).

7. Chief Lawrence expects the Homicide and Robbery staff to make Seattle narcotics people familiar with this situation so that they may develop Vancouver, B.C. narcotic contacts which might eventually develop new informants. Cliff Dawley will be out this September, (1960). The FBI, through Bellingham Special Agent Al [Alf] Gunn and by top level cooperation with the border and customs people, will try and cover the possibility of his entering into the United States.

8. Red Henderson (Wasylenchuk's former cell-mate) has been moved to the Stone River Penitentiary in Manitoba and this is considered to be suspicious because we believe Henderson was about to "talk." The FBI, through their Ottawa liaison, will investigate the circum-stances of Henderson's prison transfer.

CAR:sa

One week later, on January 20, 1960 Sergeant Waitt and Agent Crisman again met with Sergeant Morphett in the Devonshire Hotel in Vancouver. After a short discussion relative to the progress the Canadian officer was having on this investigation, it soon became evident that, for all practical purposes, Morphett had accomplished nothing since the Americans' last visit to Canada in September, 1959. Morphett still had his, "list of things to be done," which he had agreed to do for the two American officers at their last meeting. But Doctor St. Louie had not been re-contacted regarding his house-call appointment book, which could possibly eliminate Jackie Talbot as a conspiratorial suspect in the Seattle robbery. He had not located the residence of the Talbots, even though Bobby Talbot was released from the British Columbia Penitentiary on June 23, 1959 and Norman Talbot had been arrested by the RCMP in nearby Burnaby on October 29 for Conspiracy to Traffic in Drugs. Norman was out on $10,000.00 bail and was scheduled to appear in Burnaby Police Court on January 21st, the very next day, for a preliminary hearing. Morphett said the drug charge was built by RCMP and Vancouver detectives, but Sergeant Morphett had made no effort to determine which bonding agency had posted bail for the man. It was all too obvious to the officers present in Waitt's hotel room, where the three men were meeting, that no bonding company would post such a large amount of cash to bail out an ex-convict without adequate identification and/or certainty of the individual's residential address. The information leads which the Canadian sergeant had agreed to pursue four months earlier, were now of no apparent interest to the Vancouver authorities. To Waitt, this meant just one thing. The attitude of the Vancouver City Police, in reference to the Greenwood investigation was, as Chief Lawrence had said, "to forget it." It was also evident that the fault did not lie with Morphett. On October 1, 1959, the sergeant had been transferred to the Vancouver Police Department Narcotics Section and he was now under the direct authority of Inspector Pete Lamont, the man who had provided the alibi for the Talbot brothers on this case in 1954. The sergeant had spent the last fifteen years in the Homicide Division, but was now sitting in the back office of the Narcotics Unit with nothing to do but answer the telephone. However, he said that he was still free to assist Crisman and Waitt and would have no trouble getting released from his narcotics assignment.

In their first meeting Waitt inquired why Wasylenchuk's former cell-mate Red Henderson had been moved out of the province to the Stone River Penitentiary in Manitoba, when Vancouver officers knew that the Americans had previously requested permission of Warden Cummings to re-interview him on this case, and Ottawa had given their permission to do so. Morphett responded that Henderson and one of his associates were suspected of having been involved in a murder, and the Vancouver Police Department requested Henderson's transfer to keep the two suspects apart until homicide detectives could interrogate both. Waitt wouldn't buy Morphett's explanation. He could understand separating two suspects before interrogating them, but not by a thousand miles when there were a half dozen other correctional facilities within British Columbia where he could have been confined.

Waitt was annoyed upon hearing of Morphett's lack of progress in the investigation and at this point, Crisman went to call the penitentiary and spoke to Warden Cummings, who gave permission for the two Americans to visit the following day to interview the former associates of John Wasylenchuk and Dawley. These associates were serving time with the three bank robbery suspects. But these interviews were unsuccessful, even though the two investigators spent several hours at the penitentiary. As one inmate, Blondie Martin, a former cell-mate of Bobby Talbot put it, "I don't know anything about the Greenwood robbery, but don't let that lead you to believe I'd tell you anything even if I did." Martin had no other choice to respond as he did for, throughout the entire interview, a prison guard sat next to him. For the two Americans, this was the first time in any penitentiary interrogation setting, in either Canada or the U.S., that this had happened to them. They were sure this had not been done at Warden Cummings' direction, but they made no objection, knowing full well that no prisoner in a maximum security facility would inform on his fellow prisoners under these circumstances. (Looking back on this incident Waitt said it was probably a mistake on their part that they didn't bring this to the attention of Warden Cummings at the time).[4] Martin was active in prison affairs, editor of the prison paper, and chairman of the Prison Welfare Board. John Wasylenchuk was also a member of that board.[5]

That evening, upon returning to Vancouver, Waitt and Morphett re-interviewed Rose Dawley at her Beach Drive home. Crisman, who was the liaison man on this case with the RCMP, contacted the Mounties to see if any new information had been developed on the three suspects.

Rose Dawley was living with a man who was a dispatcher at the Vancouver International Airport, whom Rose described as a square. She was not happy this evening to see these two detectives. She knew Sergeant Morphett from previous visits when he was working with FBI Agent Dean Rolston. Reluctantly Rose agreed to talk to the two men. She was still married to Cliff Dawley, but was seeking a divorce so she could marry her airport dispatcher friend. Her husband was contesting the divorce. Yet she and their daughter still visited him about twice a year, because she said she felt sorry for anyone in prison.

When Waitt started asking questions about her husband's activities in 1954, Rose was unwilling to go over the case again, and became quite irritated with him when he pressed for details of Cliff's movements in March of that year. She said he had nothing to do with the Greenwood case, but did admit that when her husband escaped from Vancouver General Hospital after faking an injury at Oakalla Prison, he hid out at Peggy Teller's apartment. After ten days or more, Cliff came to her apartment here on Beach Drive, and stayed upstairs in her room until October, 1954, a period of about eight months in which she claimed he never left her room. In late October, he allegedly caught the train out of New Westminster for Toronto. She and their daughter joined him there that same month. She claimed he worked as an auto mechanic in a small shop there until his arrest by the Mounties.

Sergeant Waitt had the reputation of being able to charm suspects "right into the county jail," and now, with his casual and friendly manner, got Rose Dawley to open up. Quietly and almost imperceptibly, these two, one a cop and the other a mother and housewife who had been closely and intimately connected with several of the northwest's most vicious criminals, chatted as if they had known each other for many years. Rose told of her life with the "tough guy," as she described her husband, a man of tremendous personal talents, who could paint a portrait of a beautiful woman or a landscape, fix anything including a truck or an automobile, and he even built their own home. But slowly Waitt brought the conversation up-to-date and Rose mentioned that her husband had not always been faithful to her, that he, in fact, on more than one occasion, had taken another woman with him on out-of-town jobs. Although Waitt did not ask her to describe her husband's out-of-town activities, when he mentioned the Talbot women's names, Rose appeared to suddenly realize that she may have said too much to this officer. She appeared frightened and very quickly broke off the interview. She refused to answer any further questions and asked the two officers to leave.

The following day as the two Americans prepared to return to the States, Sergeant Morphett came by the Devonshire to meet with them to seek agreement on a course of action for him to pursue while the two officers were out of the country. Another "things to do list," for the Vancouver officer was developed. He agreed to continue to follow up the case, would again try to locate the Talbot's residence, and set up the phone tap that they had discussed so many times before.[6]

Doctor St. Louie was also to be re-contacted relative to his "lost" records on Jackie Talbot, and the Vancouver officer said that he might also be able to locate an informant or two on his own, whom he thought may be of some benefit to the investigation. When Waitt left the city, he held little hope that much would be accomplished by the sergeant in his absence.[7]

It would be nearly five months this time before the two Americans would be able to return to Canada, for shortly after returning from Vancouver, Waitt was again assigned to assist other detectives in the investigation of another dynamite bombing in Seattle.

In mid-April, Sergeant Morphett notified Special Agent Alf Gunn, the resident FBI agent at the border, that he had been reasonably successful in "turning an informant" who could shed some light on the Talbot brothers' activities. But Crisman and Waitt were still tied up on other assignments and it was not until June 9, 1960, that the two men were again able to return to Vancouver. Morphett, in the meantime, had been talking to Jack McClelland, who had been arrested on a drug trafficking charge with Bobby and Norman Talbot. The case against the three men had been set over in court several times because McClelland had agreed to inform on two other drug pushers, which eventually resulted in their arrest by Vancouver city police and RCMP officers, and the seizure of 96 ounces of pure heroin. McClelland, cooperating with the Vancouver Department, had "turned" several cases since his arrest. He was seeking a recommendation from V. P. D. authorities for leniency, should he be convicted with the Talbots on the current drug charge.

Sergeant Morphett said the suspect had admitted to his involvement in several cases with the Talbots over the past several years, including the $6,000.00 heist of the Black Ball Ferry Terminal office in late 1954 in Vancouver. He told the sergeant that he and Bobby Talbot were together almost constantly during that year, and were down on their luck so badly that they even stooped to shoplifting before the Black Ball job. He claimed there was no way Bobby Talbot could have gone to Seattle without him knowing about it. McClelland said there wasn't even the slightest hint that Bobby was involved in the Seattle job. Morphett believed his informant was telling the truth, as every other story had been checked out and the facts were as described by the suspect. The American officers agreed that the circumstances would indicate that McClelland was in fact telling the truth and that Bobby Talbot may very well be the wrong man, particularly since it looked like his wife, Jackie Talbot, now Bailey, was not the woman who set up a base of operations before the robbery at the Blue Bird Motel in Seattle. Possibly this could have been corroborated had the officers located Jackie's medical records, but Doctor St. Louie had still not found his appointment book for March, 1954.

Norman and Bobby Talbot were scheduled for trial in July and were currently living with two sisters in Burnaby, but again the Vancouver officer had not attempted to set up a phone tap at this location. Allegedly this was because the RCMP and Vancouver narcotic officers had been tailing the two brothers since their release, hoping to discover their source of drugs. Both were suspected of "hustling" drugs to pay their attorney fees and the premiums on the bail bonds. Presumably, this in itself would be justification for the phone tap, but no satisfactory reason was forthcoming from Sergeant Morphett why a phone tap hadn't been installed.

Clifford Dawley was out of the penitentiary now, released on May 23, 1960, and he registered as an ex-felon with the Vancouver Police Department the following day. Morphett had discovered that

Dawley's new address given on his convict registration form was only one block from his wife's home on Beach Drive and that he was working as a warehouseman for Maguire's Coyet Distributors in Vancouver. Dawley had obtained the job on his own, with no help from the Salvation Army or John Howard Society, the two agencies which devote considerable time and effort toward rehabilitation of ex-offenders. But the ex-convict apparently had little need of financial assistance from these two social agencies, as his first order of business was to purchase a new Pontiac automobile.

Notes

[1] Sergeant Charles K. Waitt, S.P.D. Case No. 288527 Investigators's Report, November 6, 1959, p. 2.

[2] Ibid.

[3] Sergeant Charles K. Waitt, conversations with the author, 1965.

[4] Ibid.

[5] Sergeant Charles K. Waitt, S.P.D. Case No.288527, Op. Cit, Investigator's Report No. 9, January 26, 1960, p. 4.

[6] Ibid.

[7] Waitt, Op. Cit, conversations with the author.

Chapter

9

The Interviews

On the afternoon of June 9, 1960, Sergeant Bill Morphett of Vancouver city police took FBI Agent Chet Crisman and Sergeant Charles Waitt to Clifford Dawley's apartment at 1366 Harwood in Vancouver, and the three men waited on the street for the ex-convict to return home from work. About 5:00 P.M. Dawley, driving his new car, approached the officers who were sitting in an unmarked Vancouver police vehicle. He slowed, looked the three men over carefully, and then continued on to the end of the block, turning out of sight. The officers recognized the stickup man readily from the latest penitentiary mug shots given to them by Warden Cummings. About ten minutes later, he returned, parked his car behind the officers, got out and headed toward the apartment house. As he walked by the police vehicle, Sergeant Waitt called out to him and said he would like to talk to him. Dawley came to the car and immediately protested to the three law officers, stating that he had just called Justice H. W. McInnes of the assize court and the judge told him he did not have to talk to the officers.[1] Crisman, first to respond, told the man to relax, that all they wanted to do was ask him a few questions and he asked Dawley to get into the police car. Dawley responded that he had done a lot of silly things in his life, but he wasn't stupid enough to get into a police car voluntarily. He became quite belligerent and nervous, he was perspiring even though it was a cool evening, and his hands were trembling. His whole demeanor was one of a violent man trying hard to gain control of his emotions. He said to the two Americans, "You guys have been bothering my wife and I want you to stay the hell away from my her, 'cause she knows nothing about the Greenwood Bank job and stay away from me and leave me alone. I don't know anymore about that job now than when your partner talked to me four or five years ago. (He was referring to FBI Agent Dean Rolston's interrogation of him in the penitentiary five years earlier). If you're interested in solving that job why the hell don't you talk to Corporal Nuttall as he knows everything that I know about the case."[2]

After a few minutes, the ex-convict became quite calm and finally sat down on the parking strip and appeared to relax to some degree. He denied again to the officers that he had a role in the Greenwood robbery, saying that he would never place his daughter and wife in jeopardy by taking them along on a job like that. This latter response was elicited from the man in reply to a statement made by Waitt, to the effect that Rose knew more about the robbery in Seattle than she was willing to admit. Although the officers had often thought that the woman at the Blue Bird Motel could have been Rose Dawley, until recently they had no reason to believe that it was not Jackie Talbot, as alleged by Irvin Teague in his conversation with John Wasylenchuk when the two were cell-mates in 1956. The bank robber readily admitted to the officers that he had been involved in "two or three" bank heists in Canada but "That's all behind me," he said, "and I've paid dearly for those mistakes with many years in the 'pen.'"

Continuing his questioning, Waitt asked if he would still be willing to submit to a polygraph test, as he had volunteered to do several times both to the FBI and to Seattle police detectives. With this question, Dawley stalled but finally said, "Judge McInnes told me not to take the test, nor even talk to you guys".[3] But after some further urging by Waitt, the man finally said, "If Justice McInnes gives his permission, I'll take the damn test."[4] He claimed that the judge sponsored his release from the penitentiary and he would not do a thing without the judge's OK. He was told that the officers would contact the judge and ask his permission for the test, whereupon he asked that the officers not contact Judge McInnes that evening, but wait till the next morning, before court. Waitt agreed, and the officers returned to their car. Morphett cautioned Waitt and Crisman not to expect too much cooperation from McInnes, for he was sure that the reason the ex-convict asked for a delay in contacting the judge was to give him a chance to "get to the judge" first. He said the judge had a paroled lifer living with him now and was known to be sympathetic toward the plight of ex-cons.[5]

The following morning, June 10, 1960, at 9:20 A.M. the two sergeants and Agent Crisman were admitted by a clerk to Justice H. W. McInnes' chambers in assize court. Sergeant Morphett introduced himself and the two Americans to the judge, and said that they were there to talk with him about Clifford Dawley. Judge McInnes immediately responded, "I know who you people are and why you're here, and it's about time this came to a stop. I have talked to your chief about you," he said, looking at Morphett. He then added: "You've been hounding that man long enough." Crisman interrupted by saying that Dawley had always been willing to see the officers and never once did he refuse to sit down with them and discuss the case even though he could have. Judge McInnes retorted, "I'm the man who sent that man to the penitentiary for seven years, and all the time he was there, you people have been after him until you've worn out your welcome."[6] Morphett interrupted, "That's not true, I've only been assigned to the case for about a year." The judge cut him off, "You stay out of this, Sergeant; I have a call going through to your chief about you now."[7] Waitt thought to himself that this meddlesome jurist was no credit to the Crown; his attitude was that of a typical defense attorney putting on a show for his client, but in this case the client was not even present.[8]

Waitt was visibly upset with the judge's attitude and was about to challenge him when Crisman intervened, "Your Honor, we had a little talk on the street last evening with Mr. Dawley. We did not contact him at his home or place of business as we did not wish to embarrass him. Mr. Dawley said he did not have to talk to us, as you had advised him, but he still stayed of his own free will and talked. He said he was perfectly willing to take the polygraph test if you would OK it. He volunteered to take the test several years ago, but it was never run because we thought the surroundings in the penitentiary were not conducive to an accurate test."[9] To this, Judge McInnes responded, "He's not that stupid; he certainly would not volunteer to do something like that to himself." Crisman said, "Your Honor, I don't want to argue with you, but I was there. He made the proposition himself, and I heard it." Upon hearing this, the judge apologized, then responding said, "Down in your country, all they would have to do is 'holler' the 5th Amendment - up here someone has to protect their rights. I would be the last one to obstruct justice, but you've got to stop seeing him."[10] Crisman persisted, telling the judge that they had a case that had to be investigated and thus far indications were that this ex-convict was involved and it had to be checked out one way or another. The polygraph would be a good method, if the judge would consent.

McInnes told the officers that he had recently attended a banquet in the State of Washington, where an official of the city of Seattle stated, "The murderer of the policeman and the robber of the bank is in jail in Canada and when he is released, we will deal with him. If you have that kind of evidence, why don't you get a warrant, have Dawley arrested and then try to extradite him?"[11]

Waitt could see that further conversation with this man, who was acting defensively and not like a Superior Court judge, was useless. The judge admitted that he had sponsored the prisoner's release and when queried if he were the man's legal advisor, he responded that he had appointed an attorney to assist Dawley. When pressed for the attorney's name, the judge changed his story and stated he was soon going to appoint a competent attorney to represent the man and would give Sergeant Morphett the name of the attorney.[12] During the interview, which lasted less than twenty minutes, Waitt was struck by the obtrusive attitude of this man, who was supposed to be an impartial witness in the criminal justice system, but acted as though he were more interested in protecting a vicious killer than he was in determining the truth.

When the meeting ended, while standing in front of the courthouse, Sergeant Morphett agreed that as soon as McInnes notified him as to the suspect's defense attorney, he would call Crisman and Waitt, who were now returning to Seattle.

Two weeks after the interview with Judge McInnes, Agent Alf Gunn of Bellingham, met with Sergeant Morphett while in Vancouver. The sergeant advised Gunn that Judge McInnes had had lunch with Chief Constable Archer since the three officers visited his chambers, and that the judge had apologized to the chief for his manner in talking to the three men. Morphett said that Chief Archer reported that McInnes never indicated he wanted the chief to pass the apology on to the officers; rather it appeared to be a "fence-mending" proposal. The judge, however did advise the chief that he had appointed an attorney to represent Dawley.[13]

While in Canada, Gunn received notification from Corporal Bruce L. Northrup of the RCMP Burnaby Detachment that in the Sunday edition of the *Vancouver Sun,* in the vital statistics column, there was an article which announced that Clifford Dawley was suing Rose Dawley for divorce and named Ray "Bud" Frazier as correspondent. In Corporal Northrup's memo, he asked that if it was important to Seattle's robbery and murder case, he might be able to set up a meeting with Rose through a connection he had with a mutual friend of Rose's. The agent passed this information on to his two colleagues in Seattle and, as the accompanying memorandum was only signed by Corporal Northrup without approval of higher authority, the two officers decided they would keep this on a personal basis for the time being and notified the Mountie they would contact him the next time they were in Canada.

It would be months before Waitt and Crisman got back together in Canada. Waitt had been on the case for nearly two and one-half years now, and more money and manpower had been expended on this investigation than any other in the history of the Seattle Police Department. Waitt's travel and living expenses alone had completely exhausted the Department's meager investigative fund, and Captain Rouse was having a difficult time obtaining additional funds to carry on the investigation. The city council, always more concerned about the police department's inability to bring in enough revenue through fines and forfeitures to pay its own way, was not sympathetic toward paying travel and per diem expenses for employees "holidaying" in a foreign country. Besides, they reasoned that as the Department had been at this investigation for six years, surely if they were as efficient as they should be, the case would have been solved long ago.

There were other reasons for Waitt's delay in returning to Canada. On July 16, 1960, Michael Distributors, a coin machine business dealing in pinball, cigarette, music machines and other vending equipment was temporarily put out of business by another dynamite explosion. Waitt was assigned to help out on this investigation. Since the bombings began in 1957, 35 polygraph examinations were conducted, and over 6,000 investigative man-hours were expended on these cases. Waitt's talents were badly needed. With the city's mayoralty and council election just a few weeks away, the candidates were having a field day at the police department's expense. Accusations of police inefficiency, incompetence and uncontrolled crime were being leveled at the Department by both the press and those who sought to oust the incumbent mayor and three councilmen. To counter these attacks, Chief Lawrence, with members of the press present, spoke before the Police Officers' Union in the auditorium of the Public Safety Building where, before a packed house, he told Department personnel that, contrary to media reports, the city was not experiencing a crime wave, but was certainly suffering from a newspaper crime wave. He carried with him a copy of the Seattle Post Intelligencer (PI), the city's only morning newspaper, which had for several days carried misleading data on the crime picture within the city. At the present time, per capita crime in Seattle remained consistently below other major cities of comparable size in the U.S., yet repeatedly the "PI" carried large headlines implying just the opposite.[14]

In the mayoralty, Gordon S. Clinton was elected to office, and shortly thereafter Jimmie Lawrence stepped down as Chief of Police, and his former aide, Captain Frank C. Ramon, was appointed as his successor. Captain Rouse was elevated to Assistant Chief by Ramon and Lieutenant A. A. Kretchmar was promoted to Chief of Detectives, to replace the retiring Vic Kramer. Lawrence and Kramer were not the only highranking officers to go; several others were given the choice of demotion or retirement, all accepting the latter. The old adage that a new broom sweeps clean held true as dozens of top level personnel chose retirement.

These combined events were directly responsible for Sergeant Waitt's delay in returning to the business of uncovering the identity of those who were responsible for the robbery of the Greenwood bank and the death of Officer Frank Hardy. Although the sergeant remained in contact by telephone with Sergeant Morphett in Vancouver and he, on one occasion, came to Seattle to brief the Americans, for all practical purposes the investigation came to a standstill. Chet Crisman continued to carry on the investigation for the FBI, as time permitted, but his contacts and sources of information in Canada were principally with the RCMP. However, in dealing with Clifford Dawley and John Wasylenchuk, he recognized that the Vancouver city police were still the best source of information. Without a Seattle police presence, this source was not readily available to the FBI. Too many Vancouver officers remembered Dean Rolston's earlier attempts to gather information which, if made public, would have blown the lid off the elaborate criminal conspiracy which involved Vancouver and RCMP officers and their political leaders. Their purpose was to protect and aid local criminals in carrying out unlawful activity. Although some of this was aired by the press as a result of Sergeants Leonard Cuthbert and Robert Leatherdale's testimony before the Royal Commission, most of the corrupt officers and politicians merely went back to work, being more discreet in their contacts with known criminals. As Paddy Sherman, publisher of The Vancouver Province observed, "The Royal Commission hearings were a travesty, and not all of the 'bad apples' had been plucked from this barrel."[15]

It was not until September, 1961 that the Seattle homicide sergeant returned to Canada to take up where he had left off on the Greenwood case. In mid-September, Sergeant Morphett called and told Sergeant Waitt that their prime suspect had "fallen" again, this time for trafficking in drugs, and that he was scheduled for a Municipal Court appearance on September 26, 1961 at 10:00 A.M. Waitt immediately notified Agent Crisman, but Crisman was tied up on another case and said he would get back to Waitt. However, it wasn't Crisman who called back, it was Agent Dean Rolston. Rolston, who had been pulled off the case in May, 1959, was now reassigned to this investigation by the new FBI special agent in charge of the Seattle office, J. Earl Milnes.

When Waitt and Agent Rolston arrived in Vancouver on the morning of September 25, the Vancouver sergeant met them at the Doric House Hotel at 1:30 in the afternoon. Morphett described the drug case that his department had built against Dawley over the past year. Word had come to the V.P.D Narcotics Squad in August that the suspect was pushing heroin and detectives of the unit raided his apartment. All they found for their trouble was a handful of empty capsules and balloons. They had missed their opportunity. Dawley thanked the detectives, and they left. But he wasn't prepared to match wits with the young detectives assigned to the drug unit who later located and "staked out" his cache, where they found 150 capsules of what proved to be high-grade heroin. About ten days after the detectives first set up the "stakeout," the suspect was observed when he returned to the site and removed about 75 capsules. The detectives moved in on a very much surprised man, taking him into custody and seizing all of the drugs. He was charged with trafficking under a new statute and bail was set at $30,000.00. Larry Hill, a prominent Vancouver attorney, was appointed by the court to represent him following the arrest.

Sergeant Morphett next briefed the two Americans on Mrs. Dawley's recent activities. Her divorce became final shortly after her husband's release from the penitentiary. She then married "Bud" Frazier. They were living on West 19th Street in Vancouver. Rolston and Waitt thought it might be best to re-interview Rose before talking to Cliff Dawley, so the three men drove to her home. She was not cooperative. When she saw Waitt and Rolston at the door with Morphett, she said, "Oh no, not you people again." Although she had made a new life for herself, she was still loyal to her ex-husband and declined to answer any questions about his activities.

The three men next went to a run-down hotel on Hamilton Street in downtown Vancouver. The Canadian sergeant explained that he would like the two officers to talk to Joe Richard, an associate of Dawley and Wasylenchuk and a close friend of Steve Polanski's. Polanski, who was to be released from prison in a couple of weeks, had gotten time off for good behavior, and his brother had made arrangements for Steve to stay at Richard's hotel. Morphett had persuaded the man earlier that it may be "financially worthwhile" for Joe to cooperate with the American authorities in this investigation, referring to the reward offered for the arrest and conviction of the bank robbers in the Seattle case. Richard agreed. Also by this time, those who were at all familiar with the fact that the Americans were still pursuing the investigation in Canada, were well aware that there was money available from both the FBI and the Washington Banker's Association for the "right kind" of information in this case.

Joe Richard was easy to talk to and he was closer to one of their prime suspects than even the Vancouver detective realized, for Cliff Dawley had called Richard just before the officers' arrival with a request that Joe put up the necessary cash to enable his friend to make bail. The prisoner was to call Richard again the following day regarding this. But Joe said he wouldn't put up $300.00 on Dawley, let alone $30,000.00, as Dawley's options were limited to flight or face a fourteen-year sentence. Joe knew which route Cliff would go. The convict was fifty-four years old and Joe said: "Cliff will skip the country rather than go back to prison."

Richard told the officers, "If John Wasylenchuk was in on the Greenwood robbery, Dawley had to have been along on the job." He said "J.W.," referring to Wasylenchuk, and Dawley were very close in the mid-fifties and it was common knowledge in his circle of friends that the two men were responsible for at least a dozen bank holdups in western Canada during that time. When Dawley called Joe, he said that he had $4,000.00 in the bank which he would give to Joe for the premium on his bond, plus another "twenty and six stashed." Joe explained the twenty was $20,000.00 Dawley had picked up in a heist from a bank at Pryor and Main in downtown Vancouver. He didn't know where the $6,000.00 came from unless it was part of the loot taken in the Seattle robbery. Joe told the officers his friend was exaggerating just a wee bit about his financial status, as everyone had laughed about the Vancouver job, for the man had buried the loot in Burnaby and, while he was in the pen, someone had built a housing project over the spot where he had hidden the money.[16] Richard wasn't inclined to go along with the convict's request even though he was sure Cliff had a few thousand on hand. He was aware that some of the man's "loot" could have come from the sale of his house, as he and Rose had recently split the $13,000.00 realized from that transaction.

The man also told the two investigators something that neither had heard before; he said two or three weeks after the Seattle robbery, Steve Polanski came to him with $3,000.00 in American currency, which he tried to fence for fifty cents on the dollar. He didn't remember the denominations of the bills carried by his colleague, but said he saw Steve several weeks later and asked him about the money. Polanski told him he had exchanged it for Canadian money at a B. C. bank.

At the conclusion of the interview, Waitt for the first time in the years since he had been assigned to this case felt the pieces of this giant puzzle were slowly falling into place. For Rolston had earlier discovered that shortly after the robbery in 1954, Wasylenchuk had tried to fence the Greenwood bank loot through a carwash operation in downtown Vancouver. Now nearly seven years later, the officers came up with the same story from a different source, only their source said that the owners of the carwash, Danny Brent and Joe Hall, both of whom were involved in trafficking in narcotics, were running with Joe Richard at the time. Here, then, was a witness to the fact that Polanski was also trying to fence American money shortly after the Seattle robbery.

Waitt realized they were still a long way from an indictment, but at least some hard evidence was now being developed, and just maybe Steve Polanski, who had been "sent up" for five years in 1959, would figure that with Dawley facing a fourteen year sentence, he could use that $50,000.00 reward. The reward, which Vancouver Police Inspector Archie Plummer had told him, was available for any one who had the "right" information on this case. Although Plummer had deliberately exaggerated the amount of the reward, the story served its purpose, as every ex-con who had done time in a British Columbia prison was well aware that for "the right story" they could collect a handsome reward. The story had been given such wide circulation throughout the prison system that several American criminals who had become familiar with two of the suspected principals in the case, from their Canadian counterparts, were trying to cash in on it.

On September 26, 1961, the morning following their interview with Joe Richard, Sergeant Waitt, Agent Rolston and Sergeant Morphett went to the fifth floor of the Vancouver city jail to again interview Clifford Dawley. The man was being held at Oakalla prison in Burnaby, but in the early morning hours he had been brought into Vancouver for a remand hearing and was scheduled to appear in court at 10:00 A.M. The officers had little time to talk to him after they arrived at the jail.

Waitt was immediately struck by Dawley's physical appearance. He was well-tanned, his eyes were sharp and cold, and he had the physical appearance of a man half his age. His left arm was still crippled from the gunshot wound he had received in a robbery in San Francisco many years before. The bullet severed two tendons in the arm and he could not open or close two of his fingers, nor move his wrist from side to side. He told Waitt that he kept the hand from withering by constantly exercising it with his other hand. Waitt observed that the defect was not especially noticeable and that Dawley had done a good job in covering it up. The officer was hoping that someday he would have the pleasure of seeing Dawley in an American courtroom, where as a defendant in a murder case, he would be asked to slip into a pair of gloves, such as the bandit with the .45 automatic and a crippled hand had done before he killed officer Frank Hardy at the Greenwood bank.[17]

The prisoner told the officers he was not represented by Barrister Larry Hill any longer and was due in court in half an hour. Nor was he glad to see the two visiting officers, both of whom had interviewed him before, when he was confined in the British Columbia Penitentiary. But his outward appearance was one of complete composure, so much different than when Waitt and Crisman talked to him a year and a half ago on the street in Vancouver. It was almost as if the man, who had spent most of his adult life in prison, was more at ease with the officers in this custodial setting than on the outside.

The officers' time was limited so they immediately launched into an intensive period of questioning of the prisoner. He responded to all their questions readily. He even reiterated his willingness to take a polygraph examination if it were approved by his attorney. He said the reason he could not keep his promise to Waitt and Crisman to take the polygraph test a year earlier was because of a parole condition imposed on him at that time by his parole benefactor Mr. Justice McInnes. He claimed that he was not involved in the Greenwood bank robbery. He knew Wasylenchuk was in Seattle at the time of the robbery and that Mary Peters (a friend of John Wasylenchuk) had told him that "J.W." had pulled the job there. He also added a new twist to the case; he said, "Mary made the arrangements for Wasylenchuk to stay in Seattle, but not at the Blue Bird Motel." He thought it may have been at a house someplace in the city rather than at a motel. He added that Mary handled the money for "J.W.," but wouldn't elaborate whether this meant that she fenced the money or handled Wasylenchuk's necessary expenses before the robbery. He had also heard that Mary had not gone to the Greenwood bank with Wasylenchuk on the day of the stickup.

The interview was cut short as the suspect was taken out on the "chain" for his trip to court. The American officers accompanied him to the courtroom with the hope of talking to his attorney, as Sergeant Morphett headed for the British Columbia Penitentiary. Waitt felt this would be a good time for Sergeant Morphett to approach Jack McClelland who was "stooling" for the Vancouver detectives and was currently in prison with The Farmer. If McClelland were able to pick up additional information, relative to Mary Peters' activities, either through rumor or possibly from "J.W." himself, it may corroborate Richard's and Dawley's statements of Wasylenchuk's and Mary Peters' involvement in this case. The Vancouver sergeant was unsuccessful at the penitentiary and returned to Vancouver. McClelland had said there was no doubt in anyone's mind that the officer's two prime suspects pulled the Greenwood job, but if Mary Peters had any part in the robbery, he hadn't heard about it in the "pen".

When the two officers arrived at the courtroom, they were surprised to see Patricia Novis, who was being arraigned on two narcotics and one petty theft charge. She was the wife of Pete Novis, whom Irvin Teague had said had driven one of the suspects to Seattle before the Greenwood robbery. She entered a plea of guilty to the charges and received an eighteen-month sentence. Her attorney turned out to be Larry Hill and, contrary to Dawley's earlier denial that Hill didn't represent him, the barrister did in fact represent him and obtained a continuance for his client. The case was set over two weeks, to October 5, 1961. The man's denial of legal representation by the attorney Larry Hill appeared to Waitt to be consistent with his past. When talking to the police, the prisoner would continue to lie or fabricate any story relating to his personal life even though it was not clear even to him that there may be some personal advantage gained by doing so.

During the court recess, the two detectives talked briefly with Hill, who said that he had represented Dawley for the past five or six years, and that he had heard that Dawley may have been involved in their investigation. He had not pursued it as there were no charges pending against his client. Besides he had read that RCMP Sergeant Ernest Nuttall had come up with evidence which put Dawley in the clear in the Seattle case. When asked if he would permit his client to take a polygraph examination, Hill replied that he saw no reason why he should not take it if he wanted to, if he were not involved, but if he were involved, he said he would advise his client not to take the test.

But it was too late now to broach the subject of the polygraph test with Dawley, for after his court hearing, he was immediately taken back to Oakalla prison. Hill agreed to talk to his client at the prison and let the officers know one way or the other about the polygraph. He thought that it was quite possible that he might be able to get the man's bail reduced and get him out for a while. If Dawley were to ask him what he should do then, Hill said he would have to advise him to leave for South America as the Vancouver Police Department had him "cold" on the narcotics charges. He was sure the man would receive at least a fourteen year sentence on these charges because of his extensive criminal record.

During the remainder of this day and most of the next, the two Americans continued their search for Mary Peters. Morphett had located a marriage license record for her and Arthur Smith with an address on McKercher Avenue in Burnaby, British Columbia, but no one knew the Smiths at that address. Finally, through the British

198 • *Cops, Crooks & Politicians*

Columbia Electric Company, he located the residence of Art Smith, but neighbors knew little of the man's movements and could not recall the last time he had been seen in the neighborhood. The Officer told the two Americans that he would probably be able to locate Peters in time if she was still in the city, and would notify them when he found her.

En route back to their hotel, Waitt and Rolston stopped off to see Joe Richard again at his hotel on Hamilton Street. They were curious if Dawley had called again regarding the premium on his $30,000.00 bond, but the prisoner apparently had changed his mind for he never called.

When Waitt arrived at the Doric House, there was a message there to call Sergeant Morphett at police headquarters. He placed the call and the Canadian told him that he had located Mary Peters Smith living in the 5200 block of Grimmer Street in Burnaby, a suburban area east of downtown Vancouver. He said there was a car registered to Art Smith parked in the driveway and there appeared to be someone living in the house. The two men left for Burnaby immediately, but they could have saved themselves the trouble, Mary Smith was no more cooperative with the officers than Rose Dawley had been. About all she would admit to was that she knew "J.W." as she called Wasylenchuk, and Cliff Dawley and had talked to them at one time many years before. When pressed for further information, Mary terminated the interview by asking the officers to leave.

The day following this interview, the two Americans were ready to go home, for there was little left for them to accomplish in Canada unless someone else "talked." They held little hope that Dawley would take the polygraph and less that he would say more than he already had about the robbery. Morphett agreed to stay in touch with the man's attorney and said he would call the officers when and if he heard whether the prisoner would agree to take the polygraph test. He also agreed that before Steve Polanski was released from the penitentiary he would see what could be learned from Polanski's partner, Joseph Hall, one of Vancouver's busiest drug peddlers. Hall was convicted of "Possession of Drugs for the Purpose of Trafficking" in July, 1960. He appealed his conviction and a new trial was scheduled for January, 1962. The officers thought he would be looking for a favor as he could still receive a minimum fourteen year sentence for this offense and Waitt thought that this could be "the route" to Polanski, the man who allegedly fenced the American money taken in the Greenwood robbery.

On October 2, 1961, Sergeant Morphett called Sergeant Waitt, who had returned to Seattle, to inform him that he had just heard from Mr. Hill, and the attorney said that his client told him Ottawa had made a full investigation of the American case and found him (Dawley) innocent of any wrongdoing. Therefore, they saw no need for him to take the test. He also said that Judge McInnes had advised his client not to take the test as the judge knew he was innocent and the polygraph machine could very well make a mistake, thus jeopardizing his future. Waitt, upon hearing this, thought to himself that such a complete reversal by Dawley after all his promises that he would take the test, certainly was another sign of Dawley's probable implication in the Greenwood robbery. The Seattle detective was fully aware of the limitations of any polygraph examination, but he was firmly convinced, unless he could establish for the Canadians some visible indication that Dawley was the mastermind of the Greenwood robbery in Seattle and the killer of officer Frank Hardy, that the Canadians would soon withdraw from the investigation. Without the support of the Vancouver police and the RCMP, their investigation in Canada would have to come to an end. With Judge McInnes still protecting this prisoner, it was even more doubtful that the Canadian police would want to stay involved in this investigation.

The American officers were fortunate that individual lower ranking RCMP and Vancouver officers were doing their best to help the two Americans. However, Judge McInnes' continuing attempts to intervene on Clifford Dawley's behalf had not gone unnoticed in either the Vancouver or RCMP police commander's offices, and neither Chief George Archer, nor the RCMP Headquarters Staff relished the thought of renewed charges of corruption arising within the local law enforcement community. Although neither agency would publicly admit it, their combined command staffs also dreaded the thought of the adverse publicity which would follow an American trial of a Canadian bank robber, for it could well expose one or more conspirators who wore a Canadian police officer's uniform. An officer outside of his own territory could not be protected by his own people if it became known that he was covering up, or had been involved in planning criminal activities with some of Canada's worst criminals. Were this to become public, it would reflect very unfavorably upon both the RCMP and V.P.D., particularly if it were to occur so soon after the Royal Commission hearings.[18]

Sergeant Morphett's only other news concerned his interview with Joe Hall, who was being held in the penitentiary awaiting trial. But Hall wasn't talking either. He would make no statements one way or the other about his long-time associate Steve Polanski, in reference to fencing American money in 1954.

Later in Seattle at a meeting between Waitt and Deputy Chief of Police Charles Rouse, who continued to maintain a close interest in the progress of the investigation although no longer directly responsible for it, the sergeant expressed his apprehension that the solution to this case was slipping from their grasp. He remarked that working with a foreign police agency that certainly was not sympathetic toward the investigation made it that much more difficult, for it was now a known fact that officers of both the Royal Canadian Mounted Police and Vancouver Police Department "set up scores" for local criminals and covered for them "for a price," while they "capered." Some even provided alibis for a twenty-five percent cut of each "job." It appeared to Waitt that his task was hopeless. Besides, Waitt reasoned, if the two principals in their case could escape or buy their way out of prison by bribing guards, or obtain "for a price" an early release, whatever made the FBI or Seattle Police officials think that the Canadian authorities would allow these criminals to be extradited?

Waitt was completely exasperated over the actions of the Canadian officials, including his honor Judge McInnes, and again expressed to his former boss his concern for the outcome of the investigation.[19] Charlie Rouse tried to reassure Waitt. He told him that just because road blocks were being thrown in front of them by the Canadians at almost every turn, he should not become discouraged. Rouse said, "Most of the problems you have laid out here are behind us; the Canadians recognized their own internal problems and, for the most part, they have been resolved. The Royal Commission took care of many of these and the real bastards have left the Vancouver Department. But most of all, Chief Archer is a respectable and professional policeman and those problems are pretty well behind us."[20] He added a comment that Wasylenchuk and Dawley were both still in the penitentiary. Wasylenchuk for several years now and his partner, because he couldn't raise his bail and no judge saw fit to reduce it, would probably stay there. Waitt responded, "It would be political suicide for any judge to reduce that son-of-a-bitch's bail. Even McInnes wouldn't intervene this time on behalf of Clifford Dawley."[21]

Although Rouse had hoped to reassure Waitt, the detective sergeant, who normally was a cheerful and optimistic individual, left the meeting with a foreboding sense of failure. Waitt had hoped to retire soon, but before he left the Department, his wish was to bring this case to a satisfactory conclusion; however, the possibility of this occurring seemed more remote than ever.

It was three months before Waitt and Rolston would return to Canada. Waitt had been reassigned to the vice squad after the shakeup in the command structure of the police department, with the appointment of the new Chief of Police. Now, no longer responsible to the chief of detectives, the time he could devote to this eight-year-old homicide and robbery case depended upon the demands of his new assignment and the concurrence of his new boss, Chief of Staff M. E. "Buzz" Cook. But Cook was agreeable that Waitt should continue to pursue the Greenwood case as time would permit, and on January 28, 1962, Waitt and Rolston again returned to the Doric House Hotel in Vancouver.

Sergeant Morphett had called and told the American officers that Dawley would remain in Okalla Prison because he hadn't been able to raise the $30,000.00 bail on the narcotics charge, as his friend Joe Richard had refused to come up with the money. Under these circumstances the Vancouver officer thought that it may be an opportune time to re-interview the prisoners and possibly Steve Polanski. Neither Polanski's "good time parole," nor his hoped for sponsor materialized and he too was doing "hard time" in the penitentiary. Waitt agreed that this was an opportune time to return to

Canada as he was sure there wouldn't be any interference from Justice McInnes as the judge wouldn't dare interject himself into the interview as long as his "protege" remained in Oakalla prison.

The following afternoon at one o'clock, the two Americans began a vigorous three-hour interrogation of Clifford Dawley at the Oakalla Penitentiary. The man's case had been continued for trial to February 27, 1962, about a month away and he had changed attorneys since his last visit with the officers. When questioned about his refusal to take the polygraph test, he said attorney Larry Hill lied about his unwillingness to take the test, and that he had never told Hill that Ottawa had cleared him in the Greenwood case. When pressed for a yes or no answer as to whether he would take the test, Dawley hedged. He said he was no longer represented by Hill but by Ann Sutherland, and if he beat these current charges and she approved, he would submit to a polygraph examination.[22] He further qualified this by adding that he was willing and anxious to take the test and would sign a statement to that effect even if convicted on the drug charges, provided he was sentenced to Oakalla and not the B. C. Penitentiary with his former partner. Word had gotten around that he had been too "friendly" with the American officers, and he was afraid of retaliation from Wasylenchuk.

Waitt was having a difficult time concealing his excitement upon hearing that Dawley was now fearful of Wasylenchuk. He was sure their repeated interviews of the principals in this case had created an atmosphere of uncertainty and distrust between the three prime suspects. During prior interviews of the two suspects, the officers intentionally, but in as subtle a way as possible, advised that the party other than the one being questioned had made statements that were damaging to the person being interrogated. Dawley was now ready to talk. He responded to questioning by the officers as one who was completely familiar with the circumstances of the crime. He said "J.W." or The Farmer, as he frequently referred to Wasylenchuk, had told him personally that he planned the Greenwood job and pulled it off with the help of Bobby Lewis, Alphie Pais, Mary Peters, and her younger brother, who acted as the pick-up man. "The Farmer claimed he did all of the shooting at the bank and the little man who crashed through the window was Bobby Lewis, who 'lost his head' when the police arrived. He dived through a bank window. Mary Peters, who was Wasylenchuk's girl friend, made arrangements before the robbery for a place to stay for herself and the other members of the gang and 'J.W.' hid out with her for a week after the robbery. The two of them had made several trips to Seattle before the robbery to buy heavy equipment and automobile parts for the Peters Garage in Vancouver, and she was crazy about him and they were together frequently in Seattle. It was during these trips that The Farmer "cased" the Greenwood bank and made plans to 'knock it over'."[23] He said he didn't recall the name Blue Bird Motel as the place Wasylenchuk and an accompanying female had stayed before the robbery, but he was sure it was a cottage-type motel. He said, "'J.W.' claimed to have stolen the getaway car and license plates and made arrangements for transportation with a 'cool car after dumping the stolen one. The stolen plates came from Peters' garage, and Wasylenchuk claimed that he had access to these as there were always a large number of vehicles and plates around the building for the taking."[24]

The prisoner said "J.W." told him he had another bank job planned near Portland; but when he killed the cop in the Seattle job he called the second one off. If he got "nailed" in the States they might tie him to the killing in Seattle. After the robbery, Dawley claimed that "J.W." said he hid the money and the guns in Seattle for several weeks, and then sent one of his girlfriends to pick them up. Wasylenchuk, according to Dawley, came up with the idea to use the false noses and horn-rimmed glasses as he and Bobby Lewis were both too well-known to the police. Wasylenchuk always used an Oldsmobile on his jobs, Dawley claimed, as no one could catch him in this type of get-away car and he always "punched" the ignition and hot-wired the vehicle.

The prisoner expressed his dislike for Wasylenchuk. He said he thought the man used Mary Peters, as she was young and impressionable, and that he just couldn't be trusted. He had a reputation for being dishonest and, when splitting any loot with his partners, always got the first and largest count. "Besides, he had no guts," Dawley said, for he needed several shots of whiskey to build his courage before going on a job. But what really turned him off was the fact that "J.W." had told some people, "I was in on the Seattle robbery and I was the trigger man that 'nailed' the three cops at the bank." When asked by Waitt if this were true, Dawley vigorously denied participating in the robbery.

So there it was. After eight years, the story of the robbery of the Greenwood bank and the shooting of the three officers was at last being told by one of the principal suspects of the crime. However, he continued to deny his part in the crime, implicating his former partners instead. Dawley's story corresponded with what was told to Irvin Teague by Wasylenchuk when they were cell-mates in the British Columbia Penitentiary in 1956. The only difference is that Wasylenchuk's story named Dawley as the robber and trigger man who killed Officer Frank Hardy and shot Sergeant Howard Slessman and Officer Vernon Chase.

Waitt had been working on this case for nearly four years and now, upon hearing of Dawley's allegations, was gratified that at long last he and Rolston had, in their opinion, obtained sufficient evidence to enable the United States Attorney to present a case before a Federal Grand Jury in Seattle requesting the indictment of Clifford Dawley and John Wasylenchuk for robbery and murder. Just a few weeks earlier, Waitt had expressed his misgivings about being able to bring this case to a satisfactory conclusion, but he was now elated. Not since being assigned to the case in 1959 by Deputy Chief of Police Charlie Rouse (formerly Captain), had he experienced a moment such as this. Here, sitting across the table from him was, as Sergeant Bill Morphett said, "One of the toughest criminals in the whole of Canada," casually discussing his participation in some of the most serious crimes ever committed. And Dawley wasn't finished talking.

He told the two officers about other bank jobs and payroll robberies in which he, "J.W." and Bobby Lewis were involved. He said Wasylenchuk, Lewis and Danny Brent had planned a payroll robbery in North Vancouver. The job was set up by an RCMP sergeant from the Vancouver detachment. Brent was a close friend of the sergeant and had made arrangements in which the Mountie was to direct the Vancouver and RCMP patrols away from the scene of the stickup. But Wasylenchuk didn't trust the Mountie so he made Brent go inside on the job with him. After going into the building where the robbery was to take place, The Farmer became suspicious of Brent and called the whole thing off. Some time after this, Dawley said, Danny stole a drug cache belonging to Joe Celona, a narcotics trafficker in Vancouver. As a result, Celona had Danny "knocked off" and his body dumped on a local golf course.[25] This started a full-scale drug war with several shootings and bombings and finally, according to the prisoner, a great deal of heat was brought on these people when a "pusher" had his leg blown off by a bomb in his car and the police started making wholesale arrests. During this time, Celona reportedly was dealing with the RCMP sergeant until they became suspicious of one another and parted company. The prisoner told of the sergeant's connection with criminals in the Vancouver area and his continuous involvement with young girls. He said "J.W.'s" alibi for the Greenwood job was "tailor-made" and arranged with the Mountie before the robbery and now he's stuck with it. He couldn't back out of it for fear that Wasylenchuk would put the finger on him. He knew the sergeant collected $3,000.00 to $5,000.00 from The Farmer for the alibi, but it wasn't all gravy, as the underworld people who the sergeant had been consorting with were putting pressure on him and the Mountie was in a trap. If he continued to provide alibis' for stickup men, he would eventually be found out by his own organization. If he didn't do it, he ran the risk of someone like Wasylenchuk turning on him.[26]

The two American officers broke off their interrogation of Dawley at dinner time and drove back to their hotel in Vancouver. Waitt was mentally exhausted. They had just uncovered not only a story of one robbery and murder, but were briefed by an eye witness to many serious crimes which Dawley had either participated in or had learned of because of his association with those who were directly involved. The two men took time out for dinner, returned to their hotel and spent the remainder of the evening preparing reports for their respective agencies and for Bill Morphett. These included information relative to Dawley's admissions and statements of his involvement in criminal activity in Canada, including the names of four Canadian police officers, three Vancouver officers and a Mountie, who were allegedly working with him and John Wasylenchuk and their partners in either "setting up a score," (bank robbery) or providing false alibis.'[27]

The following day, January 30, 1962, Waitt and Rolston met briefly with Sergeant Morphett. Morphett had been off sick for several days and just stopped by the hotel on his way to a doctor's office. The two Americans briefed him on the results of their interview with Clifford Dawley the day before. Morphett was pleased but had little to add to the investigation. He agreed to try and locate Bobby Lewis and Alphie Pais before the officers came back to Canada.

After lunch, the two officers drove back to Oakalla Penitentiary to again talk to Clifford Dawley. They agreed that this interview should zero in on the specifics of the crime itself, and they hoped to obtain a statement relative to the identity of the third man in the bank. The prisoner had told them that The Farmer and Lewis were inside the bank with a third man and Alphie Pais, Mary Peters and Mary's younger brother were present but not inside the bank during the robbery.

The prisoner, upon being brought to the visitor's room in the prison, again was very cordial as he had been the previous day. His complete composure in the officers' presence reminded Waitt of his first interview with the prisoner in a custodial facility, and he mentally compared this with his visit with Dawley last year on the sidewalk in Vancouver in front of the convict's apartment. In the latter visit, the man appeared to be on the verge of a complete nervous breakdown, but now, again in a custodial setting, he appeared to be completely at ease.[28]

During this second visit, the officers went back over the story of the Greenwood robbery. There were a few minor discrepancies in Dawley's story, but basically it was as he told it the day before. When the officers pressed him for the name of the third man in the bank, he said he knew the man, but for his own personal safety he dared not tell the detectives who it was. Waitt kept at him and asked for a description of the man. Dawley replied that he was a tall, lanky blonde kid Wasylenchuk had been capering with in Canada. But Waitt continued to press him for a name and finally the man responded, "His name is Wilson, Warren Woodrow Wilson." With this obvious fictitious name laid on the table, Waitt believed the convict was about to terminate the interview, for he obviously could go no further without implicating himself and he did not wish to name others. The sergeant changed the subject by asking him if he knew when Wasylenchuk would be released from the British Columbia penitentiary. He responded, "The grapevine has it that he will be up for parole next year. He got the "big bitch" (Life sentence as a Habitual Offender), but the Mountie that shot him on his last bank job in Burnaby is going to "go to bat" for him. The Mountie operates the Coconut Grove Lounge in Vancouver, and will provide a job there for "J.W." when he gets out. The Mountie has done this for other parolees in the past."[29]

At the end of the interview, as the two officers exited from the visitor's room, they ran into Rose Frazier, Dawley's ex-wife. She exchanged amenities with the Americans and said she was fine. Upon checking with the guard at the entrance, the officers found she had registered as "Mrs. Dawley - wife."

Later that afternoon on their way back to Seattle, the two men stopped by the Smith residence on Grimmer Street in Burnaby to talk to Mary Peters Smith, but they found no one at home. The same large German Shepherd dog that had been there on their last visit was in the back yard and a letter addressed to Mr. and Mrs. A. Smith was in the mailbox, so they assumed Mary Peters was living there.

Returning to Seattle, the two law men briefed their superiors on the results of their latest trip to Canada, and then undertook the tedious job of tying the loose ends of the investigation together and preparing a case summary which would hopefully allow the U.S. Attorney for Western Washington to present sufficient evidence before the Grand Jury with a request for indictment of the two principals in the case. The bulk of the preparation was left to Rolston and Waitt provided resource data. But when the case was presented to the U. S. Attorney, there were some unanswered questions which he wished explored before presenting the case to the Jury. First, where were the witnesses who could place Dawley and Wasylenchuk at the scene of this robbery? Were they available and would they now give testimony to support their knowledge of the crime? And where was Teague and Daniel Ault? Were they available for court? Of equal concern to the U. S. Attorney was RCMP Sergeant Ernest Nuttall. If he were to testify on behalf of Wasylenchuk and the testimony were believed by the Jury, the chance for a conviction of this criminal would be remote indeed. More importantly, although there was plenty of eyewitness evidence obtained from those present at the crime scene and over 200 items of physical evidence, there was no specific piece of this evidence linking Dawley, Wasylenchuk, Bobby Lewis or Mary Peters to the crime.

Both the U. S. Attorney and the case officers were well aware that a less than thorough job of searching the crime scene at the bank had been undertaken by the police at the time of the robbery, and it was too late to correct that flaw in existing police training and crime scene procedures.[30] The eye witness testimony was also shaky because of the disguises worn by the three stick-up men. There were multiple statements linking the two suspects to the robbery; but cold, hard, impartial physical evidence was lacking. What was needed was to place one or more of the subjects in Seattle before and during the time of the robbery. This in conjunction with the other evidence would in all probability, be sufficient to convince a Grand Jury that at least the two principal suspects in this case, Clifford Dawley and John Wasylenchuk, had committed the offense and an indictment should follow.

After several meetings which included Waitt, Rolston, Charlie Rouse, Chief of Detectives A. A. "Al" Kretchmar, the U.S. Attorney for Western Washington and FBI supervisors, it was agreed that the two officers should again return to Canada to gain this additional evidence if possible. It was also not known if the Canadian Government would honor an extradition request of subjects who were currently under sentence in Canadian prisons. This was to be explored by the U. S. Attorney's Office. In the meantime as the names of all suspects in this case were now known and something of their movements and contacts in the United States had been uncovered, it was agreed that additional follow-up investigation in Seattle was warranted, and an attempt would be made to place one or more of the suspects in the city on the day of the robbery. S.P.D. and FBI supervisors agreed that Waitt and Rolston should pursue this part of the investigation also when they returned next from Canada, rather than assign additional personnel to the case.

Notes

[1] In 1954, Justice Harold W. McInnes of the Assize, (Superior) Court of Vancouver, was a newly appointed judge from Penticton, British Columbia, Canada. His decisions relating to several of the suspects in the Greenwood bank robbery investigation in Vancouver would soon come under attack by several of the investigators in this case.

[2] Sergeant Charles K. Waitt, S.P.D. Case No. 288527 Op. Cit., Investigator's Report No. 12, June 11, 1960.

[3] Ibid.

[4] Ibid.

[5] Ibid.

[6] Ibid.

[7] Ibid.

[8] Charles K. Waitt, conversations with the author, 1968.

[9] Op. cit. Waitt, June 11, 1960

[10] Ibid.

[11] Ibid.

[12] Waitt, S.P.D. Case No. 288527, Op. Cit., Investigator's Report No. 12., June 11, 1960, p. 3.

[13] Waitt, S.P.D. Case No. 288527, Op. Cit., Investigator's Report, June 24, 1960.

[14] City of Seattle Police Department, 1959-1960 Annual Reports. Contrary to the stories in the Seattle press at the time, Chief Jimmie Lawrence's observations about crime in Seattle were quite correct; in 1959 Seattle experienced a four percent reduction in major criminal offenses reported to the police, which was also the first significant decrease in major crimes reported to the police in recent years. In 1960, major crimes in the city increased one percent. Annual Report, 1959, p. 5., 1960, p. 5.

[15] Paddy Sherman, The Vancouver Province, editorial response to the Royal Commission's *Final Report of the Vancouver City Police Force Inquiry*, February 17, 1956.

[16] Charles K. Waitt, S.P.D. Case No. 288527 Op. Cit., Investigator's Report, September 29, 1961, p. 2.

[17] City Police Department, Vancouver, B. C. Criminal Identification Bureau, Record No. 10263, p. 1. Also see "POLICE SHOT ENDS CHASE FOR FUGITIVE," The San Francisco Chronicle, September 20, 1930, Section 11, p. 2.

Clifford Dawley was arrested on a theft charge in 1930 in Penticton, British Columbia and sentenced to 15 months in the penitentiary. On August 22, at the age of nineteen, while waiting transfer to the Penitentiary, he escaped and fled to the U.S. On September 18, using the name Clifford Dixon

[Dixen] he was arrested in San Francisco, California after being wounded in the left arm by a San Francisco police officer. The San Francisco Chronicle reported at the time: "Climaxing a hectic fist fight with Police Lieutenant George Richards, Clifford Dawley, alias Clifford Dixon, 21 [Actually 19], Canadian jail breaker, was shot and later captured at Sixth and Natoma streets late yesterday in a battle which was precipitated by Dawley's identification from a police circular.

A bullet from Richards' revolver splintered Dawley's right [left] forearm. Dawley had thrown Richards to the sidewalk and the policeman drew his weapon as he lay prone on the sidewalk. Dawley tried to strike the gun from Richards' hand as the bullet jarred into his forearm at the wrist. The bullet ended the battle." Dawley was deported to Canada in October of that year where he entered Oakalla Prison under the name of Clifford Dawley, alias Frassier, the name used at the time of his earlier arrest in Penticton, B.C.

[18] Charles K. Waitt, conversations with the author, 1968.

[19] Ibid.

[20] Charles K. Waitt, conversations with the author, 1968.

[21] Ibid.

[22] Charles K. Waitt, S.P.D. Case No.288527, Investigator's Report, January 29, 1962, p. 1.

[23] Ibid. p. 1.

[24] Ibid. p. 1.

[25] Ibid. p. 2.

[26] Ibid. p. 5.

[27] Waitt, Op. Cit., conversations with the author, 1968.

[28] Waitt, Op. Cit., conversations with the author, 1968.

[29] Waitt, Investigator's Report January 29, 1962, p. 3.

[30] Although the crime scene search at the bank was flawed for many reasons, the lack of proper technical training on the part of FBI and S.P.D. personnel was not the only reason given this day for the failure to properly collect physical evidence at this incident. In critiques which followed this investigation it became only too obvious that no one individual assumed responsibility for managing this entire process at the crime scene. Nor did any one have the foresight or courage to control the actions of either the press or their own staffs in and around the bank, consequently most of the physical evidence collected at this crime was as described by both FBI and S.P.D Laboratory personnel as "valueless." However, Seattle detectives Kelson and Mitchell, and Special Agent Millard M. Bush who processed the getaway vehicle, did an outstanding job in the collection and preservation of physical evidence in and around the recovered stolen vehicle. Unfortunately, this evidence, which was examined by S.P.D. Sergeant Max Allison, the Seattle Police Department's sole crime laboratory specialist, was not sufficient in and of itself to convict the perpetrators of this crime.

Chapter

10

The Business Connection

On April 30, 1962, the two American officers again returned to Vancouver. Sergeant Bill Morphett met the two men shortly after they checked in at the Doric House Hotel. He quickly brought the Americans up-to-date on Clifford Dawley's current problems with the law. The suspect had still not been able to raise his bail on the drug trafficking charge so had remained confined in Oakalla Prison since his arrest in August. He had gone to trial on April 26th, just four days prior to their arrival, had been found guilty of possession of drugs and the case had been remanded for trial in June. Under Canadian law, Morphett explained the burden of proof had now shifted from the Crown to the accused and it was up to the prisoner to prove he had not been trafficking in drugs. The sergeant said, "He will have a hell of a time doing that. The police department has an air-tight case and the consensus is that Dawley will get a minimum of ten years in prison on this conviction."[1]

Sergeant Morphett was sorry he couldn't help the Americans at this time as he was busy with the ceremony for retiring Chief Constable George Archer, but promised he would drop by the Doric again before the two officers returned to the States. Again it appeared to Waitt that this excuse was the sergeant's way out of saying that V.P.D. would no longer officially participate in this investigation.

That afternoon, the two investigators met with Sergeant Jack Purdy of the RCMP Vancouver detachment. Purdy was now attached to the Alien Squad. The RCMP man was a friend of Morphett's and had followed the developments of the Greenwood case closely over the last four years, since first being contacted by FBI Agent Chet Crisman and Sergeant Waitt in 1959, relative to the location of Mary Peters. Purdy had been briefed on the case by Sergeant Morphett at Waitt and Crisman's request, and the Mountie was well aware of Irvin Teague's role in this crime. In June of 1959, Sergeant Purdy located Art Smith and Mary Peters, who had been living together on Sussex Street in Burnaby, and found that Peters' most frequent hang-outs were the Astor Bar and the Canadian Legion hall on Kingsway. He found Mary and Smith were now living at the Grimmer Street address in Burnaby and that her brother Allan ran Peters' Auto Parts on the same street, just a short distance from the Smith home.

The Mountie had kept tabs on all those who were connected in any way with this case, including Justice McInnes, Dawley, Wasylenchuk and particularly Ernest Nuttall, who had been promoted to sergeant within the Vancouver detachment. Nuttall had suffered a serious heart attack and had retired shortly after the promotion. Waitt was disappointed to hear of Nuttall's departure as he was counting on the sergeant's appearance, if not before the Grand Jury, then in federal court, where the two Canadian criminals would be tried. But without a direct order to do so from the RCMP, Waitt thought it would be doubtful that the Mountie would ever appear voluntarily in court in the United States.[2]

Sergeant Purdy was suspicious of Nuttall's cover stories for Wasylenchuk. He could understand that such an incidence as described by his colleague could occur once, but to provide an alibi twice within a few months for the same suspect was more than coincidence. Purdy didn't "buy it," particularly he said, "since Nuttall appears to be living beyond his means as a Mountie."[3]

The sergeant said Justice McInnes was still showing an interest in Cliff Dawley. He thought it was a good bet that the judge would do all he could to protect the bank robber and would continue to try to block the American's investigation and extradition of this criminal to the U.S.[4]

John Wasylenchuk had been transferred from the British Columbia Penitentiary to Honor Farm at Agassiz, about eighty miles east of Vancouver, and the officer said he was considered by some to be a "model prisoner." He expected a parole hearing soon. But as "J.W." had been sentenced to life on a Habitual Criminal charge, Purdy was doubtful that the prisoner would be granted parole. RCMP Constable Larry Hanson was sponsoring the parole and had promised employment for the bank robber if he were released. Hanson had resigned from the RCMP and was out for a couple of years, but had since been reinstated. While he was away, he operated the Coconut Grove Restaurant in Vancouver and had employed ex-cons there before without serious problems. Purdy believed that Hanson felt sorry for the robber, as he was one of the officers who shot and captured him after a bank robbery in Burnaby several years earlier.[5]

Charlie Talbot, the older of the three Talbot brothers, who had "capered" throughout western Canada, was now at William Head Penitentiary at Victoria, a minimum security facility. A transfer to this custodial facility generally meant that a parole would soon be forthcoming. Charlie had been "sent up" in 1955 on a drug trafficking charge.

The Mountie was aware of the problems the Seattle Police Department and the FBI were having in gathering reliable information in this investigation. Problems which were aggravated because of a desire of the Canadian authorities to conceal the fact that several crooked cops and other public officials were involved in illegal activities both with the suspects in the Seattle case and with other British Columbia criminals. This included both Vancouver police officials and the Royal Canadian Mounted Police, and since concealment of their unlawful conduct was mandated from the highest levels, cooperation was impossible. (When the author, in gathering data for this story, interviewed several former Canadian officials who had been connected with this case, most said they could not remember the circumstances surrounding Dawley or Wasylenchuk's involvement with public officials. When this fact was mentioned to retired FBI Special Agent Dean Rolston, he responded, "They don't want to remember.")[6] But Sergeant Jack Purdy was not one of these. His cooperation with the American officers was of enormous value to the investigation and he vowed to do everything within his power to bring this case to a satisfactory conclusion.

Later that afternoon, the two officers drove to Mary Peters Smith's residence in Burnaby where they found Mary and Art Smith at home. She was not glad to see the two Americans, but agreed to talk to them for a few minutes in their car, as two painters were busy working inside her home. She told her husband to come with her as she led the way to the officers' car. Once in the vehicle, Mary said, "Well what do you want this time?" When informed that the officers were continuing with the Wasylenchuk-Dawley investigation Mary responded, "Oh, for Christ's sake, are you still on that? I wasn't there, and I know nothing about it." Rolston replied, "Mrs. Smith, we can prove that you were in Seattle at the time of the robbery of the Greenwood Bank." Mary shot back, "I don't give a shit. Make your hardest lick, and I'll make mine." Rolston responded, "Will you go along and testify to what you've just said?" With this, her face flushed and she responded with great indignation: "I won't go any-where with you people." With that, she got out of the officers' automobile and headed into the house. Looking back and seeing her husband still with the officers, Mary yelled, "Come on Art, get out of there." Art stated, he knew nothing about the case, exited the car and followed his wife into the house.

The following day, May 1, 1962, the officers paid a return visit to Clifford Dawley at the Oakalla Penitentiary. The prisoner was in good health except for his left hand which he continually exercised, and Waitt was again impressed with the man's ability to continue, at his age, the vigorous physical fitness routine he described. He appeared to be in high spirits and, as before, gave an outward appearance of complete composure. He smiled when he said that, although he had been found guilty on the drug possession charge, his case was continued to June 11th and it was then his turn to prove that he was not trafficking in drugs. He didn't think Judge McInnes would go to bat for him this time as he had done in the past, because he had let the judge down. He told the officers that, when he was a child, McInnes had been a close friend of his father's (the former chief constable at Esquimult, British Columbia), and that's why he tried to help Dawley.

Referring to the two operations on his nose which the prisoner had undergone while in the penitentiary, Waitt inquired why they were necessary. Dawley replied that the operations were to correct a severe sinus condition and not to alter his appearance as Waitt had intimated. Waitt pressed the issue further by asking why he didn't have an operation performed on his hand as well, as it probably would have been successful. The man agreed but changed the subject and began to tell the officers about his daughter and of a painting he was doing of her. He said his daughter and his ex-wife visited him occasionally at the prison.

Waitt turned the conversation back to the prisoner's earlier story of Wasylenchuk's admission, that Mary Peters accompanied the three robbery suspects to Seattle. Dawley said, "The story stands the way I told it originally, both Wasylenchuk and Mary had told me that "J.W." and Lewis were in on the job." When informed by Waitt and Rolston that there was no tall, lanky blonde individual in on the bank robbery, nor a Warren Woodrow Wilson, as earlier claimed, the prisoner staunchly denied that he lied or that he participated in the robbery. He said he was not the third man, nor was he involved in the crime in any way. At this point, the officers informed him that the U. S. Attorney was going to seek an indictment for robbery and murder against him and Wasylenchuk, whereupon Dawley replied: "I'll abrogate anything I ever said to you people about your case if it goes to court."

After three hours of intensive questioning, the officers terminated the interview. The man had been polite and cordial throughout, even after the Americans had informed him that the United States Government was about to charge him with robbery and murder.

The officers' next stop was Peters' Auto Parts on Grimmer Street. This, they surmised, was the "garage" where Dawley's partner was supposed to have obtained the stolen license plates used in the Seattle robbery. However, sometime between March 8th and the date of the robbery March 12, 1954, the plates used on the getaway car had been stolen off a 1937 Packard sedan in custody of Nix Auto

Wreckers in Northwest Seattle, not in Vancouver, . Therefore, Peters garage could not have been the source of the stolen plates for the getaway vehicle, unless there was some connection the officers were unaware of between Nix Auto Wrecking in Seattle and Peters Auto Parts in Vancouver. Peters Auto Parts was owned by Allan Peters, the brother of Mary Peters, now Mrs. Arthur Smith.

Upon entering the store, the two men introduced themselves to Allan Peters and immediately announced that they would like to discuss with him the relationship his sister may have had with a person they were investigating. Peters greeted the officers cordially and took them into his private office. He said he was sorry, but he only had a few minutes to spare as he was just leaving for an Auto Parts Dealers luncheon. Waitt came right to the point and asked, "Do you know John Wasylenchuk?" The auto parts dealer, who was already acting very nervous, lost his composure for a moment and then replied, "Yes, I know him." It appeared to Waitt that with that answer, Peters breathed a sigh of relief, almost as if he had been waiting for someone from the law enforcement community to ask the question. He responded readily to the rest of the investigator's questions. "Yes," he had known Wasylenchuk for several years. "Yes," his sister Mary Peters went with the suspect. "Yes," he accompanied Mary and John Wasylenchuk to Seattle on several occasions, And "Yes," he and Wasylenchuk were together in Seattle in 1954. They were there to buy auto parts and Wasylenchuk went to Wittenburg Motors in the Ballard area in Northwest Seattle to look at a truck he was contemplating buying. Finally, Waitt asked Peters if he done business with Nix Auto Wreckers in Ballard. Peters replied, "Yes," he had. He had done business with Ed Prestek, the owner of Nix, for several years and knew Ed and his brother Ernie Prestek quite well. Waitt, who many times in the course of this investigation had experienced moments when he thought it useless to continue the quest for a solution to the case, was now happy to see that the thousands of hours he and other officers had expended on this investigation were beginning to pay off. Peters was the connection with Nix Auto Wrecking in Seattle, so it was possible, he surmised, that the stolen license plates which were used on the getaway car in the Greenwood robbery, came from Peters' garage, as Dawley had told Waitt in

January. But, thought Waitt, it was much more probable that Wasylenchuk stole the plates off the 1937 Packard some time before the robbery, possibly while he was in Seattle on an auto parts procurement trip with Allan Peters, thinking that no one was apt to report the loss of a set of license plates from a seventeen-year-old vehicle about to be junked.

In response to further questioning, Allan Peters claimed he had not been to Nix's Auto Wrecking for several months and had not heard from the Prestek brothers during that time. He said his sister Mary Peters was living just a few blocks down the street on Grimmer and she was working in a broom factory in the city. Peters then quickly terminated the interview, saying he was late for his luncheon meeting and would have to leave.[7]

Shortly after this interview, the officers discussed over lunch their good fortune in learning of Allan Peters' direct association with one of their prime suspects and of his admissions which, for the first time, placed that suspect in Seattle at Nix Auto Wrecking in Ballard prior to the robbery of March 12, 1954. Nix's was only about fifty blocks from the Greenwood bank. More importantly, the license plates used on the getaway car were stolen from Nix's and the getaway vehicle was abandoned within five blocks of the wrecking yard. Here, then, was that direct evidence placing one of the principal suspects in Seattle, that the U. S. Attorney wanted, before he would proceed to the Grand Jury with this case.

The officers' next stop was the Agassiz Correctional Camp east of Vancouver, where they first interviewed Correctional Superintendent John Maloney. The superintendent told the two men that John Wasylenchuk had been in the camp for about a month now, having been transferred there from the British Columbia Penitentiary in early April. Prior to this, the man was considered a maximum security risk prisoner and now, suddenly, he was placed in a facility that had no security whatsoever. Maloney said he thought there had to be some error in judgement on this one as the prisoner, in his opinion, was not to be trusted under any circumstances. The warden said the "Cons" at other Canadian prison facilities had always considered Wasylenchuk a big wheel and the same pattern was developing here at Agassiz. However, the warden said the custodial staff were keeping an eye on this, but as yet nothing serious had come of it. The man tried to give the impression that he was a model prisoner, but the staff had seen through his act and were not taken in by it, particularly since Wasylenchuk had escaped from custody before and would not be eligible for a parole hearing until June of 1963. The warden reiterated that there must have been a lot of "soul searching" by someone high up in the Bureau of Prisons to have placed this particular convict, a lifer and known bank robber and suspected cop killer, in a minimum security facility.[8]

The superintendent made arrangements for Wasylenchuk to be brought to his office and, for the next two hours, the two officers, after exchanging amenities with the prisoner, conducted an intensive interrogation of the man, whom they now believed they could prove had planned and executed the Greenwood bank robbery and who was aided in this venture by Clifford Dawley and yet-to-be-identified third party, thought to be Bobby Talbot.

John Wasylenchuk insisted that the Americans were on the wrong track and were again wasting their time questioning him; besides, he said Ottawa had conducted an official investigation into his activities on the day of the robbery and found that he had taken no part in it. He reminded the officers that Corporal Nuttall came to his home and found him working in his backyard on March 12, 1954, at about 11:00 A.M. the day the robbery occurred. He said he recognized the Corporal, but had never spoken to him until the Mountie approached him as he was working on his boat. According to the prisoner, the officer said, "Hello, John, I see you are home today. Where's Dawley?" Wasylenchuk said he responded that he did not know where Dawley was and ordered the Mountie off his property. With that, he said the cop took out a notebook, made an entry in it, turned and left the yard. The man said the reason he ordered Nuttall off his property was that he did not want the neighbors to see him talking to a Mountie. However, when it was pointed out to the prisoner that the Constable was in plain clothes and it was very unlikely the neighbors would take him for a police officer unless they saw him arrive in a marked police vehicle, Wasylenchuk had no response. Nor did he make a comment when the officers pointed out that it was the rare officer who would not wait until he returned to his police vehicle before making a short entry such as this into a notebook. But the bank robber stuck to his story. There was little doubt that it had been well-rehearsed, as the same story was told by Corporal Nuttall, even to the notebook entry which he claimed was made while questioning Wasylenchuk.

The officers went into other areas of the case with the prisoner, hoping for a response or word that would give them additional evidence that this was the man they wanted. But the stickup man was "con wise" and, as each question was asked, he would deny even knowing what the officers were talking about. Waitt asked him if he would agree to take a polygraph examination. The prisoner responded, "No,'cause I'm innocent. And I don't trust the damn thing. I've read a lot about that machine and it's been proven wrong in too many cases."[9]

The officers shifted the questioning to getaway cars and mentioned that, when Wasylenchuk was captured in Burnaby after robbing a bank there, he was driving a stolen Oldsmobile. The prisoner readily admitted he was the driver in that robbery and that he always used an Oldsmobile on bank jobs as they were the most dependable car on the road, easy to handle and easy to steal. "All you have to do is 'punch' the ignition and it's all yours," he said.

With this latter statement, the officers had gained another bit of circumstantial evidence linking the man to the Seattle case, recalling that the Oldsmobile used in the Greenwood job was hot wired after the ignition had been "punched." But this and the statement about the entry in Corporal Nuttall's notebook were all the officers were going to learn from the suspect this day. This man was an intelligent and devious individual who knew that his life may well depend on what he said or did not say during these interviews.

At the close of the interview, the two Americans expressed their appreciation to Superintendent Maloney for his cooperation in the case and said good-bye. The warden agreed to keep Sergeant Morphett at Vancouver Police Headquarters advised of the prisoner's status and, as they left, he gave Waitt Wasylenchuk's wife's address in Burnaby. The warden said the prisoner's wife and two teenage daughters were frequent visitors to the penitentiary and maintained a

222 • *Cops, Crooks & Politicians*

relatively close relationship with the husband and father during his confinement.

The two investigators returned to the United States. They had done all they could. Mary Peters wasn't talking, her brother Allan had been helpful, but he would have to be re-interviewed. In the meantime, the owners of Nix Auto Wrecking in Seattle, the Prestek brothers, were due to answer some hard questions regarding their relationship with Allan Peters. Now the former RCMP Sergeant Ernest Nuttall's statement would be reviewed again to learn just how close it matched with John Wasylenchuk's, relative to their meeting and discussion in the stickup man's backyard on the day of the robbery. As Waitt recalled, both the Mountie's statement to his own commander and the suspect's story, where the officer explained what had occurred in the meeting that day, were identical, including the notebook incident and even the greeting exchanged between the two men. This was too perfect.

The Prestek brothers at Nix Auto Wrecking were interviewed, and readily admitted that they knew Allan Peters and that the Canadian was a frequent visitor to Seattle in 1954. Ed Prestek said he had very little contact with Peters except for the sale of used auto parts for the man's company in Vancouver.

When Ernie Prestek was questioned, he said that he and Allan Peters frequently got together with their colleagues when Peters was in Seattle or when he went to Vancouver on business. He may have seen Allan's sister, Mary, and her friend John Wasylenchuk, but he couldn't be sure that the picture shown of the suspect was the man he saw with Peters. Neither Rolston nor Crisman would "buy" the Prestek brothers story, as it was just too much of a coincidence that the license plate which was used on the stolen getaway car was stolen from a vehicle belonging to the two brothers. Allan Peters, a friend of John Wasylenchuk, was doing business with them and even stayed at the same motel as Ed Prestek while in the city. This, coupled with the fact that Clifford Dawley said the stolen plates came from Peters' garage, led the officers to believe that if the brothers were not actually accessories to the crime, they knew more about the stickup trio than they let on.[10]

During the following weeks, police homicide detectives and Agents Rolston and Crisman paid several visits to Nix Auto Wrecking, sometimes just to observe the clientele, recording license numbers and determining the name and business of their customers, but also to ask the same questions: Did John Wasylenchuk and Mary Peters accompany her brother on business trips to Seattle in March of 1954, when Allan came to purchase auto parts from their yard? After repeated questioning, the two brothers became more and more defensive of their position. Soon, both denied even knowing anything about Wasylenchuk, as they did not want to be implicated in any way in the case.[11]

The owner of the National Auto Court was also questioned by the agents and readily admitted that Allan Peters was a regular customer of his, having stayed at the motel many times over the last six or eight years. He claimed the Canadian frequently brought guests with him while he was in town, but he knew very little about these people except that one woman was the man's sister. An attempt was made to determine if Allan and Mary Peters were registered at the motel on the date of the robbery, but hotel registration cards for Peters, Wasylenchuk or John Wesley, the bank robber's well-used alias could not be found. The motel owner explained this could be accounted for by the fact that the auto parts man was such a frequent customer the clerk may not have had him fill out a registration card. He said he recalled that on the night of the bank robbery, both FBI agents and Seattle detectives visited the motel; but no mention was made of possible involvement by Canadian visitors and it never came up until now. By now, too much time had passed to state definitely that either Allan Peters or any of his friends were in town on March 12, 1954. The agents had run into this same problem at the auto wrecking yard, as eight years had elapsed since the robbery, and businesses involved in salvaging used vehicle parts were not prone to retain voluminous and unnecessary records of auto parts sales. Thus no records of such sales eight years earlier were available.

During these weeks, Charlie Waitt tried to stay abreast of the investigation through Dean Rolston and Chet Crisman, but the summer of 1962 was a hectic one for members of the Seattle Police

Department. Tourists were coming into the city for the World's Fair in greater numbers than ever before in the history of the city. And the vice squad, with Sergeant Charles Waitt as its only supervisor, were very busy trying to respond to an avalanche of complaints of vice activity. However, on August 20, 1962, Rolston notified Waitt that Sergeant Morphett called and advised that Clifford Dawley had been sentenced the day before to nine years in the penitentiary on the earlier drug trafficking charge. The sentencing judge, County Court Justice W. D. Ferry, told the bank robber that trafficking in drugs was a vicious crime that affected so many innocent people's lives, and with the defendant's extensive criminal background his nine-year sentence was certainly appropriate to the charge.[12]

During the months that followed, Special Agents Rolston and Crisman continued, as time permitted, to work the case between other high priority case assignments. Witnesses who had been contacted during the initial investigation had to be relocated and interviewed for the second time and for the third and fourth time in some cases, in preparation for the upcoming Federal Grand Jury, for the agents were now able to convince the U. S. Attorney's Office that there was sufficient evidence to indict and convict both Clifford Dawley and John Wasylenchuk on the charges of bank robbery and murder.

Many witnesses, however, had moved out of the city and some were difficult to locate. Kenneth McElhaney, the former manager of the Greenwood branch of the Seattle First National Bank, was now president of the Yacolt State Bank in Clark county on the Oregon border. He would soon assume the presidency of the Vancouver National Bank, in Vancouver, Washington. Several young detectives became involved in this limited role of locating witnesses who no longer resided in Seattle. This would be their only contribution, in what was the culmination of the most extensive investigation the Seattle Police Department had ever undertaken.

Waitt remained in frequent contact with Rolston and Sergeant Morphett, but it was not until the early part of December, 1962 that the three men again got together at Vancouver police headquarters, and this time FBI Special Agent Alf Gunn was also present. The Vancouver sergeant had earlier advised Gunn's office in Bellingham that Steve Polanski would be released from the British Columbia Penitentiary on December 14th and the convict's family was trying to get Joe Richard to put him up in his hotel in Vancouver. Joe wanted nothing to do with his former friend.

After a brief discussion at Morphett's office, the sergeant called Joe Richard and made arrangements for the Americans to interview the "money changer" in person. The four officers were cordially greeted by the hotel owner upon their arrival at the Delmar Hotel on Hamilton Street; however, they lost little time in coming to the point of this visit. They wanted current information on Steve Polanski and his relationship with their two principal suspects. Richard said he had been notified by the Polanski family that Steve would be out of the penitentiary in three or four days, but he wanted nothing to do with this convict. According to him, Polanski was a "pusher" and he didn't want him around his hotel. Besides, the word was out that Wasylenchuk would be released soon and he foresaw trouble if these two were together at his hotel, particularly since the press was still complaining about the inability of the cops to curtail the activities of drug traffickers who allegedly had been frequenting his place of business.

Richard, in response to a barrage of questions from the Americans, said he had better shed some light on information which he neglected to tell Sergeant Morphett and the American officers on their earlier visit. Four years before, he had told the officers that Polanski exchanged a large amount of American currency for Canadian money shortly after the robbery at one of several downtown Vancouver banks. He now said he actually took $2,500.00 of the money from the suspect himself in exchange for Canadian currency. This was something that Waitt had not expected. During earlier interviews with Richard, Waitt and the agents had no reason to doubt the hotel man's story that his friend Polanski fenced the American currency for Wasylenchuk. Now to find that one of their chief sources of information was himself an accessory to the money exchange, knowing it came from the bank robbery in Seattle, made the officers wish more than ever that they could have taken the principal Canadian witnesses to this crime before a grand jury in Canada to assist them in uncovering the truth of these seemingly endless conspiracies. But the power of the American legal system was not available to them here and they were forced to rely solely upon their ability to elicit the truth through skillful and persuasive interrogation. In most cases, the witness was fully cooperative, but if he or she were involved as a principal in the investigation, Sergeant Waitt believed an entirely truthful response was seldom obtained.

Richard, in response to a question from one of the Americans, said he was sure Polanski was in the States at the time of the Greenwood stickup. By his actions and admissions afterward, Polanski knew more about the job than anyone else. Without prompting, he repeated the statements he made to Waitt and Rolston years before, that he still believed the two Canadian bank robbers pulled the Greenwood job and that, "Cliff was the trigger man inside the bank." This was common knowledge in his circle of friends he said.

While discussing Clifford Dawley's present status, the hotel man said, "I know that Cliff Dawley paid Justice McInnes $1,000.00 to get him out of prison one year ahead of his scheduled release date, and it will now cost him $2500.00 to get McInnes to 'front' for him again. But there was no way that guy will be paroled during the next four or five years."[13]

When the Americans continued to press Richard about the currency exchange, Joe could offer no excuse for not mentioning this transaction with Polanski, except that he didn't want to become involved any further in this incident. He thought that if the money was "hot" he may be in trouble with the Vancouver authorities.[14]

The officers' next stop was the Burnaby address where Mrs. Wasylenchuk, who was also known to the officers as Mrs. E. M. Wesley, was residing. Although she had always been pleasant to Waitt on previous visits, she was not happy to see the officers. She refused to discuss anything with Waitt or the other officers present. She appeared frightened and nervous and Waitt found himself feeling sorry for this woman, the mother of two teenage daughters, whose husband he was determined to send to the hangman at the state penitentiary in Walla Walla.

The following day, Waitt and Rolston left Vancouver before daylight for Williams Lake, in the British Columbia interior, three hundred and fifty miles north of the city, to interview Paul McRay, brother of Kris McRay and owner of McRay Transport, one of the biggest independent trucking operations in western Canada. McRay, an ex-convict, had worked hard since getting out of the penitentiary in 1953. He was a close friend of Danny Danahur, the used car dealer whom the officers had reason to believe loaned the two suspects the car used in the Seattle robbery. McRay was a respected and prosperous businessman in Williams Lake who apparently knew the trucking business well. During questioning, he commented that when he got out of the penitentiary he left that part of his life behind him and was now running a legitimate trucking business. He left Vancouver sometime in 1953 and only returned after receiving a telegram advising him of Danahur's death on March 11, 1954. He could give the officers no help on identifying a vehicle which the two stickup men may have obtained from Danahur.

Late the following day, December 13, 1962 while en route back to Vancouver, Waitt and Rolston stopped again at the British Columbia Correctional Camp at Agassiz to check on the current status of Wasylenchuk. In talking to Superintendent John Maloney, the warden said that: "Judge McInnes is again 'fronting' for Wasylenchuk and he carries a lot of weight." The officers were not surprised to hear this, after all the prisoner was Cliff Dawley's running mate and it was obvious to them that the Judge was taking more than a casual interest in two of Canada's most vicious criminals. According to the warden, "The judge helped Alan Babcock, John Bertlson and Bobby Lewis. These guys are all heavy 'cons' and former partners of Wasylenchuk. The judge makes a practice of handing out heavy sentences while on the bench and then at a later date he'll go to bat for the prisoner to get him out on an early parole. But in The Farmer's case, as they call him here, I find it more than unusual since McInnes wasn't the sentencing magistrate. Your man is still playing the part of the model prisoner; he was sentenced to life and was eligible for a parole hearing a year ago, after seven years. It's underway now. He's been in for eight years, but his 'friends' in high government circles are working hard on the outside for his release, so I assume he'll be out soon. This guy is a sharp 'con' and has a way of doing things which always make himself look good in the eyes of the custodial staff, but as I told you before my staff are not fooled by this."[15] He explained that after the officers' last visit, the prisoner contacted the superintendent in person to assure him that he was not a security risk and said he would always cooperate completely with the correctional staff.[16]

The Superintendent said Mrs. Wasylenchuk continues to visit her husband frequently at the camp. She was always very pleasant, dressed well and generally wore a fur coat. This, coupled with the fact that she drove a late model automobile and was not employed, led Maloney to think that her husband still had plenty of money "stashed" somewhere.

The two officers saw no reason to re-interview the suspect again, even though, since their last visit, they had learned of the fencing of American currency through Joe Richard shortly after the Greenwood robbery. En route back to their hotel in Vancouver, the two men discussed what they had accomplished on the investigation thus far. Both were confident that they had gathered all the evidence they could on the case and the investigative phase of this case was coming to a close. Charlie Waitt had few regrets; he was satisfied that the investigation was complete. He recognized that the investigation was not as cut and dried as the U. S. Attorney would like, but there certainly was sufficient evidence to lead a reasonable man to believe that Clifford Dawley and John Wasylenchuk were guilty of robbery and murder. If he had any regrets, it was that there was little chance that they would ever positively identify the third man in the robbery.

Within the Seattle Police Department, there were others who were glad that this investigation was coming to a conclusion. The Canadian end of this investigation had severely depleted the police department's limited criminal investigation funds, and within the police department hierarchy it was common knowledge that Charlie Rouse had diverted vice investigative funds into the Greenwood Bank robbery and murder investigation, contrary to the wishes of the Mayor and City Council. Rouse made no apologies for this, he was adamant that the Department needed to solve this case, and if he had to manipulate the bureaucracy of city hall to accomplish that goal he was perfectly willing to do that. Yet no one chose to challenge Sergeant Waitt's continuing assignment in Canada because it had the blessing of Rouse's close friend Frank Ramon, the Chief of

Police. Waitt was not concerned about either the internal departmental or the political skirmishes for that matter relative to his responsibilities in this case. He laughed about what this investigation had cost him financially, for the city continually failed to provide the necessary funds to pay his full expenses and no money at all for informants. Any money that was paid out to ex-cons or others who had been helpful in the investigation or were down on their luck, came out of Waitt's own pocket or from the federal government through the FBI.[17]

Upon returning to Seattle, Sergeant Charles Waitt filed his final report on the Greenwood Bank Robbery case with the newly appointed Chief of Detectives Robert M. Green. Waitt told Green that he would still be around to assist in gathering the physical evidence, which had been retained in the Seattle police property room, and he would be available to testify at trial; but this would be his last official responsibility toward this investigation, for he planned to retire on January 14, 1963, which was just thirty days away. Waitt had his twenty-five years of service behind him and it was time for a vacation, a short trip with his wife and then on to another career, for he had been offered a job as an inspector with the Washington State Liquor Control Board.

With Waitt's retirement from the force, for all practical purposes, the Seattle Police Department's involvement in the Greenwood bank robbery and murder investigation came to a close. Charlie Rouse had been briefed by Sergeant Waitt before he left for his new job. Both were satisfied that the Bureau could and would continue with the investigation, if the U.S. Attorney's Office needed any additional information on this case before the Canadian suspects were brought to trial. But Rouse was concerned that, with Waitt gone, there was no other man on the Department that could be expected to pick up the pieces and continue to pursue the investigation in the event that federal officers decided not to carry the case forward to a satisfactory conclusion. Waitt had been the middle man, the go-between, an officer who was respected by both Canadian and American officers who got to know him as they worked with him on this most troublesome investigation. He, with FBI Special Agent Alf Gunn, the resident FBI agent assigned to Bellingham, Washington, were instrumental in bringing about an open, cooperative working relationship between the FBI and the Vancouver police authorities. Rouse had great faith in the FBI agents' investigative abilities, particularly Agents Rolston and Crisman, who had been assigned to the Greenwood case from the very beginning. He was assured also that the local FBI-SAC from the Seattle Office was firmly committed to bringing the criminals involved in this case to trial. But, as he thought back to the problems the agents encountered in Canada in 1954 through 1958 with the local British Columbia police and the RCMP, he was concerned that, for the first time in nine years, no Seattle officer was directly assigned to the case who would or could work with the Canadians. In the U.S., much was yet to be done in the task of second interviews of those who had actually witnessed the robbery and shooting at the Greenwood Bank. This was not his direct responsibility and, after discussing the case with the Chief of Detectives where he expressed his concerns, Rouse took no further active role in the investigation.[18] FBI agents, in the meantime, continued to work on the case. They located and re-interviewed many of the witnesses who would be called before the federal grand jury in Seattle, and much of their time was spent working directly with the United States Attorney's Office and Brock Adams, special assistant to the U.S. Attorney, and his staff in laying the groundwork for the grand jury. The investigation was complete. Now it was just a matter of hearing from witnesses and waiting for the release of Dawley and/or John Wasylenchuk. The prisoners could not be extradited while serving time for a criminal offense in their own country.

Meanwhile in British Columbia, shortly after Waitt's retirement, Walter H. Mulligan, the man who must share some responsibility for impeding, if not directly obstructing this investigation, was back in Canada. On February 17, 1963 Vancouver's former chief constable slipped quietly across the border into Canada virtually unnoticed. Mulligan settled in the small community of Oak Bay on the outskirts of Victoria, on Vancouver Island. Here he hoped to avoid the publicity from his past and live out the remainder of his life quietly with his wife, Violet, in the country he loved.

In the intervening years between Chief Constable Mulligan's self-imposed exile in the U. S. (1956-1963), he had settled in Southern California. At first he tried his hand in the nursery business, but as he was still "good copy' for the press, he had a difficult time in holding onto a steady job. Finally, he obtained employment as a security guard at Los Angeles International Airport, a job he held for four years. From there he went on to a variety of security or guard jobs in private industry, but unfortunately, the Royal Commission investigation followed him wherever he went. Now it was time to come home, for the former chief constable was tired, he was nearly sixty years old, and he wanted to retire and settle down. He would work in his garden, a hobby he truly loved, and he and his wife would be able to survive on his police pension. He would also collect a few dollars a month from a modest investment and, at age sixty-two, would be eligible to receive a small Social Security check from the U. S. for his years of employment in Southern California.[19]

Notes

[1] Waitt, Investigator's Report, May 4, 1962, p.4.
[2] Waitt, Op. Cit. conversations with the author, 1968.
[3] Waitt, S.P.D. Case No. 588527 Op. Cit., Investigator's Report, May 24, 1962, p. 1.
[4] Ibid.
[5] Ibid.
[6] Agent Dean C. Rolston, conversations with the author, 1968.
[7] Waitt, Op. Cit., May 4, 1962, p. 3.
[8] Ibid.
[9] Ibid. p. 4.
[10] Ivey, Op. Cit., conversations with the author.
[11] In an interview with the author on August 30, 1974, Ernest and Edward Prestek expressed their resentment toward the agents, particularly of Crisman's implications that the brothers knew more than they were willing to tell about this case. And Ed Prestek said that it appeared to him that the case had been mishandled by the FBI. This may have been reinforced by a statement attributed by Ernie Prestek to Detective Gene Ivey, who mentioned that the "Bureau blew the case," through an overly aggressive action in dealing with Canadian officials and potential witnesses in Canada. According to Ernie Prestek, Detective Ivey told him, "If it hadn't been for the way the FBI handled the whole thing in Canada, the case would have been settled years before; but not

now. The Canadians resented the FBI and because of this they won't cooperate in the investigation."

12 The Vancouver Sun, August 20, 1962.

13 Ibid.

14 Waitt, Op. Cit., Investigator's Report December 14, 1962, p. 1.

15 Ibid. p. 4.

16 Ibid. p. 4.

17 Waitt, Op. Cit., conversations with the author, 1968.

18 Rouse, Op. Cit., conversations with the author, 1972.

19 Paddy Sherman, "Ex-Chief Mulligan is Back," The Vancouver Province,
Victoria Bureau, Victoria, B. C., April 11, 1963.

Chapter

11

The Indictment

On March 12, 1963, the ninth anniversary of the Greenwood Bank hold-up, an article about the robbery, written by reporter Dick Saltonstall appeared in the Seattle Times[1]. This story created a small flurry of activity for Seattle police homicide detectives. Several readers called the police department with some long forgotten bit of news about this crime. The information relayed was thought to be of little value by the Department; but, nevertheless, it was faithfully recorded and routinely forwarded to the FBI by the detectives, almost as if to say, "The responsibility for continuing this investigation is yours, not ours." Unfortunately, this was a fact of life, as no-one from the Seattle Police Department had been assigned to the case to carry on where Charlie Waitt left off upon his retirement in January.

On a routine homicide, it was the custom of the Department to assign one homicide sergeant and two detectives to each case and they would remain with the investigation until they left the unit, or the case was brought to a satisfactory solution. But this was by no means a routine case; this was the cold blooded killing of one of their own officers and the shooting of two others. It appeared, however, as if agency personnel were completely oblivious to these facts and no one within the homicide and robbery section was now charged with the responsibility for continuing this investigation. Yet there was no deliberate decision made by anyone within the unit *not* to pursue this near decade-old case. It appeared more as if the sheer weight of information, evidence and accumulated paper, now over two filing cabinets full to the brim, was too much for anyone to comprehend, let alone to willingly volunteer to take this case on, along with their current investigative caseload. Many of the supervisors and detectives were new to Homicide and even the Chief of Detectives, Bob Green, was a novice to this type of policework, having been recently assigned from his Traffic Division responsibilities to replace the transferring Chief of Detectives A. A. "Al" Kretchmar. But the shift commanders knew full well that, if the case were assigned to their watch, they could "write off" the services of at least one full-time detective. It would take the man at least six months just to review the accumulated investigative case files, let alone the anticipated time lost in the pursuit of what most experienced homicide supervisors thought was a hopeless cause. To use the vernacular of S. P. D. personnel, this was a "loser," the term routinely used by the detectives in referring to unsolved homicide cases.

On March 26, 1963, the news Chief Rouse and the now retired Charlie Waitt had waited for came. John Wasylenchuk, The Farmer, had been released from the British Columbia Correctional Camp at Agassiz and paroled to Vancouver. After receiving a life sentence for a 1955 bank robbery in Burnaby, British Columbia and an additional two years for his escape from Oakalla Penitentiary in November of that year, Wasylenchuk was out in eight years. It was a high price to pay for a robbery and short-lived escape which ended when captured by the Mounties. Rouse was anxious for the U.S. Attorney to proceed with the grand jury. The investigation was as complete as was humanly possible; the evidence was clear, although the physical evidence, or lack thereof, left a lot to be desired. No one wanted to address the issue of the failure of both the FBI and the Seattle Police Department to properly collect, identify and preserve the abundance of physical evidence left at the scene of the crime. It was too late for that. Yet, in retrospect, those who had worked closely on this case for any period of time knew full well that both agencies dropped the ball on this.[2]

Most of the witnesses to this crime were available and it was time for the federal government to act. However, the wheels of justice were slow to respond; it was six months before the indictment of John W. Wasylenchuk was forthcoming. Finally, on October 17,

1963, United States District Judge William T. Beeks released the secret indictment of the Canadian bank robber, at the request of the Special Assistant to the U. S. Attorney, Brock Adams. Wasylenchuk was named in a five count indictment charging him with the robbery and theft of $7,000.00 from the Greenwood Branch of the Seattle First National Bank on March 12, 1954, with the murder of Seattle Police Officer Frank Hardy and with the shootings of Officer Vernon Chase and Sergeant Howard Slessman.[3] At almost the same moment that the indictment was announced publicly, RCMP Sergeant Bruce Northrup, accompanied by FBI Special Agent Alf Gunn from the FBI's Bellingham Field Office, arrested Wasylenchuk on his job in Vancouver. Upon notification of the arrest, the U. S. Attorney's office in Seattle undertook plans for the immediate extradition of the stickup man to the United States.[4]

With the arrest of this bank robber and suspected killer, Seattle Police personnel took a new interest in the case and the newly assigned Homicide Section Captain Dean Phillips, at the request of the U. S. Attorney's office, reopened another investigation which they hoped would place the two principal suspects together in Seattle on the day of the robbery, nine and one-half years before.

Detectives Larry Webb and Eugene Ivey re-interviewed Ed and Ernie Prestek, the owners of Nix Auto Wrecking, even though both had denied earlier to the officers and before the Federal Grand Jury that they knew John Wasylenchuk, stating that they could not identify Wasylenchuk or Clifford Dawley, as friends of Allan and Mary Peters. Sam Hoff, the owner of the National Auto Court, was also re-contacted by the two detectives. He admitted before the Federal Grand Jury that Allan Peters stayed at the Auto Court on the night of the robbery in 1954 and that another man whom he could not identfy was with Peters. He also readily admitted that Ed Prestek was a resident of his motel in the early 1950's, and although it was learned that Ernie Prestek socialized with Allan Peters and his Canadian "friends" in the city in 1954, Hoff again said he could not identify either one of the suspects as being in Seattle during the week of March 12, 1954. Unfortunately, the prosecution was unable to get anyone else to admit that they had seen these two men with Peters[5] and Ernie Prestek.[6]

With the publication of Wasylenchuk's picture in the local papers, a new aspect of this bizarre case unfolded when the manager of a large south-end grocery store "positively identified" Wasylenchuk as the robber of his store on February 8, 1954, a month prior to the Greenwood job. Although the detectives were skeptical of this "positive identification" of a robber from a newspaper picture of a robbery that occurred nine years before, what intrigued them was the fact that the store was just a few blocks from the Blue Bird Motel, the motel Irvin Teague named as the base of operations for the two Canadian criminals in 1954. Although the effort was made, solid evidence which would link the Canadian with the grocery store robbery or place him at either the Blue Bird Motel or the National Auto Court was never found.[7]

On November 7th, three weeks after the suspect's arrest in Canada, his extradition hearing got underway in the Supreme Court of British Columbia in Vancouver with Justice James G. A. Hutcheson presiding. Included among the many witnesses to testify were Vernon Chase and Kenneth McElhaney. McElhaney was now the president of Vancouver National Bank in Vancouver, Washington. Harry Strong, the former assistant manager of the Greenwood branch of the Seattle First National Bank, now assigned with the same firm in Bellingham, was also present in court. In addition to several others, Dean Rolston, Gene Ivey and Charlie Waitt were there along with Assistant United States Attorney Douglas Fryer and Brock Adams who would try Wasylenchuk in federal court in Seattle. Although the suspect was the focus of the extradition proceeding, the man who commanded the attention of all witnesses and law enforcement personnel present in the courtroom was Clifford Eugene Dawley.[8] He was brought to court from the British Columbia Penitentiary at New Westminster, hand-cuffed between two Mounties. He was dressed neatly in a dark pin-stripped suit, white shirt and tie, with a neatly folded white linen handkerchief protruding from his suit coat pocket. As Waitt watched the Canadian enter the courtroom, he compared himself with this man whom he had so frequently studied and questioned. Dawley, now fifty-one, appeared much younger; he was as trim as ever, although his dark hair was turning grey at the temples. Had he not been hand-cuffed to the Mounties, no one would have taken this

Clifford Dawley was led into the Vancouver Courthouse to testify at the John Wasylenchuk extradition hearing. Handcuffed to a Royal Canadian Mounted Police officer, Dawley put a hand up to hide his face. (Richard S. Heyza / The Seattle Times, Nov. 7, 1963)

man for "the toughest criminal in the whole of Canada," as described by Sergeant Bill Morphett many years earlier. Dawley looked directly at Waitt, but he gave no sign that he recognized the former officer and, as he passed, Waitt noticed that the two fingers of the prisoner's left hand were still drawn up into the palm as a result of the San Francisco police officer's bullet in that city many years before.

Vancouver barrister Hugh McGivern, retained by the U.S. Attorney to represent the United States in the extradition proceedings, opened the government's case by reading aloud the affidavit of Irvin Teague. In the affidavit, Teague repeated the story he had told Charlie Rouse and Dean Rolston in 1958, when he was confined in the King County Jail in Seattle for forging stolen Canadian money orders. He said Wasylenchuk admitted to him that he, Dawley and Bobby Talbot had robbed the Greenwood branch of the Seattle First National Bank on March 12, 1954. Teague was told by his cell-mate, that Dawley, armed with a .45 caliber automatic, shot three of the police officers who had responded to the bank alarm. Teague's affidavit explained in detail how he recalled the story, told to him in the penitentiary by his cell-mate, of the planning that went into the job, including where they obtained the guns, the false noses and horn-rimmed glasses, and the getaway car. He described in the affidavit Wasylenchuk's description of Talbot's "hurried exit" through the side window of the bank after being surprised by the early arrival of the police officers.[9]

McGivern next called to the stand several of the bank's employees and customers. Kenneth McElhaney described to the court the circumstances surrounding the robbery, but admitted he could not positively identify any of the suspects as participants. But other witnesses identified both suspects as members of the trio of robbers. William Vance identified Dawley as an occupant of the green Oldsmobile seen leaving the bank at a high rate of speed, and Mrs. Frank Beattie, a customer inside the bank at the time of the robbery, said she believed Dawley was one of the three bandits and that he was the one who shot the approaching officers.

Mrs. Virginia Nonis, another customer, also stated by affidavit that Wasylenchuk was one of the three bandits. She identified the stickup man from a picture of him taken in 1954. Another witness,

Mrs. Hilda Robinson, testified that she saw Wasylenchuk at the Union Arms Apartments at 604 East Union Street in Seattle the day before the robbery. It was from this apartment that the getaway car was stolen.

The next witness to be heard from was Vernon Chase. The crowded courtroom was hushed as the retired officer described his response to the alarm at the Greenwood bank. Although his testimony was repetitious in part, his description of the events which surrounded the robbery, the death of officer Frank Hardy, the shooting of Sergeant Slessman and himself, left no doubt in anyone's mind that the robbers were hardened criminals who would let nothing stand in their way. Some who heard this testimony said that Chase's testimony undoubtedly influenced Justice Hutcheson's decision to release the prisoner to U.S. authorities more than did any of the other persons who testified that day.

Finally, it was the investigating officers turn. They, through questioning by the government's attorney, retraced the steps of their investigation in Canada. They explained how, after first being advised that Vancouver police, upon hearing of the crime, immediately suspected Clifford Dawley and his associates of the robbery. This, Waitt said, precipitated Detective Superintendent Jack Horton's call from Vancouver to the Seattle Police Department shortly after learning of the bank robbery and murder in Seattle. A series of officers, including Waitt, Rolston, Gunn, Ivey, Superintendent Horton and Sergeant Northrup described how subsequent investigation lead the police to the three Canadian suspects, one of whom was Bobby Talbot.

Waitt and Agent Rolston testified of their findings in their interviews with Teague, who tied together the two principal criminal suspects in this case. Finally, both testified about Dawley's statement made to them in the penitentiary in 1962 that he knew, "Wasylenchuk planned and carried out the robbery of the bank and that the man was aided by Bobby Lewis and others."

After nearly two full days of testimony, McGivern rested the government's case and Wasylenchuk's attorney, Thomas R. Braidwood, immediately began by calling his key defense witnesses, beginning with retired Royal Canadian Mounted Police Sergeant Ernest Nuttall.

Under skillful questioning by the defense attorney, the Mountie told the story, so frequently heard by Waitt and Rolston, beginning with the sergeant's visit to the defendant's home approximately one hour after hearing at Vancouver Police Headquarters that three police officers had been shot in a Seattle bank robbery that morning. The Mountie said, "I found Mr. Wasylenchuk working on his boat in the backyard of his residence in Burnaby at twelve o'clock noon that day and I inquired of him about Clifford Dawley's present location." During this interview, he said he entered into his notebook the date and time of the visit. On cross-examination, McGivern hammered away at Nuttall's credibility, for this was the second time the retired Mountie had appeared in a Canadian court on behalf of this bank robber. The barrister brought out that the sergeant was the only defense witness that testified on the defendants behalf in May, 1956, when the suspect was convicted of participation in the robbery of the Royal Bank of Canada in Burnaby earlier that year. When McGivern suggested that the ex-convict used the former Mountie in the 1956 trial as an alibi witness, the former officer flatly denied it. He said that his testimony on behalf of the defendant in the earlier trial was misunderstood by the prosecution and he, in effect, assisted in obtaining a conviction of the defendant in that holdup.

Returning to the Mountie's statement relative to recording his visit, and the date and time of this visit to the suspect's home on the day of the robbery, McGivern elicited testimony that the entry did not follow other incidents which the former sergeant found necessary to record in the normal performance of his duties. As the questioning continued relative to the sequence of events recorded in his notebook and of the corresponding discrepancies in his formal report to his agency, the officer became highly excited and his responses became evasive, disjointed, almost unintelligible, and it became more difficult for him to control his responses. Finally Justice Hutcheson interceded by admonishing the former officer, "Mr Nuttall, it should not be difficult to respond directly to counsel's questioning, yet your testimony is so confusing that the court cannot accept it."[10]

The second witness to testify for the defense was also a retired Mountie. Former Sergeant Frederick Saunders was called by the defense to testify relative to the picture taken of Wasylenchuk at the

RCMP barracks by the American officers in 1954. It was from this photograph that the man was later identified as one of the robbers by the witness Virginia Nonis. Saunders, a highly respected former member of the force, was called upon by the defense to cast doubt on the ability of a witness to identify a robbery suspect from a picture, taken under such circumstances. Upon cross-examination, however, McGivern was successful in eliciting testimony from the officer which cast doubt on the accuracy of Nuttall's notebook entry, specifically that portion which related to his fellow officer's visit to the defendant's home on the date of the robbery. When it was pointed out to Saunders that the entry in the notebook relative to Sergeant Nuttall's visit to Wasylenchuk's residence shortly after the robbery in Seattle was not in chronological order with other officially recorded police data, Saunders agreed with McGivern that it would be "very strange" that any entry of information of a major crime in a police officer's notebook would be out of sequence with other data.[11]

The third defense witness was Elizabeth Wasylenchuk, the ex-convict's wife of twenty years. Mrs. Wasylenchuk told the court she was at their home in Burnaby on the day of the bank robbery in Seattle, and at approximately noon she saw Sergeant Nuttall talking to her husband in their back yard. McGivern made no attempt to challenge her testimony.

Finally, Braidwood called on Wasylenchuk himself to take the stand. To a series of rapid-fire questions, the man denied participating in the bank robbery in Seattle or of telling Irvin Teague or Cliff Dawley that he was involved. On cross examination, the government's attorney brought out that Teague and Wasylenchuk were cellmates in the penitentiary in 1956, when Teague claimed the defendant told the story of the robbery. During this examination, he reluctantly admitted that he and Clifford Dawley were frequent companions prior to his arrest in the 1955 Burnaby holdup. McGivern next elicited testimony from the defendant exposing a police record of at least ten prior convictions for crimes ranging from auto theft at the age of seventeen, to his most recent conviction as a habitual criminal and bank robber, and the fact that the criminal had served eight years of a life sentence after escaping in 1955 from the British Columbia Penitentiary.

At the end of the third day of the hearing, both sides rested and Justice Hutcheson ordered that the court would hear final arguments on the requested American extradition of John Wasylenchuk the following afternoon.

As the court recessed, Detective Ivey who had accompanied Vernon Chase to Canada to attend the extradition hearing, approached Ernest Nuttall in the hallway outside the court chambers, where he introduced Chase to the former Mountie. Ivey had not seen the man since he had worked on the case here in Vancouver, nearly eight years before. He recalled his last meeting with the retired officer when he had taken him out to dinner one evening and bought several drinks hoping that the man would be indiscreet enough to admit that he had criminal ties to Wasylenchuk. However, no such admission was forthcoming during their evening on the town, but Ivey was sure that the former Mountie lived in fear of winding up in the penitentiary himself with those whom he had associated.

In his introduction of Chase, Ivey made no effort to hide his belief that, were it not for the ex-Mountie, Clifford Dawley and John Wasylenchuk would have long since stood trial for murder in a U.S. court, nor did he conceal his contempt for the man when he said to him, "I just wanted you to meet the officer who had his guts blown out by those two bastards in there," referring to Dawley and Wasylenchuk. Nuttall responded, "Well, we really don't know if they were responsible, do we?" As he walked away, Ivey could not help but reflect on the discredit that this man had brought upon the Royal Canadian Mounted Police and "poor old blustering George Archer," as Ivey described the former commander of the RCMP Vancouver detachment, whom he viewed as an RCMP professional who could not admit that some of his men had "gone wrong." Were it not for these two and other Canadian police and public officials, Ivey was convinced a closer working relationship would have existed between the American officers and the Canadians. He was pleased, however, for after all these years, at least Nuttall had been discredited, and Archer, whom Ivey believed was culpable for allowing members of his command to operate outside the law, had now been retired from the Vancouver Police Department. Ivey was convinced that the Americans' investigation of Dawley and Wasylenchuk in

Canada had been partially instrumental in bringing to light the corruption that existed within the Vancouver department under Chief Constable Mulligan, and the RCMP had since taken some steps, as he put it, "to clean-up their own organization."[12]

The next day, Thomas Braidwood directed his assault on the government's case against his client by attacking Irvin Teague's affidavit, taken in 1958 at McNeil Island Federal Penitentiary in Washington. The attorney insisted that to believe the uncorroborated statement of a convicted felon, now held in the Federal Correctional Institution in Sandstone, Minnesota, an institution which housed federal prisoners awaiting psychiatric care, would be a miscarriage of justice. (Teague had been transferred to Sandstone from Leavenworth Penitentiary for his own safety before the government released his testimony). In closing, the barrister insisted that, before granting extradition, Justice Hutcheson must find the evidence to be such as to satisfy a careful and prudent man that the defendant was guilty of the offense charged and this, he maintained, had not been accomplished by the prosecution.

In response, McGivern's summation was direct and to the point. The attorney said that the evidence necessary to decide the issue of extradition need not be sufficient in and of itself to lead one to conclude that the defendant was guilty of the crime; but only that it be sufficient to convince one that a jury should decide the fate of the defendant after a careful review of all the facts of the case.

Unfortunately for John Wasylenchuk, Justice Hutcheson concurred with the government. He ruled that the issue of guilt or innocence of John Wasylenchuk could only be settled by a trial of the facts in the appropriate jurisdiction, and that the conflicting testimony heard in this case should be settled in this manner. He also indicated that the evidence presented at the hearing by the government would have been sufficient to commit the accused to trial had the crime been committed in Canada. "Therefore," he said, "it is my duty to allow this case to go to a jury." Shortly thereafter in his chambers, the judge signed a Warrant of Committal and Wasylenchuk, escorted by two uniformed Mounties, was taken back to Oakalla Prison to await review and approval of Justice Hutcheson's decision by Canada's Minister of Justice in Ottawa.

Before leaving the court, Braidwood notified Justice Hutcheson that he would seek a writ of habeas corpus, challenging the decision of the court. Unfortunately for his client, the writ under Canadian law limited the challenge to one of jurisdiction and the barrister admitted there was little doubt but that the United States government had jurisdiction. With this the Clerk of the Court issued the warrant. [13]

WARRANT OF COMMITTAL
CANADA
PROVINCE OF BRITISH COLUMBIA
COUNTY OF VANCOUVER
CITY OF VANCOUVER

TO WIT:The Peace Officers in the said City of Vancouver, and to the Keeper of the Common Gaol of the County of Vancouver, in the said County of Vancouver at Oakalla in the County of Westminster. BE IT REMEMBERED that on this 9th day of November, in the year A.D. 1963, at the City of Vancouver, Province of British Columbia, is brought before me, James G. A. Hutcheson, a judge under the Extradition Act, John Wasylenchuk, who has been apprehended under the said Act, to be dealt with according to law, and for as much I have determined, that he should be surrendered in pursuance of the said Act, on the grounds of his being accused of the crimes of:

knowingly and unlawfully and by force and violence and intimidation taking from the persons and the presence of employees of a member Bank of the Federal Reserve system and from the said Bank, the sum of approximately $7,000.00 belonging to, and in the case, custody, control, and possession of the said Bank and in committing the said offence or offences and in attempting to avoid apprehension for the commission of such offence or offences did knowingly, wilfully and unlawfully kill a person, to wit: Seattle Police Officer Frank Hardy (in violation of Section 2 and 2113, of Title 18 of the United States Code.)

THIS IS THEREFORE TO COMMAND YOU, the said peace officers in Her Majesty's name, forthwith to convey and deliver the said John Wasylenchuk into the custody of the Keeper of the Common Gaol at Oakalla Prison Farm, in the Province of British Columbia, and you the said Keeper to receive the said John Wasylenchuk into your custody, and him there safely to keep until he is thence delivered pursuant to the provisions of the said Act, for which this shall be your warrant.

Notes

[1] Dick Saltonstall, "Policeman's Slaying Nine Years Ago Still Unsolved," The Seattle Times, March 11, 1963.

[2] In 1954, police agencies throughout the U.S. routinely charged the field detective with the task of collecting evidence at crime scenes; but in most large metropolitan police agencies, few homicide detectives had ever been formally trained to handle these responsibilities. Within the Federal Bureau of Investigation at the time, many agents were even less skilled than the average large city detective in the investigation of violent deaths. In more recent years, both the FBI and local police in the U. S. and in Canada, have utilized crime scene specialists and/or trained laboratory personnel to collect evidence at the scene of a violent crime. In 1954, these services were not generally available. Sixteen years would pass (1970) before the first S. P. D. Homicide Unit Supervisor, Lieutenant Richard Schoener, would be assigned to attend a formal training program for homicide investigators. Forensic scientists and medical-legal-pathology experts from around the world were employed by the Southern Police Institute in Louisville, Kentucky for these very informative and hands-on instructional training programs, training which had been available to all police agencies in the U.S. for a number of years. Unfortunately, it would be many years before the city got around to providing the police department's other first line police supervisors with even the most rudimentary management training, which most police experts believed to be necessary to properly fulfill one of the most difficult and demanding supervisory/management roles ever faced in any occupation. Supervisory training, for Seattle Police Sergeants first got underway at the State Training Academy in 1975. Several S.P.D. managers who were assigned to attend this very basic and rudimentary course had been employed in a supervisory/management capacity for more than twenty years, never before having attended a supervisory training course sponsored by the city administration.

[3] Constantine Angelos, "B.C. Man Indicted in 1954 Greenwood Bank Robbery," The Seattle Times, October 17, 1963, p. 1.

[4] Charles Dunsire, "Greenwood Bank Holdup Slaying Suspect Arrested," The Seattle Post Intelligencer October 18, 1963, p. 1.

[5] In a 1992 interview with the author, Allan Peters, who by now had become a very successful Vancouver business man, continued to deny any knowledge of this 1954 crime in Seattle. He readily admitted knowing John Wasylenchuk in the 1950's but he said he never associated with the man and certainly never traveled to Seattle with this criminal. He claimed he knew Wasylenchuk to be a gardener and later he was in the roofing business. He said Wasylenchuk came to his business establishment on Grimmer Street in Vancouver only on a few occasions and that was to buy parts for his truck. Peters accused the FBI, the Vancouver police and members of the RCMP of lying when they alleged that he was in Seattle with Wasylenchuk at the time of the Greenwood bank robbery.

Mary Peters Smith was reluctant to be interviewed. Still married to Art Smith, she was living in Burnaby in 1992. Allan Peters had told the author that his sister was unable to talk as she had suffered two disabling heart attacks and a stroke; but when her husband was interviewed he advised the author that Mary would consent to an interview only if her brother Allan approved of it. In a second attempt to interview Mary Smith, it was apparent her brother Allan had not approved the interview.

[6] Detective Larry W. Webb, S.P.D. Case No. 288527, Op. Cit., Investigator's Report, October 24, 1963.

[7] Webb, S.P.D. Case No. 288527, Op. Cit. October 29, 1963, p. 1.

[8] The Seattle Times, November 7, 1963, p. 22.

[9] Ibid.

[10] The Seattle Times, November 9, 1963, pp. 1, 4.

[11] Ibid.

[12] Detective Eugene F. Ivey, interview with the author September 3, 1974.

[13] Charles Dunsire, "Judge OK's Extradition in Bank Slaying Case," The Seattle Post Intelligencer, November 10, 1963 p. B. Also see Constantine Angelos, "Canadians Extradition is Ordered," The Seattle Times, November 10,1963, pp. 1, 32.

TIMES 3-1-74

Citizen review board for police demanded

Leaders of a citizens committee presented Mayor ...

Bank robbing is a loser's crime   T- 12-3-75

REVIEWING its experience with the Bank Protection Act of 1968, the federal Justice Department laments that "there is very little good news to report.

It isn't that the act is a complete failure. It's because the act has been a disappointment in curbing the growth of robberies.

Where ...

selves confronted with a pistol, and that the "country club" atmosphere which banks create for their branches may be a factor.

On that latter score payment suggest bank pla...

B 9 The Seattle Times

Sunday, June 9, 1974

THE beginning of the end. That was the year that to police principally from prompted a lengthy Times in Marshal Wilson and John ...

Sunday, March 17, 1974   The Seattle Times B 9

Interim police chief has changes in mind

'Philosophical differences' with Tielsch are cited

BY DAVE BIRKLAND AND ROSS ANDERSON

Robert Hanson's appointment as interim police chief appears to have heightened police fears that outsiders would again be involved in city police affairs, ...

HANSON said the ...

Officers fear more politics   T 3-15

BY DAVE BIRKLAND

Robert Hanson's appointment as interim police chief appears to have heightened police fears that outsiders would again be involved in city police affairs, ...

Payoff scandal wouldn't go awa[y]

THURSDAY, MAY 1, 1969

An End to Gambling Hypocrisy

The Times' opinion and comment:

Cool thinking needed to avoid police walkout   T-3-22-74

AN ugly confrontation appears to be threatening over police disciplinary procedures and whether Officer Ed Fjerstad should be dismissed from the force.

John Sullivan, president of the Seattle ...

and demands have been voiced that outsiders be permitted to participate in the division's proceedings hereafter. Uhlman is opposed to the side of parti...

---

71 Police, Firemen May Face Budget Ax   T-26-74?

BY CHARLES ...

Exams Are Mailed Sweepstakes On For Police Chief

Police seeking proof Dawley 3rd man in fuel barge blast

The Seattle T[imes]

AN INDEPENDENT NEWSPAPER
Founded August 10, 1896

Alden J. Blethen, 1896-1915   W. K. Blethen, 1949-196[ ]
Elmer E. Todd, 1942-1949
John A. Blethen, Publisher
W. J. Pennington, President

FRIDAY, MAY 24, 1974

The Times' opinion and comment:

City Hall's ploy with police-manpower slashes

WE seriously question that deep cuts can be made in the size of the force without impairing its public responsibilities. ...

TIMES - 1-28-74

Herb Robinson:

Value of police air patrol questioned

Former Officer Gets Jail Term

GRAND JURY

Uhlman Says Police, Gaming Linked Here

Herb Robinson:

New talk of city-coun[cil]

Chief Tielsch Leaves Job After Clash With Uhlman

Dispute Over Firing Case

BY CHARLES DUNSIRE

Capt. Hanson Takes Charg[e]

BY GEORGE FOSTER

One, big conspiracy must be proved, judge rules

BY LARRY BROWN

Evans OK's limited social card games

Chapter

12

Extradition

With the announcement of Justice Hutcheson's approval of John Wasylenchuk's extradition to the United States, subsequent publicity brought about a renewal of activity in Seattle for Captain Dean Phillips and his homicide detectives. One caller to Phillips identified himself as R. James Malone, who asked if Wasylenchuk was right or left handed. When queried by Phillips as to Malone's interest, the man responded that he had some "real hot information" which would break a major United States kidnapping case wide open, but he had to know whether Wasylenchuk was right or left-handed. Phillips advised the man he would check this out and get back to him. The FBI was contacted and told Phillips that their reports indicated that Wasylenchuk was right-handed. In his return call to Malone, the homicide section captain again asked what Malone's interest was in this case. Malone responded that his information hinged upon the suspect being left-handed; he would not further elaborate, but said he would discuss it with Phillips if he would come to his home. Phillips indicated he would send an S. P. D. Homicide detective to see the man.

The following day, Detective Frank W. Jones and FBI Agent Pat Coyne visited James Malone at his Queen Anne hill apartment. Malone said he was John Philip Weyerhaeuser's brother-in-law, Weyerhaeuser, being the largest lumberman in the country and reportedly one of the richest, had paid $200,000.00 ransom for the return of his nine-year-old son George, who was kidnapped in Tacoma on May 24, 1935, and released nine days later. Although the kidnappers were subsequently arrested and convicted of the offense and the crime had occurred twenty-eight years before, Malone was sure that John Wasylenchuk was one of the men involved.[1] But his identification of the man rested upon whether Wasylenchuk was right or left-handed. Upon obtaining a signature from one of the kidnapping suspects when acting as an intermediary and delivering the package of money to the kidnapper, the man was left handed.[2]

Although Malone's story was discounted, this was not the case when Detective Harry Schneider at Phillips' direction, accompanied Dean Rolston to Mrs. Frank J. Beattie's home in response to a threat on the woman's life. Mrs. Beattie had testified three days earlier at the extradition hearing in Justice Hutcheson's courtroom in Vancouver that she believed Clifford Dawley was the man who shot the three officers during the Greenwood robbery. Following this, both the Vancouver and Seattle papers published pictures of Mrs. Beattie and listed her home address in Seattle[3]. The tone of the calls to the Beattie residence following this were extremely disturbing to the family, but it was impossible to determine whether they were initiated by someone connected to the Greenwood case or were merely crank calls. Schneider hooked a crudely made recorder to the telephone, and Mrs. Beattie was instructed on how to activate the machine in the event that the calls continued[4]. Although the family members were alarmed at the nature of the original calls, Rolston and Schneider assured them that the district patrols would, "keep an eye on the family." Fortunately there were no other calls of this nature to the Beattie residence.[5]

Meanwhile in Canada, acting within the fifteen day limit in which Wasylenchuk was allowed by law to contest Justice Hutcheson's order of committal for extradition, Attorney Braidwood petitioned the Supreme Court of British Columbia on November 20th, for a Writ of Habeas Corpus for the release of his client. The defense's motion not only challenged Irvin Teague's testimony, but also the Justice's authority to issue the order of committal. [See *Appendix*.]

Three weeks after listening to Mr. Braidwood's argument on behalf of his client for dismissal of the warrant and order of extradition, Supreme Court Justice J. G. Ruttan denied the petition. Thus the only remaining hurdle for the release of Wasylenchuk was approval of his surrender to American authorities by the office of Federal Justice Minister Lionel Chevrier in Ottawa. This was accomplished routinely. And on December 18, 1963, nearly ten years after the crime of bank robbery and murder in Seattle on March 12, 1954, the warden at Oakalla Penitentiary surrendered John Wasylenchuk to two FBI agents. He was immediately brought to Seattle in chains to stand trial for robbery and murder.[6]

In Seattle, meanwhile, the U.S. Attorney's office presented to the newly impaneled federal grand jury a report of the evidence which was received by Justice James Hutcheson during the extradition hearing of Wasylenchuk, including the identification in the courtroom in Vancouver of Clifford Dawley by witnesses William Vance and Mrs. Beattie. Shortly thereafter, the twenty-three-member jury returned a six-count indictment charging that Clifford Dawley conspired with John Wasylenchuk in the robbery of the Greenwood branch of the Seattle First National Bank and, in so doing, killed Seattle Police Officer Frank Hardy and wounded Officers Vernon Chase and Sergeant Howard Slessman.[7] Unfortunately, under Canadian law, Dawley could not be extradited while confined in Canada for a criminal offense, and he faced eight more years of confinement for trafficking in narcotics.

But some Canadians were reluctant to turn over to the Americans their notorious citizen John Wasylenchuk. A week before his release a group of "Wasylenchuk's friends" convinced B. C. Liberal Party leader Ray Perrault that "J.W." or "The Farmer," would not receive a fair trial if extradited to the United States, but would in effect, "be railroaded to the gallows for a crime he did not commit."[8] It soon became obvious that some of these "friends" were attempting to block the extradition of Wasylenchuk to continue to conceal the ongoing alliances which existed between several Canadian officials and John Wasylenchuk and Clifford Dawley. (The Mounties also weren't anxious to have one of their own officers placed in the position where he could further embarrass the Royal Canadian Mounted Police on the witness stand in the U.S., for Sergeant Nuttall was sure to be invited to testify in U.S. District Court in Seattle). Perrault took it upon himself to block this extradition by

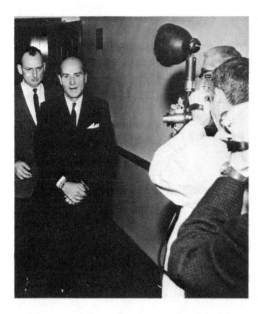

John Wasylenchuk arrives in
chains in Seattle on December 20,
1963. (Photo courtesy: Seattle
Post-Intelligencer Collection
Museum of History & Industry)

asking Justice Minister Lionel Chevrier to investigate the propriety
of the actions of the parties involved and to direct the RCMP to
undertake a full-scale investigation of the facts surrounding this case
before allowing the prisoner to leave the country. Mr. Chevrier
responded that, in view of Perrault's concern, he would again discuss
the case with the department solicitors, but he was not sure how far
his office had progressed with the extradition request, for it had
considered the case as routine. Unfortunately for Perrault and
Wasylenchuk, Chevrier's office had already approved the bank robber's extradition and had notified Oakalla Prison Officials and the
U.S. Attorney's Office in Seattle that the prisoner could be released
to the American authorities. By the time this information reached
Perrault in Vancouver, Wasylenchuk was already en route to Seattle.
The politician's attempt to halt the transfer of the prisoner came too
late.[9]

In Seattle, on December 19, 1963, the suspect was brought
before United States District Court Judge William F. Lindberg for
arraignment, where Braidwood's associate, Vancouver Barrister
Thomas A. Dohm, vigorously protested the extradition of his client,
contending that he had been taken from Canada illegally by the FBI,
as the order of surrender had been signed inadvertently. He asked

for and was granted a continuance until he could arrange for a member of the American Bar to represent his client in his effort to forestall the actions taken thus far. Judge Lindberg agreed to the continuance and set the arraignment over to January 7, 1964. Shortly afterward, Dohm released a prepared statement to the press protesting the actions of the FBI in "spiriting" his client out of Canada without the opportunity for the man to consult with his attorney or even to say good-bye to his wife and family. He said, "The FBI acted with undue haste, when legal action was being prepared to insure that my client would receive the full protection of the law."

In the nation's capitol at Ottawa, Wasylenchuk's hurried exit from British Columbia to the United States brought about an angry debate in the House of Commons in which a member of parliament accused Prime Minister Lester Pearson of failing to protect the rights of Canadian citizens accused of criminal acts in foreign countries.[10] Frank Howard, New Democratic Party (N.D.P.) in an obvious attempt to embarrass the prime minister from the floor of parliament, asked whether in view of the way the extradition of Mr. Wasylenchuk was handled, he planned to dispose with the services of Justice Minister Chevrier and clean up the Justice Department. The Prime Minister angrily retorted that he would not dignify Howard's question with an answer. But the Justice Minister did not take lightly the charges that his office had not complied with the Extradition Act in handling the Wasylenchuk case. Ray Perrault questioned whether, under the Extradition Act, a man under sentence could be extradited and under the Parole Act, "asking if Mr. Wasylenchuk were still technically under sentence." Chevrier responded that his office had investigated the Wasylenchuk case fully and that he had no alternative under the law but to sign the extradition warrant. He maintained that he couldn't understand what all the uproar was about over this "lifer," who had been given every opportunity and protection that one's government could grant one of its citizens, nor could he understand those who took the position that one on parole could not be extradited. If this were true, he added, persons on parole in both countries could cross the border and commit crimes at will without fear of extradition.[11]

In discussing the minister's statements with American reporters, Perrault said his only concern was that the justice minister had not followed the provisions of the Extradition Act; but now that Wasylenchuk had been taken to the United States, he said, "I merely suggested to the Justice Minister that his office keep an eye on this case to insure that Mr. Wasylenchuk receive a fair trial." He also told the reporters that he had talked to the prime minister personally and that Mr. Pearson assured him that he would take a personal interest in the case. But, in later conversations with Canadian reporters in Vancouver, Perrault was critical of Chevrier's action; he told them that the justice minister had mishandled the entire case. Referring to Chevrier's approval of the extradition warrant, Perrault said, "Chevrier could have signed his own death certificate that day and wouldn't have known the difference by the way this case looks."[12]

Thomas Dohm, meanwhile, did not doubt that his client would receive a fair trial in Seattle, but he had other problems; his star witness, former RCMP Sergeant Ernest Nuttall, had allegedly suffered a heart attack and was confined to a Vancouver hospital and apparently would not be available to testify. Upon hearing of the ex-Mountie's "sudden attack," a homicide detective who had worked on the case expressed his feelings toward Wasylenchuk by stating, "We'll see that son-of-a-bitch hang yet." Charlie Waitt, upon hearing the news that Nuttall would not testify for the defense, was relieved. For, had the former officer (now retired) remained with the Royal Canadian Mounted Police, he undoubtedly would have been forced by his own organization to honor a request from the U.S. Attorney's Office to testify in the United States, where Waitt was sure he would have cracked under cross-examination relative to his association with John Wasylenchuk. Had this happened, the accused would unquestionably be convicted; but, in obtaining the conviction, the reputation of the RCMP would have suffered terribly. Of greater concern to Waitt, were this to happen, was that the gulf between the law enforcement agencies of the two countries may well have widened and the seeds of distrust and suspicion have flourished anew.[13]

At noon on January 7, 1964, as Charlie Waitt headed toward the Federal Court House in Seattle for the 1:30 arraignment, he caught the tail end of a news report in which there was speculation that

Sergeant Ernest Nuttall had recovered sufficiently to appear at trial on the bank robber's behalf. Waitt was skeptical of the report. Upon his arrival at the courthouse, he was asked by reporters if he was aware that Sergeant Nuttall was reported to be in good condition and had been released from the hospital in Vancouver. Waitt suggested that the reporters ask that question of the U.S. Attorney's Office or Erle W. Horswill, Wasylenchuk's court-appointed attorney. The former S.P.D. homicide sergeant gave no indication that he was keenly interested in Nuttall's activities, but of one thing he was sure, Ernest Nuttall would never again voluntarily appear as a defense witness for John Wasylenchuk or any other criminal.

As the arraignment got underway, failing to obtain a dismissal of the charges against his client, Horswill argued that under the existing provisions of the Extradition Treaty between the United States and Canada, the charges must be limited to those for which his client was extradited and as the charges of entering the Greenwood bank with Intent to Commit Larceny, Committing a Larceny and Assault with a Deadly Weapon were not specified in the original extradition request, they were not prosecutable offenses. Although Judge Lindberg refused to dismiss the larceny and assault charges, he did agree to hold them in abeyance until conclusion of the trial on the murder and robbery charge, for which the defendant had been extradited. Horswill also requested a delay in the trial date, explaining that a key defense witness was ill and currently unable to testify on his client's behalf. Agreeing to the request, Judge Lindberg set the trial date for March 24, 1964.

Notwithstanding that Wasylenchuk's key defense witness was apparently too ill to travel to Seattle to testify, the former Mountie was willing and able to tell his story to any and all who would listen to him in Vancouver. In an interview subsequent to the arraignment in Seattle, the former officer told a reporter from the Vancouver Sun that he was extremely ill, suffering from a heart condition and had been ordered to rest at home.[14] He said he would stick by his testimony that the accused could not have robbed the Greenwood Bank in Seattle, because he was home in Vancouver one hour after the robbery, and that if he were able to travel to Seattle, he would so testify to this. When asked whether he may be recovered enough by the end of March to travel south, the man responded that if he improved, he could possibly attend the trial, but insisted it would be necessary to have a nurse accompany him. If not, he would give a deposition, not just for Mr. Wasylenchuk's sake, he explained, "but that justice may prevail. From my recruit days I learned a good Mountie must state the evidence both for and against the accused."[15]

But another former Mountie apparently hadn't learned the lesson in recruit school that justice was dependant upon a careful scrutiny of all the evidence both for and against the accused. Larry Hanson who, at 37, once again resigned his commission in the Royal Canadian Mounted Police and was now operating a catering business in Burnaby, British Columbia, came to Seattle to offer his services to John Wasylenchuk. Hanson, like Perrault, was unhappy with the turn of events which surrounded the ex-con's extradition from Canada, stating he believed that the prisoner was not guilty of the crime charged and that, "Mr. Wasylenchuk is a model citizen."[16] With this, the man announced that he was raising money from "Wasylenchuk's friends" for a defense fund for the accused. Although the defendant's court-appointed attorney, Erle Horswill, expressed his surprise at the former Mountie's announcement to the American officers, Hanson's actions only further intensified the suspicion and distrust which had grown between them and their Canadian counterparts as a result of the Dawley-Wasylenchuk investigation. Notwithstanding Hanson's intentions, his actions were suspect and Waitt was fed up with "Canada's finest" again found "fronting" for this convicted thief and bank robber who was now facing a murder charge for the death of a police officer. Even though Hanson was one of two RCMP Constables who captured Wasylenchuk in 1955 after his escape from Oakalla Prison, where he was being held awaiting trial on a bank robbery charge, it cut no ice with Waitt. In his twenty-five years service, he had never heard of a case in which an officer would place his trust in a convicted habitual criminal let alone a suspected cop killer. A social worker may frequently take such action and a judge, occasionally, but a law enforcement officer, never.

After Hanson announced his plans to raise funds for the prisoner, Horswill advised him that his client needed money to defray

John Wasylenchuk (c) with his attorneys Thomas Dohm and Erle Horsiwell — 1964. (Photo courtesy: Seattle Post-Intelligencer Collection Museum of History & Industry)

the cost of transportation for witnesses and other costs for stenographers, depositions and court transcripts. However, the former Mountie did not appeal directly to the public for money, but indicated he was gathering funds strictly from "Wasylenchuk's friends" and other "interested parties." Who these were, was not revealed by the ex-Mountie. Waitt continued to be amazed at those whom he had found to be "interested" in this ex-con's wellbeing. But the Canadians who were so concerned that their " model citizen" receive a fair trial in the United States, did not need to worry about attorney fees, for the American taxpayer not only paid these, but with Erle Horswill, the court appointed attorney, he received the services of one of the best trial lawyers available.

Whereas the American officers were skeptical of Hanson's motives, to some observers, the ex-Mountie's actions were a logical outgrowth of the ramifications and adverse publicity which arose over the defendant's extradition from Canada. Many Canadians were upset with the manner in which he was removed from Canada by the FBI. And Erle Horswill again publicly expressed his concern that the Bureau "may have taken advantage of the defendant by spiriting him across the border," before his client was able to again seek legal assistance or even to say good bye to his family.

Notes

[1]   Byron Johnsrud, "Crime in a Bygone Era." The Seattle Times, June 13, 1974, p. G-2.

[2]   Detective Frank W. Jones, S.P.D. Case No. 288527 Investigator's Report, November 20, 1963.

[3] The media's practice of providing a witness' home address continues to this day. This type of publicity makes it more difficult for the police to obtain voluntary statements from witness in criminal cases and witnesses, on occasion, are harassed, threatened or even killed by one or more of the parties involved in the original crime.

[4]   Harry L. Schneider, conversation with the author, November 7, 1991. The former S.P.D. Commander suggested that this crudely made recording device was yet another example of budgeting "shortfall," for most of the Police Department's specialized equipment was either homemade, federal government surplus or antiquated World War II military equipment "jerry rigged" to meet the Department's needs. He remembered this device well, describing the two buttons that the victim of such telephone calls had to activate simultaneously to turn the machine on after picking up the telephone handset, thus creating a clearly audible electrical sound which could be heard by the calling party.

[5]   Detective Harry L. Schneider, S.P.D. Case No. 288527 Investigator's Report, November 20, 1963.

[6]   The Seattle Times, December 19, 1963, p. 6.

[7]   The Seattle Times, December 12, 1963, p. 1.

[8]   "Parole Law Cited For Wasylenchuk," The Vancouver Sun, December 18, 1963, p. 16.

[9]   "Wasylenchuk Extradition Stirs Angry House Debate," The Vancouver Sun, December 19, 1963, p. 1-2.

[10] Ibid.

[11] Ibid.

[12] Ibid.

[13] Charles K. Waitt, conversations with the author, 1968.

[14] The Seattle Times, January 25, 1964.

[15] Ibid.

[16] The Seattle Times, January 11, 1964.

New Book Details Seattle Corruption of 1960s

By Larry McCarten

A new book that hangs out for public view some of Seattle's moldering dirty laundry is now on sale at stores here.

Author William J. Chambliss' "On The Take: From Petty Crooks to Presidents," details the era of Seattle's police payoffs and the graft that once that operated the corrupt corrupt corrupt.

Chambliss, now a sociology professor at the University of Delaware, paid a similar price at the University of Washington in 1967 when he began investigating corruption that gripped the Seattle Police Department and ran higher-up public figures.

The best thing about this book is the feelings is that it provides a capsule account of Seattle's most notorious system of ... latter-day corruption. Newcomers will find the history fascinating.

Careful readers will wince at the book's errors. Chambliss confuses, for example, the ownership of the city's dominant newspapers, the Times and the P-I, and faints on "old reporter" rather than the proper "skid road."

The book treats supposed corruption in the administrations of several U.S. presidents, including Richard Nixon, but the emphasis is on that dark period of the 1960s and 1970s when the police payoff and pinball systems flourished here.

In 1982, five years before the present hiatus alluding to a police payoff scandal, the professor droned in a courthouse and frequented Skid Road and the police joints, playing poker, looking and betting.

He says he discovered without luck the payoff system. Names differ, but he also conferred with various with with who were aware of the corruption but couldn't get their papers to print stories, and with investigators who ran into the payoff information but from the other network.

Basically, the system involved police mobs shaking down businesses who didn't want to peddle their wares. The payoff were passed up to the police chiefs or joints with each level taking its cut. The pinball bush also flourished under a monopoly b

...an accident.

Gonzo says the P-I article produced plenty of "hue and cry".

"There was an uproar, we got stacks of indignant letters. There was a citywide outcry to get rid of Charlie O. Carroll and it showed up in the next election, when he was soundly ...to the private," the Washing...

Gonzo says Chby had an appointment to talk with a competing reporter the day he drowned and that "drowning was a favorite method for debunking investigations."

Chambliss asserts that crime and graft figures don't fit a "profound seeing around. He says he was set to for blackmail by being plied with money for looking into. He says his case

Crime-ring indictments tied to Seattle

Colacurcio brothers charged

Times staff and Associated Press

Two brothers of Seattle racketeer Frank Colacurcio and a former employee have been indicted by a state grand jury that charges at least 14 men and other crimes at four topless dance clubs in Tucson and Phoenix, Ariz.

According to documents obtained in Maricopa County Court and Pima County Court filed worked out for Frank Ochan, who had worked for several former clubs, and Romile Moore from of four topless bars in Phoenix and four topless bars in Tucson, have been put Tucson, have been put the forf...

Patrick Colacurcio, as members of Western Consultants, a management firm owned by Phoenix. Thomas Strite owned by Phoenix. Ochan as a general stockholder and management at a management firm were charged.

Gary Schietman, state Liquor Department investigator, said the documents at a corrupt agent for the department, used liquor laws to dismiss charges of liquor law against the violations the clubs. He sought forfeiture for the cl...

in racketeering.

Frank Colacurcio at that time said not to be defendant in the indictment that faces him. He do know that from Rime to the indictment faces him. He did know that from Rime to the indictment he regularly.

The clubs are Bourbon Street Circus and Cheetah I in Phoenix and Bourbon Street Circus and Drown Street in Tucson, Drown Street in Tucson, said.

Tucson police undercover Officer LaMont Novak says a document that from him had he after officers from him that he at an after officers from him then met in Oregon and Washing ton met in discuss alleged 1984 Olympic carriers drive by the Colacurcios and developing family in the Seattle and slightly operating complex affairs since Frank Cola curcio after alleged of their family. He now operates the private skimming profits from the business affairs on an also after owned this prison in He in Transacted a federal a four.

Frank Colacurcio served time in a state of Alaska in 1960 and 1961. Is taken receiving a check bank in two because a state and obtained about half the 230,000 a decree, according to ...versed 50 appeared

He now operates an employment agency in Lake City Way ioe. Gilbert Talenta, a former owner of the Seattle Talenta a former owner of the Seattle and several other topless club operating authors by their organization authors by their organization back and Washington profits from after alleged the organization told investors that profits have come from their alleged members have come of the sharing proceeds and over for pointing proceeds and over for theft.

When Pauole also landed ...

victims in a contract murder case, and his organization about. Mentioned the authorities about Alaska clubs he Colacurcio is part by clubs he Colacurcio is part by state's Liquor partment, in the state's Liquor partment, witness procedure, with Colacurcio views and inves believed through story Colacurcio views and inves the the organization himself rick through views his belief through story himself complete list of large bills, with story himself complete list organization his belief through story himself states detect cameras their authorized inve the office and another devices in can in Tucson Stream is manager can in Tucson Stream is and observed the weekly clients the Colacurcio make his Colacurcio.

The others says, a groups of and stuffing the money in his shoe and pockets, the officers says

Police Chief Won't Be
Selected Before June

It will be at least June before a new Seattle police chief is named. Benneil Feigenbaum, chairman of the selection committee, said to day.

However, Feigenbaum said his seven-man committee has agreed on the testing procedures for candidate and that the committee was appointed by Mayor Wes Uhlman last year to search out candidates nation-wide.

Feigenbaum said that applications for the job will be taken another three

Applicants then will be given a 3½ to 5 hour written test. The top 16 to 15 from that list will be invited to Seattle for oral examina...

Each candidate will be questioned two hours by each of two five - member panels. The panels will be made up of the seven committee members, two police chiefs and a consultant.

Feigenbaum said interviewbackground investigations will be made of the 999 four or five candidates and then the names of the top three will be submitted to Mayor Uhlman who will make the final choice.

The new man will replace Frank C. Ramon, who cred last November. Frank Moore has been acting chief. Moore said he plans to apply for the permanent appointment.

Feigenbaum said the selection has been the ...

hard to come to a consensus on how to pick a new chief.

"There just is no way to shorten it," he said.

Arsonists Cause
$500 Damage

An arson fire caused an estimated $500 damage last night in an unoccupied business building at the pier Way 5.

The fire, reported before 8 p.m. started on the first floor of the former Way's Way spread ...estimated ...

Retired policeman tells of 1969 attack by protester Bissell

By Steve Mikkelsen

See BISSELL Page A5

Police explore a vote of 'no confidence' against the chief

No top officers seek chief's job

The Seattle Times

Seattle narcotics squad under fire

Other agencies lose confidence

Give the police more drug tools

Seattle has become one of several Western cities targeted in the last year or so by Los Angeles-based gangs as a lucra-and relatively low-risk market to peddle police here have in-...number of felony...year on drugs...

It would serve two purposes...permit monitoring of drug dealers when there is "real" evidence of illegal drug sales taking place at a particular location, and provide trial evidence.

At present state law prohibits what is known as "one-party consent" to recorded conversations in drug cases, although it is permitted in federal law. One result is an inability of Seattle police to work closely with federal drug agents in some narcotics cases.

Of the three bills under legislative consideration, we favor House Bill 1966, which provides the greatest protections against improper search and seizure and require police to file a written report with the courts for review, following each incident in which a conversation is recorded.

Other bills would permit abatement of proven drug rock houses as public nuisances and, under the most aggravated circumstances of drug sales or manufacture, allow dwellings to be seized and sold by the state.

One barrier to the timely prosecution of drug offenders is a terrible backlog of cases in the state crime laboratory, where confiscated substances are tested to verify that they are illicit drugs. This has resulted in delays in felony drug prosecutions of up to six months.

The Legislature, Gov. Booth Gardner, must act to alleviate the crime lab problem, which has become a serious obstacle to effective law enforcement.

Seattle has become endangered by the menace of illegal drugs and all that accompanies them, including gang violence and wide-spread burglary and theft as the means of supporting drug habits. The city needs and deserves the state's assistance to help rid it of this scourge.

Serious crime is back on the rise

st ser

f I call the ort someh fficer to ...g... "There a ...Worse w...

Ex

Chapter

13

The Trial

On March 24, 1964, at 9:30 A.M., notwithstanding Erle Horswill's objections, the trial of the United States of America vs. John W. Wasylenchuk got underway in Seattle in United States District Court for the Western District of Washington, District Judge William J. Lindberg presiding. Assistant United States Attorney Douglas M. Fryer was assigned to try the case along with Brock Adams, appointed as a special government prosecutor for this case. Adams had recently resigned as United States Attorney for the Western District of Washington to run for Congress from the Seventh Congressional District, and had been appointed as Special Prosecutor because of his familiarity with the circumstances surrounding the case and with the principals involved. Horswill, appearing on Wasylenchuk's behalf, was assisted by Vancouver barrister Thomas Dohm.[1]

As Charlie Waitt entered the courtroom, he recognized several Canadians whom he or Bureau agents had interviewed at one time or another over the last ten years, but retired RCMP Sergeant Ernest Nuttall was not present, nor had he expected to see him here. Several Mounties who had been requested to testify and were willing to see this case come to a satisfactory conclusion were present. These included RCMP Sergeants Edward Murton, Ellis Domay and Bruce Northrup. Officer Vernon Grace of the New Westminster Police Department, John Wasylenchuk's home town, was also present. Grace was to report back to his command on the results of the trial, including whatever new information may be disclosed through testimony of this criminal's continuing activities in Canada. Near the rear of the packed courtroom, sat Mrs. Wasylenchuk and her seventeen-year-old daughter, both of whom would testify for the defense before this trial was over. Accompanying the family, were the wife's brother, Donald Ross of Burnaby and brother-in-law Richard Alton of Vancouver. In the back of the courtroom, almost unnoticed sat Vancouver Police Superintendent Jack Horton. Horton's testimony would be critical to the government's case for it was he who first suspected Clifford Dawley, John Wasylenchuk and the Talbots of this crime, notwithstanding the fact that his own colleagues in Vancouver would be quick to establish alibis for two of the three principal suspects involved. Horton had survived Sergeant Leonard Cuthbert's allegations of corruption before the Royal Commission and he continued to occupy the office of Superintendent of the Criminal Investigations Bureau. In the courtroom on this first day of trial, in addition to the Seattle officers who were subpoenaed to testify, there were dozens of detectives and uniformed officers, both on and off duty, plus several high-ranking officers, including Assistant Chief of Police Charles A. Rouse.

Wasylenchuk sat between his American and Canadian counsel dressed conservatively in a black suit with white shirt and narrow red tie. To the unsuspecting, he could have passed himself off as a businessman or a farmer, the nickname Waitt first heard him called several years before by Mary Peters. But a farmer he wasn't, and Waitt found himself thinking back to Sergeant Bill Morphett's description of both this man and Clifford Dawley as, "The toughest criminals in the whole of Canada," with a whole string of bank robberies, assaults and burglaries to their credit, including the suspected murder of two police officers, one in the U.S. the other in Canada.

By noon, a jury of five women and seven men, plus two alternates was established with twenty-eight prospective jurors having been excused or peremptorily challenged, many of whom opposed the death penalty on moral or religious grounds. Prior to recessing for lunch, both the defense and the prosecution informed the court of prospective witnesses, Horswill stating the defense would be presenting by deposition the testimony of retired RCMP Sergeant Ernest F. Nuttall.[2]

As the court convened after lunch, Brock Adams began presentation of the government's case. Speaking in a loud voice, he commanded the attention of all those in the courtroom. Beginning with the robbery of the Greenwood bank, the shooting of the officers and the tragic death of Officer Frank Hardy, Adams recited the story of the investigation of the case in Canada, describing the difficulties which were encountered by the investigating officers, but which inevitably led to the defendant. The baby-faced attorney who had lectured in the Seattle Police Academy to many of the Seattle officers present, appeared at first to have difficulty in expressing himself, but there was little doubt that he commanded the attention of the entire court, if for no other reason than the fact he articulated a story of an investigation fraught with intrigue and contradiction.[3] In rapid order, the government's witnesses followed, responding in turn to questions from Adams or Assistant United States Attorney Douglas M. Fryer. Kenneth McElhaney, after describing the events which occurred inside the bank on March 12, 1954, freely admitted under cross-examination that he could not positively identify the defendant as one of the robbers. However, when shown a photograph of Clifford Dawley, he said he believed he was the leader of the trio that robbed the bank and was the man who shot the three officers.

The bank manager was followed by Mrs. Patrick J. Kennedy, employed as a bookkeeper by the bank at the time of the robbery. Mrs. Kennedy testified that, "The gentleman in the red tie, sitting next to counsel was one of the robbers," pointing at Wasylenchuk.

On cross-examination, the defendant's attorney asked her if she was positive in her own mind of her identification, taking into account the fact that FBI agents had shown her a picture of his client and that ten years had elapsed since the robbery. She responded, "I'm sure in my own mind that your client and the robber are one and the same."[4]

Vernon Chase and Sergeant Slessman were called to the stand in succession. Both repeated their stories relative to responding to the alarm at the bank and the subsequent events which led to their injury. Chase had told the story so many times in these past ten years that he could recall to mind and recite the circumstances surrounding his response and the facts of the shootings without hesitation or support from the government's attorneys. Neither man could, however, identify the defendant as one of the robbers.

The following day, as court convened, the prosecution called three women, two of whom witnessed the robbery and all three unhesitatingly pointed out the suspect to the court as one of the subjects in this crime. Mrs. Winifred J. Rouleau, a former bank employee, identified the accused as the "lookout" who positioned himself near the back door of the bank during the robbery. In response to a request from Adams, Mrs. Rouleau stepped down from the witness chair and pointed at a scar on the defendant's face which she said was an abrasion or cut, when she saw the robbery suspect on the day of the crime. The scar was now only faintly visible on the left side of the man's face. To counter this testimony, Horswill positioned his client immediately before the jury asking for them to form their own conclusions about this mark on the man's face, "The large red scar Mrs. Rouleau described to you today in her testimony as running from the top of the eyebrow, to the cheek bone on the one who robbed the bank is not visible on my client. The injury she has described certainly would have left a more noticeable scar than that which you now see. A mark which is not even discernable on my client's face from where you sit in this courtroom."[5]

Another bank employee, Mrs. Sheila Stangvik, stated on direct examination that the defendant looked exactly like one of the robbers who stood in front of her in the bank on the day of the hold up. Walking over to where Wasylenchuk sat, she pointed at the man and said, "That's the gentleman there in the black suit."

Mrs. Hilda Robinson followed testifying that, the day before the robbery, she saw the defendant and another man at 604 East Union Street, Seattle in the basement garage of the Union Arms Apartments. It was from this garage that the getaway car was stolen, prior to the robbery. But upon cross-examination, Horswill brought out the fact that when she testified in Vancouver during his client's extradition hearing five months earlier, the witness could not positively identify his client as the man at the Union Arms Apartments.

And finally Mrs. Mary A. Beattie was called. Mrs. Beattie was a customer in the Greenwood Bank on March 12th when the robbery occurred. She could not identify the defendant as one of the robbers, but when handed a picture of Clifford Dawley, she identified him as the leader of the trio and the one who fired on the approaching officers.

Sergeant Ellis Domay of the Cloverdale, RCMP detachment in the British Columbia lower mainland testified next. The Mountie was involved with the defendant shortly after the man was alleged to have been at the Greenwood bank. He said from his own recollection, when John Wasylenchuk was arrested by the Mounties in 1954, he did in fact have an injury to his left cheek. This was supported by an RCMP record made at the time of his arrest. The record was admitted into evidence at trial.

As the trial continued into the third and fourth days, Special Prosecutor Adams and Assistant United States Attorney Douglas Fryer placed on the stand over two dozen of the fifty prosecution witnesses who had been subpoenaed, with little and sometimes no cross-examination from the defendant's attorney.

Mrs. Pearl Marsden Thompson, another bank employee, identified the accused man as one of the trio of robbers. She was followed by Frances Huson, a customer in the bank at the time of the robbery. Mrs. Huson identified Clifford Dawley as the leader of the group of bandits, but said she could not identify the defendant because his back was turned to her in the bank. And William Vance, who testified, at the suspect's extradition hearing in Vancouver, again identified Clifford Dawley as a passenger in the bank robber's getaway car.

The prosecutors traced the flight and recovery of the getaway vehicle through the witnesses' testimony. Edward Prestek's admission, of the theft of the license plates (later recovered on the getaway car) from a vehicle awaiting wrecking at his place of business, a vehicle taken from the Union Arms Apartments, supported the tie between the accused and the stolen car[6],[7].

But of the sixty-five witnesses who were subpoenaed to testify in this case (fifty for the prosecution), no one held the attention of the courtroom audience more than did Irvin Lester Terrance Teague. Teague, brought to Seattle from the federal correctional facility at Sandstone, Minnesota, had served six years of his eight-year sentence for forgery. He was due to be released on parole in less than five months. He was the perfect witness, for where else would you find a witness's alternatives limited to cooperating with the police or face continued confinement for at least two more years.

The man repeated the story which he had first told Captain (now Assistant Chief of Police) Charlie Rouse and Agents Dean Rolston and Chet Crisman in 1958, in the King County Jail. He stated that he and the defendant, as cell-mates in the British Columbia Penitentiary in 1956, after drinking a smuggled bottle of whiskey between them discussed the story of the Greenwood bank robbery. He said the accused claimed the Seattle robbery was his "score," that he had planned it and carried it out with the aid of Clifford Dawley and Bobby Talbot, that Dawley was the one who shot the three officers, that the accused claimed he fired only to scare the officers away. He told of Bobby Talbot's hurried exit through a window in the bank and the defendant's description of their flight from the bank in a stolen Oldsmobile which was acquired earlier after "punching the ignition."

As Teague continued his story in response to questioning from the Assistant U.S. Attorney, he told of Wasylenchuk's arrangements made with retired Sergeant Ernest Nuttall to, "cover him on this job," in the event that suspicion was later directed toward the accused for this crime. Teague testified that the defendant told him the Mountie was to receive $3,000.00 after the robbery for providing the alibi, and all the officer had to do was claim that he had found the defendant at home at the time of the robbery. When Teague finished his story, the prisoner was excused without cross-examination for the government wished to recall him at a later time.[8]

As the court concluded its activities for the day, Charlie Waitt and Chief Rouse, who had listened to the testimony of Teague and the other eye witnesses to the robbery, were both satisfied that Wasylenchuk would be convicted on the charges, based upon the evidence which had thus far been placed before the jury. Rouse was pleased with Brock Adams and Douglas Fryer's handling of the case, for Horswill was an able antagonist, but in discussing the course of the trial with FBI agents, they were reminded that Horswill was a very capable lawyer who was yet to have "his turn at bat." Rouse agreed and, upon reflection, wondered just how Teague would hold up under cross-examination by Horswill.[9]

When Teague's testimony became public knowledge, the Canadian press from Vancouver to Ottawa headlined the story and reporters converged on RCMP headquarters for a story. After receiving a "no comment" from the RCMP Vancouver detachment commander, reporters contacted retired Sergeant Ernest Nuttall at his home in North Vancouver. Upon hearing of Teague's testimony of his alleged acceptance of the bribe of $3,000.00 to provide the alibi for John Wasylenchuk, the former Mountie was incensed and, in righteous indignation, denied any criminal involvement with the bank robbers. As reporters from the two leading newspapers in Vancouver, The Province and the Vancouver Sun, pressed Nuttall for a story, the man exploded in a tirade against Teague and the American officers. He called Teague a liar and a mental case, a small-time crook who was seldom successful in stealing enough to eat, let alone being involved with "the big people" in the Canadian underworld. Of the FBI, Nuttall was even more critical, accusing the American officers of importing the Canadian criminal to discredit the RCMP.

Of Wasylenchuk's trial, the former officer described it as, "a farce, as phony as a three dollar bill; the whole thing from start to finish has been rigged." When asked a question relative to the eye witness testimony of Mrs. Kennedy and other witnesses, who identified Wasylenchuk as one of the robbers, the ex-Mountie ridiculed the American court system stating, "Such testimony would never hold up in a Canadian court. Everyone knows Wasylenchuk always wore a wig and false nose when he went on a job. How anyone could have identified him in that bank robbery is beyond me."[10] Of Rolston and Crisman, the FBI Agents who worked on the case, first with Detective Eugene Ivey and later with Sergeant Charlie Waitt, Ernest Nuttall was no less critical. He told of his visit with the three American officers to the apartment of Barbara Olson in Vancouver. Olson was a friend of Rose Dawley, and it was here that the officers found the address of Clifford Dawley's Montreal hideout, which eventually lead to the convict's capture. The former officer said Rolston became agitated with him when he and Detective Ivey took the evidence to RCMP detachment headquarters, instead of turning it over to the

Bureau as the agents requested. He claimed heated words were exchanged between him and the agents and he walked out and left the two officers behind at the woman's apartment. After Clifford Dawley's capture in Montreal and return to Vancouver, Nuttall said he interrogated the prisoner personally and determined that the man could not possibly have participated in the Seattle robbery. When Rolston heard this, Nuttall said, "the FBI agent blew his top - he was raving mad and just wanted to 'book' somebody at any cost."[11]

Nor did Nuttall extol the virtues of Special Prosecutor Brock Adams. He said he would like to go to Seattle to see that justice was done in this case, as he didn't trust Adams. Referring to the trial, he said, "It has gotten completely out of hand, but I fear, were I to enter the United States, I would be arrested."

The man's fears were well founded, for Adams later confirmed that the former police officer might very well be arrested and held as a material witness if he entered the U.S.

In addition to his denials of complicity in this case, notwithstanding his inability to travel the one hundred and fifty miles from Vancouver to Seattle, Nuttall found plenty of strength to expound immodestly to the press of his exploits as a member of the much revered Royal Canadian Mounted Police. He described how during the "fifties," he was the "archenemy" of the criminal element in the Vancouver area. He related how he singlehandedly hunted and pursued John Wasylenchuk for years, notwithstanding the fact that during the fifties Wasylenchuk had spent most of his time in the penitentiary, never once having been arrested by Nuttall. Of the accusations of the Mountie's alleged improper conduct which first came to light in 1955, he said the American officers were grasping at straws due to their own inability to find the culprits involved in the robbery. Because of this, he claimed his promotion to sergeant had been delayed eighteen months, while headquarters personnel in Ottawa investigated the allegations.[12] This investigation he said, later led to his complete vindication[13]. Contacted in Vancouver, George Archer, Nuttall's former RCMP detachment commander and later chief constable of the City of Vancouver, confirmed that such an investigation had taken place, but Archer refused to comment further.[14]

As the trial continued in Seattle, Horswill began his attack on the government's case by calling five Canadians who corroborated his client's alibi. Mrs. Wasylenchuk testified she was at home on March 12, 1954 with her husband and daughter and observed her husband talking to Corporal Nuttall in their backyard at noon. Her seventeen-year-old daughter, next took the stand, identifying herself as Elizabeth Wesley. She explained that ten years before, on the day in question, she was home with the measles and recalled the officer's visit. The obvious fact that she was only seven years old at the time was not pursued. The girl was followed by Richard Alton, a diesel engineer from Vancouver, and then by Donald Ross, the defendant's brother-in-law, both of whom attempted to assure the court that on March 12, 1954, they were with the accused throughout that day, helping him fiberglass his boat. Finally Grace Ross testified, recalling that her husband left home early that morning to assist his brother-in-law with the boat repair.[15]

The following day, the defense called Henry Taylor, a former Vancouver resident, who testified that he recalled seeing the defendant at a wrecking yard in the city about noon on the day of the robbery. He was followed to the witness stand by two character witnesses who vouched for the reputation of the former Mountie. One, retired RCMP Sergeant Neils Krag of Kamloops, testified that on the day in question, he accompanied Corporal Nuttall to the defendant's residence, but remained in the patrol car while Nuttall went to the rear of the residence. This information was a shock to the investigating officers and to the prosecution, for at no time during the investigation had the RCMP command officers indicated to the American investigators that a second officer had accompanied Corporal Nuttall to the suspect's home on the date of the robbery, thus corroborating the officer's alibi story from John Wasylenchuk. When questioned relative to the man's presence, the Sergeant Krag responded: "I saw Corporal Nuttall talking to Mr. Wasylenchuk in his yard."[16]

Krag was followed to the stand by Vancouver Detective Sergeant Charles Campbell, who testified that he had known Ernest Nuttall for approximately fifteen years and that the former Mountie had a good reputation for veracity.[17] But the defendant's character witnesses were few. Carl Bollman, a roofing contractor who had employed the accused since his release from the penitentiary, testified that the defendant was a very satisfactory employee during his short time with the company. It was from one of Bollman's contract jobs in Vancouver that the suspect was arrested on the present charges by RCMP Sergeant Bruce Northrup, accompanied by FBI Agent Alf Gunn.

Two British Columbia Penitentiary officials and the prison chaplain were also called and their testimony relative to John Wasylenchuk's prison behavior was very favorable to the defense. In listening to the three men vouching for Wasylenchuk's character, Waitt couldn't help but recall Warden John Maloney's admonition that Wasylenchuk had, while in confinement, a way of responding which tended to make him look good in the eyes of the prison staff. Maloney had said, however, experienced correction officials soon saw through this convict's performance.

Horswill next called the defendant and, on direct examination, John Wasylenchuk repeated his often heard story of the then Corporal Ernest Nuttall's visit to his home on March 12, 1954. He told of the Mountie's inquiry relative to Clifford Dawley's location, claiming he knew nothing of Clifford Dawley's activities at that time. After this inquiry, he claimed that he ordered the officer off of his property. In equally strong language, he then refuted Irvin Teague's entire testimony, denying that he at any time had told his cell-mate that he and his colleagues were the ones that robbed the Greenwood Bank. In his effort to protect himself, Wasylenchuk said he erred when he said that he visited a wrecking yard in Vancouver on the day of the robbery, for it was actually later in the week than was previously reported by Henry Taylor. This, although a minor discrepancy, was in conflict with those who placed him at his home working on his boat at the time of the robbery. In response to a question from Horswill, the man denied offering or making any deals with Corporal Ernest Nuttall or anyone else for an alibi.[18]

Douglas Fryer elicited testimony from Wasylenchuk of the witness's prior criminal record, which dated back to 1930. Wasylenchuk admitted he first met Clifford Dawley in 1937, when the two of them were confined in the British Columbia Penitentiary and that he had known Bobby Talbot for about ten years. Fryer was also successful in bringing out testimony that the scar that was now faintly visible on Wasylenchuk's left cheek, was from an injury he sustained shortly before the 1954 robbery, and that the wound remained quite noticeable for several months thereafter.

The following day, in rebuttal, Dean Rolston was the first of several witnesses who were called to refute the defense's contention that the accused could not have been one of the Greenwood bank robbers because he was at home at the time of the robbery. The agent testified that, in an interview with Donald Ross in 1955, Ross could not remember the date of the boat repair at his brother-in-law's and further that Ross told him that Richard Alton was not present. Later in an interview with Henry Taylor, he said this witness claimed to have heard the broadcast of the robbery on the noon news, at a Vancouver wrecking yard, and that he could not remember whether or not John Wasylenchuk was present on the same day.

In listening to the agent's testimony in Adam's attempt to refute the direct testimony of Ross, Alton and Taylor, Seattle detectives who were present in the courtroom were surprised that FBI agents had not taken signed statements from these witnesses when they were first interviewed in Canada. S.P.D detectives were required to obtain written statements from all witnesses interviewed in major cases. Although this requirement was resisted by many officers, the procedure was insisted upon by King County Prosecutor Charles O. Carroll for the very reason that was all too evident here — witnesses frequently changed their stories between the time of the first interview with a police officer and their courtroom appearance.

Teague was called again to testify in rebuttal and this time implicated John Wasylenchuk and the RCMP officer in other criminal acts in Canada. When asked if he were aware of another bank robbery in New Westminster in which Sergeant Nuttall had also provided an alibi for the defendant, Teague responded, "I understand that he had a continuing thing with Sergeant Nuttall and had on an earlier occasion provided a similar story as in this case."[19]

On cross-examination, Horswill hammered away at Teague's credibility as a witness, bringing out the man's criminal record, narcotics addiction problem and the fact that the convict was now committed to a federal institution which housed the criminally insane. The attorney was successful in eliciting an admission that when first questioned in the King County Jail, the witness said he lied to both Seattle Police Homicide Captain Charles Rouse and FBI agents, who first questioned him relative to his former cell-mate's involvement in the robbery. As Horswill continued with this line of questioning in an attempt to discredit the witness, Teague suddenly blurted out that there were two constables, not just one, who were bribed to provide the defendant with his alibi. Horswill immediately discontinued this line of questioning and, upon cross-examination, Judge Lindberg refused to allow the prosecution to pursue the subject any further.

Charlie Waitt was called to testify relative to the defendant's relationship with Clifford Dawley and of the details of his lengthy investigation into this case in Canada. Then Seattle Police Sergeant Fred Mitchell, an auto theft specialist, testified to the method used by the stickup men to punch-out and hot-wire the ignition of the getaway car.[20]

Shortly after rebuttal, Brock Adams renewed the United States government's demand to have Ernest Nuttall's entire deposition placed before the court. Although unsuccessful, Judge Lindberg allowed, over objection, certain portions of the transcript to be read to the jury. He cautioned, however, that some parts of the deposition were too damaging to the defendant and admonished Adams that, had Ernest Nuttall been in court, many of the questions asked of the witness in the deposition, would not have been allowed in court.[21]

The prosecution was successful, however, in laying before the jury testimony from the deposition damaging to both Nuttall and the defendant, testimony relative to Ernest Nuttall's defense of the accused in the April 29, 1954 robbery of the Royal Bank of Canada in New Westminster, along with his previous involvement in an alleged bribery attempt by another Canadian criminal. These the officer claimed to have reported to his superiors. Nuttall, however, vigorously denied in the deposition, that he was to share in the profits of safe burglaries committed by Teague, for decoying Vancouver and New Westminster police officers away from buildings targeted for burglaries.

Adams was also successful in bringing before the jury, two admissions from the former Mountie, which courtroom observers thought would be devastating to Wasylenchuk's defense. First, the officer conceded that "a Canadian police officer" was in fact receiving "favors" from Mr.Wasylenchuk for protection, but he declined to name the person. When the issue was pursued by the government, he responded: "It was none of my [his] business."[22] (That this statement would come from one who had, within the past week, told reporters that he had pursued John Wasylenchuk and Clifford Dawley for years in an attempt to put them out of circulation, was hard to accept). Second, the ex-Mountie insisted in his deposition that he first learned of the robbery at 11:30 A.M. at Vancouver police headquarters. Suspecting Wasylenchuk, he immediately drove to the man's home, arriving at twelve o'clock, finding the suspect there, working on his boat. This statement was now suspect and was contradicted by the testimony of Vancouver Police Superintendent Jack Horton.

Horton produced records which indicated that the Vancouver Police Department received notification of the robbery and shooting of the Seattle officers seventeen minutes after twelve o'clock, thus placing Sergeant Ernest Nuttall, by his own admission, at the defendant's home seventeen minutes before notification of the crime was received by Canadian authorities.[23] However, the record also indicated that Vancouver detectives were notified by RCMP Sergeant Ed Murton the day following the hold up, that his subordinate, Corporal Nuttall, found the ex-con at home at 1:00 P.M., on the day of the robbery. Although Murton had been in the courtroom earlier, the government attorneys had excused him, feeling his testimony would not now be necessary. The retired sergeant left the city, not realizing that the defense would attempt to use him as a rebuttal witness. However Murton's testimony was not necessary to the defense, as Horswill argued quite convincingly that Vancouver officials could very well have learned of the incident before twelve o'clock noon via commercial radio.

With the last of the testimony before the court, Adams, in his final argument, told the jury that, because of the nature of the crimes involved, the government sought the death penalty for John Wasylenchuk, even though they did not claim he was the one who killed Officer Frank Hardy. "This crime was engineered by the defendant. It was his score. This was a crime he planned and carried out with his friend Clifford Dawley, the 'trigger man.' That was the man who gunned down the three police officers when they responded to the robbery alarm, and the man sitting here before you planned this crime and aided in it's commission."[24]

In turning to the defendant's alibi, Adams also attacked former RCMP Sergeant Nuttall's testimony from the deposition entered into trial. He pointed out that the retired Mountie claimed to have seen the defendant only three times in his entire career. Once he appeared to testify in the accused bank robber's defense in a robbery case and on the other two occasions he provided the convicted robber with an alibi. He also took issue with the sergeant's testimony relative to his visit with the defendant at home at twelve o'clock noon on the day of the robbery, seventeen minutes before, as Superintendent Horton had said, the Vancouver department received notification of the crime.[25] To several officers who were present in the courtroom, Adam's arguments in seeking a conviction and the death penalty for a crime committed over ten years before, by three masked men, whose identification was based entirely on eye witness testimony, appeared to be weak.

Horswill, in his closing argument, attacked the identification of his client by the government's witnesses. He hit hard at the fact that many of the prosecution witnesses had either seen the defendant's picture in the newspapers or had been shown a police "mug picture" of the two suspects by investigating officers. He said it was only human nature for a witness to identify a suspect after seeing a picture of him and reading of his alleged involvement in a crime such as this. The attorney next directed his attack on the credibility of the government's star witness, Irvin Teague. He called the man a liar, a drug addict and a mentally unstable person, reminding the jury that the witness was presently serving time in a federal mental institution. Of Teague's motives, the lawyer asked the jury to consider why this person would testify against the defendant, reminding them that the government's witness admitted lying to the investigating officers about the circumstances surrounding this very case, then later changed his story after receiving a promise from the officers that they would intervene for him with his parole officers.

When these arguments ended, Judge Lindberg admonished the jury in his instructions that they were to be the sole judge of the evidence and that, if they found the defendant guilty, they may, of their own choosing, direct that John Wasylenchuk forfeit his life. However, the Judge cautioned that they may not find the defendant guilty based solely upon the testimony of Irvin Teague, uncorroborated by other evidence.

At 12:20 P.M. on the afternoon of Friday, April 3, 1964, the case of the United States of America vs. John Wasylenchuk went to the jury, and the panel of five women and seven men left the courtroom to begin their deliberations. Waitt, who had remained at the court house throughout the two week trial, was tired but relieved that the investigative effort of the FBI through Dean Rolston, Alf Gunn and Chet Crisman, in addition to that of several Seattle officers, had paid off and at least one of the trio of stickup men now faced a possible death sentence. In reflecting on the investigation, he was thankful for the help that he and the agents had received from several Canadian officers in this case, for he knew full well that without them, both the Seattle and FBI officers' activities would certainly have been limited and their objective made much more difficult. In his discussions with Charlie Rouse, while the two men awaited the return of the jury, they agreed that Bobby Talbot and possibly even Clifford Dawley would never stand trial in a United States court on this case. The latter still had seven years to serve in prison in Canada on his earlier drug trafficking conviction; by that time seventeen years would have elapsed between the commission of the crime and his projected date of release. Both knew convictions were seldom obtained under these circumstances and, under the Canadian extradition act, Clifford Dawley could not be extradited while confined after conviction on a criminal charge in Canada. Bobby Talbot, although never positively identified as the third man in the robbery, was also confined in the British Columbia Penitentiary on a ten year drug trafficking and a conspiracy sentence, the expiration of which was not up until 1970. There was no hope that a criminal case would ever be built against this man.[26]

The following day, after receiving notification from the Clerk of the Court that the jury had reached its verdict, Assistant Chief of Police Charlie Rouse picked up Charles Waitt at the King County Licensing Department and the two men rushed to the Federal Court House. At 12:24 P.M., almost exactly 24 hours from the time the jury panel received the case, the jury foreman handed the verdict to the Clerk Mrs. Lois Stolson who read aloud, "We the jury find the defendant, John Wasylenchuk, not guilty."

Wasylenchuk, who had sat throughout the entire trial almost expressionless, was elated. The defendant thanked his attorney and the members of the jury, assuring them that he would not betray their trust and would show the people of the United States and Canada that he would be, "that model citizen," as he was described earlier by former RCMP Officer Larry Hanson.

At police headquarters, the news of Wasylenchuk's acquittal spread rapidly throughout the Public Safety Building. As it was Saturday, few detectives were working and those who were were mostly younger men, recently assigned who had never worked on the Greenwood case. After the initial excitement, most went back to work on their own cases without much thought of John Wasylenchuk or Frank Hardy, for they had no firsthand knowledge of either man. In Canada, the announcement of Wasylenchuk's acquittal created considerably more interest than in Seattle. At Vancouver Police Head-quarters, the news was received with some consternation by those who were familiar with Wasylenchuk's criminal activities and connections with local officials. Shortly after notification that the suspect was cleared, a Vancouver police radio dispatcher announced: "All cars, Wasylenchuk acquitted in Seattle."[27]

Throughout the police community of the lower British Columbia Mainland, including within the RCMP barracks in Vancouver, news of John Wasylenchuk's acquittal in the U.S. spread quickly. The Mounties in particular were relieved, for the men and women of this very proud organization were sick to death of the adverse publicity directed at their organization due to a half dozen officers cozy relationship with one or more of Canada's most cunning criminals was wrecking havoc on the reputation of their organization.

In Seattle, Charlie Waitt was philosophical about the not guilty verdict. Like most police officers with twenty-five or more years on the street, he worked on a lot of cases which were later lost in court. In some ways, he thought this acquittal may have been a blessing in disguise. The Canadian police organizations he had been working with had gotten rid of most of their crooked cops as a result of both the Greenwood investigation in Canada and the efforts of the Royal Commission, albeit that body in and of itself accomplished very little in this regard. Although not pleased with the outcome in court, he was relieved that the issue which had created so much friction and hard feelings between American and Canadian officers assigned to this investigation was now history. This would end it and the two groups hopefully would resolve their differences and get back to work in a cooperative and professional manner.[28]

Notes

[1] Constantine Angelos, "Jury Selection to Try Suspect in Greenwood Robbery-Murder," The Seattle Times, March 24, 1964, p. 10.

[2] Constantine Angelos, "Greenwood Case," The Seattle Times, March 25, 1964, p. 6.

[3] Although Adams was fully aware of the constraints placed upon the American investigators by several Canadian officials, he made no mention of this during the trial, nor did he acknowledge that there was often a lack of cooperation from those in the British Columbia law enforcement community who could have opened the door and provided an early solution to this case, but who for their own sometimes not so obscure reasons, chose not to do so.

[4] The Seattle Times, March 26, 1964, p. 37.

[5] Ibid.

[6] Ed Prestek, the affable, middle-aged businessman and auto wrecking yard owner, was not happy with the federal judicial system. Prestek had more than a passing interest in the outcome of the trial, for he felt his own reputation and integrity and that of his brother Ernie would again be placed in jeopardy. He had long since lost his respect for the FBI, for in his mind the federal agents were responsible for the delay in bringing this case to a satisfactory conclusion, because of their obviously inept investigative procedures and lack of common courtesy in dealing with witnesses. He maintained that, had the agents been less abrasive in their approach, witnesses would have long ago come forward

with the information sought. But Prestek's unkind attitude toward the agents may have been reinforced by one or two Seattle detectives who themselves openly expressed the premise that the case could have been solved much sooner had the FBI cooperated with Canadian authorities in the early stages of the investigation. On the other hand, with the exception of Sergeant Charlie Waitt and Detective Gene Ivey, few of the detectives were fully aware of the problems encountered by the American officers while in Canada.

It wasn't only the FBI which had soured Ed Prestek's view of the federal justice system. His appearance before the Grand Jury had been traumatic and, now in federal court again facing the former United States Attorney, Special Prosecutor Brock Adams, who had left government service and had since announced his candidacy for the House of Representatives, Prestek couldn't help but feel that Adams was using the trial of Wasylenchuk as a political maneuver to gain publicity for his forthcoming election bid. After testifying, Prestek remained in the courtroom and watched the progress of the trial, later finding himself astounded at Adams' apparent ineptness in handling the prosecution of the case. He left the federal court house that evening disillusioned with the system which allowed politics to take preference over what he thought should have been the judicious pursuit of the truth in the prosecution of this criminal.

[7] Edward Prestek, interview with the author August 30, 1974.

[8] The Seattle Times, March 27, 1964, p. 6.

[9] Charles A. Rouse, conversations with the author, 1972.

[10] The Province, Vancouver, B. C. March 25, 1964, p. 1.

[11] Ibid.

[12] Although the results of the internal probe of Ernest Nuttall's connection with John Wasylenchuk were never revealed publicly, in conversations with the Americans before this investigation was over, the Mounties were very candid and admitted that more than one of their own officers, and at least one member of the Vancouver judiciary had been working in collusion with Vancouver city police officers in fronting for a half dozen criminals involved in robberies and burglaries throughout western Canada and the U.S. This was confirmed in part by Nuttall in his deposition earlier in the year when he denied that he had any part in providing alibis for Canadian criminals. In this deposition, he acknowledged that, "somebody else was receiving favors from Wasylenchuk, but that was not my [his] business." (Seattle Times, April 1, 1964, pp. 15-16).

[13] Ibid.

[14] The Province, Vancouver, B. C. March 26, 1964, pp. 1, 2.

[15] The Seattle Times, March 31, 1964, p. 28.

[16] Constantine Angelos, "Witness Shifts Wasylenchuk Alibi to Different Scene," The Seattle Times, April 1, 1964, pp. 15, 16.

[17] Ibid.

[18] The Seattle Times, March 30, 1964.

[19] Constantine Angelos, "Wasylenchuk Case Witnesses Changed Stories, Says Agent," The Seattle Times, April 2, 1964, p. 5.

[20] Ibid.

[21] The Seattle Times, April 1, 1964, p. 16.

[22] Ibid.

[23] Ibid.

[24] The Seattle Times, April 3, 1964, p. 1.

[25] Constantine Angelos, "Time Conflict Shown in Wasylenchuk Case," The Seattle Times, April 3, 1964.

[26] Charles K. Waitt, conversations with the author, 1968.

[27] The Seattle Times, April 4, 1964, p. 1.

[28] Between the fallout of this investigation in Canada and the Royal Commission hearings, as with the soon to be convened Federal and King County Grand Jury investigations into corruption within the Seattle Police Department, public pressure to reform would force the RCMP and VPD to "clean up" their organizations. Both organizations have since improved their effectiveness and public image by adopting tighter management controls with particular emphasis on organizational performance and improved internal integrity.

Chapter

14

The Aftermath

In the aftermath of the Greenwood investigation, there were no winners, even though John Wasylenchuk was a free man. He immediately returned to Vancouver with his family; but others were less fortunate. For Irvin Teague there would be no homecoming, for the return to Canada would cost him his life. He was returned to the federal correctional facility at Sandstone, Minnesota until arrangements could be made to release him to an area removed from the northwest. For his efforts, he would soon be somewhat richer than when he came to Seattle; plans were made to see that he received the reward which the city established by ordinance shortly after the holdup in 1954, ". . . for information leading to the arrest and conviction of each of those bandits participating in the holdup at the Greenwood branch of the Seattle First National Bank on March 12, 1954, in which Patrolman Frank W. Hardy was killed and Sergeant H. M. Slessman and Patrolman Vernon R. Chase were seriously wounded, . . . The Chief of Police is hereby authorized and directed for and on behalf of the City of Seattle to post and offer a reward of $1,000.00. (Ordinance No. 82843)."

Chief of Police Frank C. Ramon, with the agreement of the U.S. Attorney's Office, petitioned the city council to have the reward paid directly to Irvin Lester Terrance Teague.

April 6, 1964
City Council
City of Seattle
Attention: Councilman Floyd Miller
               Chairman, Finance Committee

Dear Sir:

Your attention is invited to Ordinance no. 82843, attached, which authorizes $1,000.00 reward for information leading to the arrest and conviction of the bank robbers who participated in a holdup of the Greenwood Branch of the Seattle First National Bank on March 12, 1954.

In the recently concluded trial of John Wasylenchuk for the murder of Patrolman Frank W. Hardy and for the robbery of the bank, part of the government's case was based on the testimony of Irvin T. Teague. Wasylenchuk was acquitted by the jury, but Teague has complied substantially with the reward offer made by the City of Seattle. Teague placed his life in definite jeopardy by his testimony. Since he first told the authorities of his knowledge of the robbery, he has been subjected to considerable personal discomfort and harassment. He is at the present moment a prisoner serving sentence in a United States institution, but will be released within the next two months. It is my feeling that Teague has complied with the requirements of Ordinance No. 82843 as far as he is possibly capable of doing. He did supply names and information not known to law enforcement as to the perpetrators of this crime. He did testify in open court concerning Wasylenchuk's statement of the crime. It is my feeling, although I am no attorney, that had the United States Government been able to compel the presence of some of the alibi witnesses of Wasylenchuk and subject them to cross-examination, a verdict of guilty would have resulted. In any event, the federal government could not have proceeded with the prosecution of Wasylenchuk and with the pending prosecution of Clifford Dawley without the active assistance of and without the information supplied by Irvin Teague. I, therefore, recommend that the reward of $1,000.00 in the attached Ordinance be paid to Irvin T. Teague.

Yours very truly
F.C. RAMON
Chief of Police

But the chief's request for payment of the reward to Teague was denied after Chief Assistant John Harris, of the Corporation Counsel's Office, advised that it was impossible under the wording of the ordinance of 1954 for the city to grant payment. Ramon next sought approval of a new ordinance which would allow payment of Teague, "for services rendered to the city," but this too was denied him by the city council. Ramon then turned to the victim, in this case, the largest financial institution in the northwest, Seattle First National Bank, and upon receipt of the Chief's request, the bank agreed to pay the informant-witness the $1,000.00 denied him by the city[1]. In the meantime, Charlie Rouse, through a business acquaintance, obtained employment for Teague with the Todd Shipbuilding Corporation in Houston, Texas, after the U.S. Attorney's office interceded on the prisoner's behalf with the United State Immigration and Naturalization Service which allowed the informer to establish residence in the U.S. In an exchange of letters between Ramon, Adams and Teague, arrangements were firmed up in preparation for his release and transportation from Minnesota to Houston for employment[2]. The FBI notified the U.S. Attorney's Office that they too would contribute $1,000.00 toward Mr. Teague's wellbeing, thus providing the convict with a larger stake than he had ever acquired at one time through his illegal ventures. See *Appenix B*.

By mid-June and upon receipt of an airline ticket from Seattle, Teague was released from the Sandstone Correctional Institution and boarded a plane in Minneapolis en route to Houston. Teague was thirty-eight years old and, like Dawley and Wasylenchuk, had spent most of his adult life in prison. He was first arrested in Calgary, Alberta at the age of sixteen for vagrancy, and arrests and convictions followed for forgery, theft, burglary, and armed robbery, with sentences totalling over thirty years in both Canada and American prisons.

Maurice "Bobby" Talbot, still confined in the British Columbia Penitentiary, remained there for nearly four more years. Talbot was

286 • *Cops, Crooks & Politicians*

first arrested in Jasper, Alberta in 1942, at age twenty-one for illegally riding on trains and received a fine of five dollars and costs or
twenty days. A year later, he was arrested after holding up a bank in
Victoria and received a seven-year prison sentence. He, like Clifford
Dawley and John Wasylenchuk, spent most of his adult life behind
bars. He was released on parole in 1968 at the age of forty-seven. He
had to his credit a dozen convictions with accumulated sentences in
excess of thirty years.[3]

In Vancouver, after the trial, retired RCMP Sergeant Ernest F.
Nuttall continued to make headlines. Whenever the question was
raised by Canadian reporters relative to the charges leveled against
him by the American authorities in the Wasylenchuk trial he would
attack both the media and the American law enforcement agencies.
In one interview, he not only attacked the FBI but his own organization and Vancouver police alleging that they tapped his home telephone at the height of the controversy[4]. By summer, it was all over
for Nuttall; he died quietly in his car near his home in Burnaby, B.C.
of an apparent heart attack on August 5, 1964. He was sixty-three
years old.

Upon John Wasylenchuk's return to Canada, he remained on
parole for his 1955 bank robbery conviction in New Westminster
where, on October 1, 1968, he too suffered a heart attack. Shortly
thereafter, he was pronounced dead upon arrival at Royal Columbian
Hospital[5]. At fifty-five, Wasylenchuk had, in addition to the life
sentence which was imposed in 1955, been sentenced to a total of
forty-seven years in Canadian prisons and had spent most of his
adult life behind bars.

Three months after Wasylenchuk's death on November 1, 1968,
Clifford Eugene Dawley was released on parole from the British
Columbia Penitentiary after serving nearly seven years of the nine
year sentence for trafficking in narcotics imposed in 1962. In Seattle,
upon receipt of the news that Dawley was out of the penitentiary,
there was speculation within the police department that the former
convict would soon be extradited to face the murder and robbery
charges which were still pending in Washington. It was now nearly
fifteen years since the robbery of the Greenwood bank and the
murder of Officer Hardy. In discussions with Seattle Police and FBI

officials, the U.S. Attorney agreed that there was little likelihood of obtaining a conviction under these circumstances and the extradition of Dawley was not pursued.

Clifford Dawley was first arrested at the age of thirteen for highway robbery. Like John Wasylenchuk, he too had spent most of his adult life in prison. He had been arrested twenty-eight times and convicted of twenty-two separate offenses. He also escaped from prison on three occasions.

In 1971, Dawley was again in custody in Vancouver, but this time for only fourteen days as a result of a drunk driving charge. During these years he lived quite comfortably. He was seen frequently in Vancouver harbor aboard his 32-foot pleasure boat, and although several of his former partners in crime were dead or still in the penitentiary, it was suspected that he continued to traffic in drugs. However, there was nothing to tie him directly into the drug scene other than his associates. For a man who had never held a steady job, his style of living gave evidence of an income much above the average.

As Dawley lived violently, he also died violently. On January 4th 1974, he visited a friend, John Campbell, who worked on a gasoline barge in Vancouver harbor for the Home Oil Company. Campbell, an ex-convict, drug pusher and small time safecracker had served time in the penitentiary with Dawley. At 2:23 in the afternoon, as the two men were fueling the bank robber's boat, an explosion occurred on the barge. Within seconds, the entire barge, which contained nearly 50,000 gallons of gasoline, was one large mass of flame. Dawley and Campbell and a third person, a seventeen-year-old boy who was aboard the barge, disappeared in the fire. The explosion shattered windows for blocks and was heard miles away. Within minutes, nothing above the water-line remained of the pleasure boat, and the superstructure of the barge was a mass of fire. Fire boats fought the blaze for 14 hours before bringing it under control. The following day, three bodies were recovered from the water and investigators from the National Harbor's Board Police surmised that all three men must have been sucked into the inferno by an implosion effect of the fire. Identification was accomplished through dental charts. Clifford Dawley was sixty-two years old[6].

On January 5, 1974 Clifford Eugene Dawley was killed in the explosion of the Home Oil Company barge in Coal Harbor at Vancouver while refueling his yacht. Two others were killed in this same explosion, one a seventeen year old boy and the other an ex-convict narcotic trafficking partner of Dawley. (Photo courtesy of Pacific Press Library)

Seattle Police Patrolman Vernon "Bud" Chase at home two years after being shot in the Greenwood Bank robbery case (7-8-1956). (Photo courtesy: Seattle Post-Intelligencer Collection Museum of History & Industry)

With Dawley's death, the U.S. attorney for the Western District of Washington requested the dismissal of his indictment for robbery and murder in the U.S. On March 8, 1974, four days short of twenty years from the date of the robbery of the Greenwood Bank and the murder of Officer Frank Hardy, United States District Judge William J. Lindberg dismissed the indictment, thus bringing to a close one of the longest criminal investigations ever undertaken in the Pacific northwest[7].

Of others involved in the Greenwood case, Frank Hardy's widow, Rolene, gave birth to her second child shortly after her husband's death and raised her two children alone on a police widow's pension of $182 a month, plus a small income from a trust fund that was set up and administered for the family by Henry Broderick, a wealthy real estate and investment broker, and by the president of the Seattle Police Officer's Union, Officer Fred Keenan. Dave Beck, former president of the Teamsters, was instrumental in obtaining contribu-

Seattle Chief of Police Frank C. Ramon (1961-1968) and newly appointed Assistant Chief of Police Charles A. Rouse receiving a commendation from military officer colleagues. (Photo courtesy: Seattle Police Records Archives)

tions to the fund, which Rolene Hardy would later use to educate her children.

Sergeant Howard Slessman never fully recovered from his wounds, but he did return to duty, retiring in 1967 after thirty-three years on the force. Dean Rolston, Alf Gunn and Chet Crisman, the federal officers most responsible for bringing the Greenwood case to a conclusion, have since retired after many years of devoted service to the government. Rolston, will long be remembered by S.P.D. detectives, as no other FBI agent was more respected for his ability as an investigator and skilled interrogator. Rolston was one of the very few agents who ever cooperated completely in investigations which required joint participation of the police and the FBI. Although frequently denied by FBI managers, Bureau agents occasionally "neglected" to pass on to the police, information which would have, in many cases, led to the arrest of fugitives by local authorities. This was never the case, however, with Rolston and a few other experienced agents assigned to the Seattle Office of the FBI.[8] He would be missed by S.P.D. personnel.

No longer able to function as a police officer, Vernon Chase retired from the force on disability in 1963. No other Seattle officer ever survived after suffering such devastating wounds. As the .45 caliber slug from Dawley's gun traveled through his abdomen, it splintered into a dozen different fragments, each tearing their way through soft body tissue. Chase underwent twenty-two separate operations for removal of the bullet fragments or corrective surgery. In order to continue on the payroll, thus assuring continued income and medical coverage, Chief H. J. Lawrence allowed him to return to work periodically for short periods. It became a common sight to see him struggling from office to office in the Public Safety Building supported by two canes. Finally, unable to continue, he was forced to retire. He worked for a short period as an investigator for the County Prosecutor Charles O. Carroll, but when asked to campaign for the re-election of the prosecutor, Chase refused and resigned. In continual pain, he was well on his way to addiction to narcotic drugs until doctors severed several nerves in his chest which gave immediate and permanent relief from this ever-present pain. Unable to support his family on his pension, Chase held a variety of jobs from

First Lieutenant Charles A. Rouse (second from right), a B-25 bomber pilot receiving his Seventh Oak Leaf Cluster to his Air Medal from Brigadier General Robert D. Knapp. Official photo U.S. XII Army Air Force, May 1945. (Courtesy Glen Rouse)

truck driver to job broker. But alcohol soon became a bigger problem than drugs, and he lost a series of jobs due to excessive drinking. By 1968, Chase, at thirty-eight, was emaciated, completely grey, a confirmed alcoholic, and unable to find work nor able to care for himself and his family. His wife, Joyce, worked as a bank clerk, fought to hold their family together and watched helplessly as her husband lost his will to survive. However, after nearly four years of continual bouts with the bottle, Chase committed himself to an alcohol rehabilitation center and by 1976, after completing a university-sponsored alcoholic counseling program, he was employed full-time as a counselor in the County Rehabilitation program for alcoholics.[9]

On July 5, 1968, Assistant Chief of Police Charles Rouse, now with twenty-seven years police service behind him, came through the offices of his command staff to say good-bye. It was time to retire. Still in his fifties, he looked much older and the smile that always came so easy to him was gone. To those close to him, he was always jovial and he was a practical joker who delighted in being able to get a laugh out of those around him. If he had a command weakness, it was being overprotective of his staff. This finally cost him his job. One of his detectives had picked up a waitress from a local restaurant during his tour of duty and had taken her home. Shortly thereafter, she accidentally shot and severely wounded herself with the detective's gun. In an attempt to save the man's job, Rouse concealed from the chief of police the fact that the detective was on duty at the time of the incident. When this fact was revealed in subsequent civil action against the officer and the city, Charlie Rouse was given the option by the chief of police of resigning or being fired.

However, the city and federal government were not through with Rouse. Information had come to light through a series of stories in the local press, not dissimilar to those published in Toronto in 1955 in The Flash about police officers in the City of Vancouver. In Seattle, the city's Blue Ribbon Committee had issued its findings on April 11, 1967. These would directly impact upon Charlie Rouse's future, along with hundreds of his colleagues within the Seattle Police Department. The Committee, composed of four prominent businessmen, reported to the mayor that "The facts uncovered in our investigation of the Seattle Police Department to date, fall short of establishing corruption within the Department[10]." It was obvious to most members of the organization that the Committee had not done its job and, after continued charges in the media of "pay-offs" to the police and of internal corruption within the force, in late 1969 the United States Attorney's office began to take a closer look at the Department.

On January 14, 1970, a special federal grand jury convened[11] and, within three months, Charlie Rouse's successor, Assistant Chief of Police Milford E. "Buzz" Cook was indicted for perjury and, in June, during the prosecution of Cook, evidence was brought to light which unleashed a whirlwind, striking the Department a devastating blow[12]. The federal grand jury made the Royal Commission's investigation into corruption within the Vancouver Department in 1955 appear as a summer breeze. Before it was over, the lives of every single officer on the force were directly affected. However, Cook was one of the few officers of the department ever convicted of a felony and actually sentenced to prison as a result of the federal grand jury's action[13]. On August 12, 1970, Cook was sentenced to three years in the federal penitentiary at McNeil Island for perjury. He won his freedom on an appeal, but in July, 1971, he was again indicted by a King County Grand Jury, this time alleging involvement in a police vice, gambling and bribery pay-off conspiracy. In May, 1973, he was convicted in King County Superior Court on these charges. On July 27, 1976, appealing this last action, the Washington State Court of Appeals upheld the conviction.

In the Cook trial, Charlie Rouse, who had since returned to city employment as a civilian supervisor in the city jail after a change of Chiefs, was accused of bribery, and in subsequent action by the County Grand Jury in 1971, he was named as an un-indicted co-conspirator in a massive bribery, extortion and blackmail operation involving the violation of liquor, prostitution, gambling and abortion laws of the state. One hundred and eighty others, mostly Seattle police officers were named in the same Bill of Particulars, including three former chiefs of police from the Department, plus the county sheriff, prosecuting attorney and president of the city council[14]. Evidence was brought to light that payoff monies collected by the police were finding their way into the mayor's office and to members of the city council. Although the city's mayor was not indicted or named as a co-conspirator in the case he was accused by the grand jury of personally receiving money illegally through this police payoff system. The conspiracy reached all the way into the governor's office and before the grand jury abandoned its efforts, it handed down over 100 indictments for bribery, grafting, grand larceny and/or conspiracy to violate the laws of the State of Washington. Charges of fraud were also brought against four past or present members of the state Liquor Control Board, accusing them of fraudulent appropriation of liquor consigned to state liquor warehouses, some of which was finding its way into the halls of the state legislature and the governor's mansion in Olympia.

Notwithstanding the action of the County Grand Jury at this time, Charlie Rouse was never tried on the conspiracy charge. In subsequent trials of former subordinates, Rouse was again accused of accepting bribes in the police payoff scandal and, as the trials came to a close, Chief of Police George P. Tielsch, the sixth chief of police to serve in the preceding five-year period, ordered the author to direct Rouse, along with over three dozen officers of various ranks, to either resign or face disciplinary action in the form of dismissal - Tielsch had no stomach for this type of confrontation with subordinate police personnel. So once again, the man who had engineered the Greenwood bank robbery and murder investigation and who dearly loved the police department, resigned rather than face dismissal.[15]

Rouse graduated from Queen Anne High School in Seattle in 1934, where he was a star athlete and honor student, then went directly to work as a common seaman on a tug boat in Puget Sound. He joined the police department in 1941, and when World War II broke out, immediately joined the United States Army Air Force, graduating from B-25 Bomber Flight School in early 1943. He flew 62 combat missions with the 57th Bomb Wing of the 12th Air Force, flying missions over the Mediterranean, Europe, and Asia, and in support of ground troops in North Africa, France, Germany, Iwo Jima and Okinawa. He came through the war without injury and was described by the press at the time as "Seattle's Hottest Pilot," receiving over a dozen military decorations for bravery. After the war, Rouse returned to the police department, graduated from the FBI Academy, and at age 34 was the youngest officer on the force ever to be promoted to the rank of captain. He took his civic responsibilities as serious as his police work, coaching the city's boys club baseball and basketball leagues for nearly 20 years. He was president of the local Kiwanis and an active board member of the American Legion, Big Brothers of Seattle, Urban League and his local community club.[16]

On July 27, 1986, former Assistant Chief of Police Charlie A. Rouse died of natural causes. He was survived by his wife and three daughters and one son who was also a Seattle police officer. Coincidentally, his former boss, retired Chief of Police Frank Ramon, who himself had been fired by the mayor when the police payoff conspiracy was disclosed and who had fired Rouse for misconduct in

1968, died this very same day. Except for the war years, Rouse served the city he loved from 1941 to 1973.

Nor did Charlie Waitt escape the fury of the County Grand Jury. In 1967, he resigned his investigative position with the Washington State Liquor Board to become Director of Business Licenses for King County, replacing the former retired Chief of Police H. J. "Jimmie" Lawrence. Lawrence had been fired by the county commissioners and Waitt felt badly that he was to replace his former boss under these circumstances.

In the months following this appointment, Waitt remained a familiar figure around police headquarters. He could be found frequently working with both city and county detectives in the pursuit of information, searching county records, which were necessary in criminal investigation cases and which, prior to his appointment, were seldom available to the detectives.

On July 27, 1971, Waitt, too, was indicted on a multiple conspiracy charge of bribery of public officers, and for allowing illegal gambling, lotteries, violation of the liquor laws of the state, extortion and blackmail[17]. To Waitt, who was sixty-four years old and in poor health, the charges were devastating. He had raised two sons, one a captain in the Marine Corps, the other a practicing attorney, and pro-tem Justice Court Judge in Seattle. The former police sergeant and his wife were looking forward to retiring to his grandfather's old homestead in eastern Washington. That would be delayed for he would have to continue to work in order to pay his attorney's fees[18].

Waitt was no stranger to hard work. He was the grandson of one of eastern Washington's first white settlers, George Waitt and his beautiful and gifted grandmother Josephine of the Spokane Indian Tribe. Both had a major influence on the young "Chas" Waitt while he was growing up. They instilled in their three grandsons a strong work ethic. Farming in eastern Washington, as elsewhere in the 1920's, was difficult and each member of this family was expected to contribute a significant portion of their day to planting, harvesting or tending livestock. The grandparents, however, also insisted that their grandchildren continue with their education. Waitt had been a student at Gonzaga University until the Depression hit in 1929 and, during his student days, had soloed in a World War I army plane under the tutelage of Tex Rankin in Portland, Oregon. He wanted to be a pilot, but during the depression, he found that unless he owned his own plane, flying jobs were few. He worked as a truck driver, loader and warehouseman, and finally joined the police force in 1937. As a detective sergeant, his top pay before retirement never exceeded six hundred dollars a month and what little was saved was soon to go for attorney fees. But Charlie Waitt would never stand trial, for within three months, on October 15, 1971, he died of cancer[19].

In looking back over these thirty odd years since three armed men, Clifford Eugene Dawley, John Wasylenchuk and a third unknown man robbed the Greenwood Bank and left three officers for dead on the sidewalk, one cannot help but think that what was lost here was more than just one life. Outside the bank, Patrolman Frank W. Hardy was dead, and Patrolman Vernon "Bud" Chase and Sergeant Howard Slessman lay on the sidewalk with bullet wounds, wounds which would take their toll in the years ahead. Dawley and Wasylenchuk escaped with less than $7,000. They dropped almost $90,000 on their way out of the bank, and overlooked a quarter of a million dollars in their bungled stickup operation. Though never convicted of this crime, these two men would spend the majority of their adult lives behind bars.

Monetarily, it was conservatively estimated that the investigation into this robbery, which lasted for nearly ten years with its subsequent court hearings, cost the American and Canadian taxpayers well over two hundred and fifty thousand dollars. Beyond these tangible costs that can be identified, in the years that followed, the citizens of the cities of Seattle and Vancouver, B. C. paid a much higher price for their neglect of their police forces and for their failure to demand of their elected and appointed officials the highest degree of proficiency and honesty in the performance of their public duties.

That these were the facts of life in Vancouver was never made more obvious than by Dr. John Hogarth, President of the British Columbia Police Commission, in a prepared address delivered in May, 1976, before the International Association of Airport and Seaport Police Chiefs' annual conference in Vancouver. Hogarth out-

lined the status of crime in that city. He reported that British Columbia had the highest crime rate of any province in Canada. Organized crime continued to flourish there, supported by illicit drug
trafficking through the Vancouver port. Sixty percent of Canada's
heroin population resided in Vancouver, and the city had the lowest
per citizen police population and the highest police workload of any
major Canadian city. Many British Columbia constables had not yet
received the necessary basic police training which would enable them
to perform at an acceptable level in an enforcement role.[20] In a more
positive vein, however, Dr. Hogarth explained that in 1976, for the
first time in five years, juvenile delinquency rates were stabilizing,
and more heroin had been seized in Vancouver than in all of the
previous 10 years and that progress had been made in developing
community support for the police. In addition, he reported that
some improvement had been made in the last few years in local
police training efforts[21].

In a review of the criminal justice system in the City of Seattle
during these troublesome years, we may well find that the inhabit-
ants of Seattle fared no better than our friends in Vancouver. In the
thirty year period, 1960 to 1990, serious crime increased over 200
percent or at a level nearly double the national average, and the
annual crime rate in the city continues to this date to be 10-15
percent higher than the average rate for comparable metropolitan
areas in the United States. Although crime clearance rates, the police department's "report card," is somewhat better than that experienced in Vancouver in the fifties, even today, 80 percent of the
reported crime in Seattle remains unsolved. Much of the responsibility for this glaring deficiency is directly traceable to an indifferent
citizenry and the naiveté of elected officials. This is evident when
one looks at the short hundred and twenty three year history (1869 -
1992) of the city's police force. During this time, sixty-five different
police chiefs sat at the helm of the Department, some for a period as
short as three days, with a few surviving throughout the elected term
of the city's chief executive[22]. Several chiefs, however, even with their
limited tenure, were able to plot a progressive course for the Department, with some visible progress being made in reducing the rate of
crime; but for the most part, crime continued to spiral even though

the city officials had available to them an effective deterrent, in their police force, had they chose to give it the proper tools and direction.

Like Vancouver during this period, the Seattle force was underpaid, untrained and poorly equipped to meet their challenge. Training programs, other than the basic academy were non-existent, and there was never enough money available to even provide the basic equipment needs of a major police department.[23] Until recently police precinct station houses were condemned or abandoned fire stations or turn of the century city halls. Much of the police fleet consisted of vehicles that were six to ten years old and, after operating 24 hours a day, seven days a week were, as Ralph Nader would say today, "unsafe at any speed." After the outbreak of the civil disturbances of 1969-70, one or two elected officials recognized some of the Department's needs. But their answer to these very frightening times was to "hire more men" with little thought of providing for the proper training direction or equipping of those already in uniform, or for setting standards of employment which would ensure that only those persons who met the highest physical, educational and integrity standards would be employed by the city as police officers. Surprisingly, the men and women of the police department handled this challenge effectively for the most part . But during the troubled 60's and 70's, as was so often the case in this city, there was a complete lack of support and direction from "city hall" and it was not uncommon to find the mayor and most members of the city council "out of town" during the height of the anti-war civil disturbances which were sweeping the nation's largest cities at the time. (Prior to the 1969 appointment of Frank W. Moore as Interim Chief of Police, it was also not unusual that many members of the police department's top "brass" also found the need to travel "outside" the city during these very volatile times.)

Nowhere was this lack of direction from elected officials more evident than in the policy decisions affecting the police department's vice operations. Like Vancouver, the cop on the street was never fully aware of "what the hell the Department's policy was" in vice matters. In the area of gambling, which was prohibited by the State Constitution, a tolerance policy, promulgated by the city council, existed and allowed "controlled" gambling, but few officers really understood it. This policy allowed every type of gambling from dollar limit poker games to wide open "Las Vegas Nights" in private clubs. In these clubs, there was no limit on the amount or type of gambling tolerated. Bootlegging was common and "after hour" clubs flourished throughout the city. Liquor was available at any hour, day or night, in violation of the law, in the plush privately operated social and athletic clubs of the city. In many hotels, liquor was routinely sold by bell hops or cab drivers to any guest who desired it. In downtown Seattle, "abortion mills", some run by "legitimate" doctors, others by "butchers", operated without interference and with the full knowledge of the press, the public and the Prosecuting Attorney's Office. Houses of prostitution operated openly and when raids were conducted, members of the vice squad were always amused to find in the prostitute's "trick books" the names of their clients, and the type of sex acts desired by some of the city and state leading business and political leaders, including the governor.

Many houses of prostitution in Seattle continue to operate today in the guise of massage parlors. Openly operating as escort services in the leading motels and hotels in the community where "services are rendered" with payment by use of a check, credit card or cash. And the local press, who were so critical of the Police Department's vice enforcement policies freely advertise these "services," knowing full well their purposes. With this background, it is little wonder that, in a discussion with the former Assistant Chief of Police Charles Rouse, he asked a young Police Captain recently assigned to head up the City's vice squad, to let him know when he found out what the city's vice enforcement policies were. But the question asked in jest was moot, for soon the laws prohibiting gambling, abortion and illegal liquor sales were, for all practical purposes, void. The state legislature, allegedly in response to citizen demand, supported the repeal of existing statutes prohibiting most forms of gambling and a state initiative to this effect was soon approved. Since that time, gambling throughout the state has become as common as the northwest rain. Bingo parlors, cardroom, punch-boards and casino gambling and the state supported lottery are now legal. With liberalization of the state's liquor laws, "bootleggers" have been put out of business, as liquor can be obtained legally at almost any hour of day or day of the week. And the U. S. Supreme Court struck down the nation's abortion prohibitions; thus there has been little need for the police to maintain their so-called "morality squads", even though street prostitution and call-girl activities continue at a high level in both Vancouver and Seattle.

In the 1960's, every police officer on the Seattle Department (as was the case in Vancouver in the 1950's), knew that it would be just a matter of time before the corrupt "shakedown" practices of the city's politicians and certain police officers would be exposed. Those officers who tried to change the system from within frequently faced the most difficult of tests as "selective assignments" were the order of the day, with command officers being careful to keep those who refused to "go along" with illegal activity working in areas where they would not interfere with "the system." It was here that "curb-to-curb" policing, a term used to describe a system which restricted patrol car officers to policing the streets while their fellow foot patrolmen and vice squad officers policed and "collected" graft from business owners throughout the city, had its genesis. Patrol officers, who persisted in efforts to enforce the vice laws, were soon transferred to "other duties." For these men, more than others the job was most difficult, for so widespread was the corruption within the political and criminal justice system of the city, county and state government, that their allegations of illegal activities of their fellow officers fell on deaf ears. But in 1970, these men, along with the vast majority of officers of the Department were pleased to hear of the plans for the impanelling of a federal and later county grand jury to investigate corruption within the police department. Most of the officers deplored the fact that several of their own were "on the take," and it was common knowledge that at least 20 percent of the department's personnel were in this category.[24]

Unfortunately for the citizens of the city, the majority of the men and women on the force were soon disappointed with the actions of the newly appointed United States Attorney, Stan Pitkin, in his neophyte attempts to prosecute the city's corrupt politicians and police officers. Pitkin and his staff showed an almost complete ignorance of the operations of the police department and apparently had little or no knowledge of human psychology. It appeared that their purpose was not just to convict the guilty, but to smear the reputation of all the men and women of the force and in so doing, to gain the widest possible media coverage. In the criminal trials that followed the Grand Jury indictments, each police witness subpoenaed to testify, either for the defense or prosecution, was put through the most rigorous cross-examination by the government in what was an apparent attempt to discredit the entire department. In one instance, the government, in examining their own witness, an assistant chief of police, elicited testimony that the officer distributed "pay off monies" to fellow officers, with Pitkin knowing full well that the source of such funds was from rewards paid to department members for the arrest of wanted persons or for the recovery of stolen property. The receipt of these funds was certainly improper, albeit condoned by the Department, but in no sense of the word was it illegal. Other officers were treated similarly. In one case, a captain was subpoenaed by the government for the sole purpose of eliciting from him the information that, as a young police sergeant many years before, he concealed the fact that his former boss, now on trial for bribery, had been involved in an accident with a city vehicle while drinking.

As the trials continued, the news media were having a field day, with daily headlines which, when analyzed, appeared to be seeking to assist the government in destroying the reputation of all the men and women of the police department. That both the government's attorneys and the news media were unsuccessful, speaks highly for the men and women of the force, but it was this "shotgun" approach in seeking the conviction of any officer for anything, coupled with the news media's distortions and misrepresentation of the truth, which created a backlash within the Department. Those officers who originally supported the concept that the U.S. Attorney's investigation would seek out and prosecute those involved in corrupt practices within the Department were soon disillusioned. Their reactions were predictable. This group took on a very vocal and highly visible defense posture which soon gained support throughout the force and from several politicians not connected with city government. Nowhere was this support more visible for the Department's personnel than in the halls of the state legislature, as was evidenced by the passage of a statute prohibiting the use of the polygraph as a condition of continued employment for police officers. Interim police Chief Charles Gain (the former Chief of Police of Oakland and later, Chief of San Francisco, California), at the height of the grand jury investigation, issued a directive which would have compelled members of the force accused or suspected of criminal activity, to submit to lie detector examinations or forfeit their jobs.

When it was over, the grand jury investigative findings, unlike the Royal Commission investigation in Vancouver, resulted in the conviction of almost two dozen Seattle police officers on criminal charges, several of whom "did time" in the county jail or federal penitentiary. Assistant Chief of Police M. E. "Buzz" Cook received the most severe sentence. However, as with Chief Walter Mulligan's flight from Canada to avoid being held accountable for his stewardship of the Vancouver department, several Seattle officers followed his example and fled to Mexico, Europe or to Canada to escape prosecution. Some of the officers remain there to this day.

In Seattle as in Vancouver in 1955, notwithstanding the fact that many local and state (provincial) politicians were the chief architects of the police payoff system, in collusion with local business men who were accused or indicted, few were ever convicted of a criminal offense. One businessman, Adolfo Ventura "Rudy" Santos, was well known to police beat officers and vice squad members. Santos, a local Filipino-American community leader and professional gambler, was convicted of perjury in 1972 for denying before the Grand Jury that he bribed one or more Seattle police officers. He received a 15-year suspended sentence, with the judge describing him as "a victim of the payoff system."[25]

These events, however, may well have had a beneficial effect within the Seattle police force, for in the future they may well serve to discourage other officers from entering into a system of corruption and payoffs with politicians and businessmen, for they know full well that they alone will be held accountable for these activities. It became obvious to all who watched these events unfold over the years that the uniformed police officer must follow a code of conduct more restrictive and demanding, both in his personal and professional life, than that of his fellow citizen. This is as it should be. Yet, one cannot help but wonder if, had some of the local politicians and police managers of this era directed their energies away from the corrupting influences of public employment toward a truly efficient police service, the end result for many police officers would be different. Training for police officers would improve, police could be furnished the appropriate "tools of the trade," which today should, but rarely does, include the technology which can improve police capabilities ten-fold. The end result is that the public would greatly benefit because of the increased proficiency of their police officers, and fewer cops would pay the ultimate price that officer Frank Hardy paid in responding to this crime at the Greenwood bank.

Notes

[1] Frank C. Ramon, Chief of Police, memorandum to Charles A. Rouse, Assistant Chief of Police, April 14, 1964.

[2] Ibid.

[3] Repeated attempts were made by the author in 1992 and again in 1993 to interview the three Talbot brothers, Norman, Charles (called Chuck by family members) and Maurice "Bobby," relative to their personal knowledge of this 1954 criminal case, but if they had any information of this crime they were still unwilling to talk about it. All three, now in their seventies, still live in the Burnaby/New Westminster/Vancouver metropolitan area in British Columbia.

[4] The Province, August 6, 1964.

[5] The Vancouver Sun, October 2, 1968, p. 49.

[6] The Province, January 5, 1974, pp. 1, 29.

[7] See J. Earle Milnes, Special Agent in Charge FBI Seattle, letter to George P. Tielsch, Chief of Police, City of Seattle Police Department March 15, 1974.

[8] The FBI has jurisdiction in investigations of over two hundred different federal law violations, but it was the National Bank (Robbery) Act and the Federal Kidnapping Statute which gave Bureau employees nation wide public recognition, and this was exploited to the extreme under the leadership of J. Edgar Hoover. Thus the drive for public recognition in solving these violent crimes frequently took precedence over professional performance and adversely impacted the actions of an entire group of agents and their superiors. This drive for favorable publicity often led to conflict between the Bureau and local law enforcement. On repeated occasions, where local law enforcement had been instrumental in identifying a suspect or arresting a perpetrator, Bureau agents were quick to take credit for solving the crime. On one occasion,

Seattle police detectives who had learned of the location of several bank robbery suspects, notified the Seattle office of the FBI of their location and suggested joint action to take the suspects into custody. However, agents proceeded to the location, made the arrests and left the area before Seattle officers arrived at the scene.

[9] Vernon and Joyce Chase, interviews with the author, January 29, 1975.

[10] Report of Mayor's Special Committee to Inquire into Alleged Police Payoffs, Seattle, Washington, April 11, 1967.

REPORT OF THE SPECIAL AD HOC CITIZENS' COMMITTEE APPOINTED BY MAYOR J. D. BRAMAN JANUARY 20, 1967, TO INQUIRE INTO ALLEGED PAYOFFS TO MEMBERS OF THE SEATTLE POLICE DEPARTMENT AND GENERAL ADMINISTRATIVE AND SUPERVISORY PROCEDURES.

LIMITATIONS, PROCEDURES AND PRELIMINARY STATEMENT

The Mayor appointed this temporary committee to inquire into the matters above set forth and with the understanding that it would be disbanded immediately following the presentation of its report. It was instructed to establish its own operating rules in order to ascertain the truth or falsity of the charges of payoffs to police officers and to inquire into the internal procedures of the administration of the police department.

The committee derived no authority by reason of said appointment and did not have the power to compel persons to testify or attend committee hearings. Further, the committee did not have power to put witnesses under oath to compel production of records or documents. All witnesses appeared voluntarily in accordance with their own wishes as to anonymity, and in all instances it was agreed, at their request, that the information so furnished would be kept confidential.

In furtherance of a policy to encourage public participation and response to the problem as to specific incidents, the committee opened a post office box at the Seattle Main Post Office, and requested through the press, radio and TV facilities that any interested persons communicate with the committee relating to these subjects. The committee received responses concerning alleged payoffs to police officers, and much of the information given was based on rumor or hearsay.

The committee met at various places to accommodate witnesses and their attorneys, and arranged interviews with individuals having authority, accountability, or responsibility in the area of law enforcement.

The Committee started its hearings immediately following its appointment, and concluded on April 6, 1967. Recognizing that the chief of police and the vast majority of our police officers are dedicated and self-disciplined men, the committee now makes the following observations and recommendations:

(1). That the information submitted to this committee falls short of establishing payoffs to police officers. While a number of statements by witnesses indicated the acceptance of payoffs by a few policemen in isolated cases, there was no substantiation or corroboration that would permit a finding by the committee as to the truth of the statements. Police officers appearing before the committee denied receiving any payoffs.

(2). That facts were developed which reflected inadequate supervision on the command level of the police department due to insufficient personnel on said level, and loose procedures of supervision. Such a situation, in the opinion of the committee, results in the breakdown of control of department personnel and permits incidents of deviation from proper conduct by policemen.

(3). That the police departmental records, manuals and personnel files need additional updating. The control and distribution procedures should also be improved, and the members of the Department should be required to be thoroughly familiar with all police manuals and directives.

(4). That members of the police department shall not be permitted to work off duty in taverns, bars, cabarets of cocktail lounges.

(5). That members of the Department shall not, while on duty, enter business establishments as set forth above except in the strict performance of their duties.

(6). A permanent record shall be kept of all secondary employment, with payment to be made only by check.

(7). That the police department inaugurate immediately a regular maximum two-year systemized basis of rotation of patrol personnel, both on shift and area beat assignments.

(8). That a survey be immediately made by the Field Services Division of the International Association of Chiefs of Police for a study to determine the efficiency and effectiveness of the supervision and administration of the Department as presently organized, and to produce relevant statistics as to the adequacy of the number of policemen per thousand population, pay standards, and other pertinent systems which should be developed as a result of the overall study.

     Richard D. Harris, Chairman.

     William E. Boeing, Jr.

     Victor Denny

     Richard D. Auerbach, Advisor

[11] The Seattle Times, January 14, 1970, p. 1.

[12] The Seattle Post Intelligencer, April 18, 1970, p. 1.

[13] The Seattle Times, August 12, 1970 p. 1. Also see The Seattle Post Intelligencer, July 28, 1971 p. 1., and The Seattle Times July 28, p. 1.

[14] Ibid., The Seattle Post Intelligencer, July 28, 1971, p. 1.

City of Seattle early 1950's. (Seattle Police Records Archives)

[15] Charles A. Rouse, interview with the author, January 4, 1974.
[16] Glen Rouse, interview with the author, October 18, 1991.
[17] Op. Cit., The Seattle Post Intelligencer, July 28, 1971, p. 1.
[18] Willa E. Waitt, interview with the author, January 25, 1975.

[19] Robert Waitt, conversations with the author, June 13, 1991.

[20] For many of those present at the conference who were familiar with the past performance of the police in western Canada this was rather a shocking disclosure, for more than a decade earlier Chief Constable George Archer warned elected officials in Vancouver and British Columbia that many members of the local police were poorly trained and ill-equipped to handle the challenges faced by the police in Canada. When he assumed office as the chief constable in Vancouver he said he·"was surprised to learn that 'a dangerously large percentage' of the (Vancouver) force had no police training whatsoever." See G. M. "Joe" Swan "A Century of Policing - The Vancouver Police - 1886-1986, Vancouver Historical Society and Centennial Museum, Vancouver, B.C. Canada 1986, p. 84.

[21] John Hogarth, Ph. D., LL.B., Chairman, British Columbia Police Commission-Aspects of Their Work, May 15, 1976, pp. 19-26.

[22] Michael Johnson, History of the Seattle Police Department, from an unpublished manuscript, Seattle, Washington 1972, pp. 4-10.

[23] One need only look at the history of police communications in large cities to determine the level of technological expertise within the Seattle police force. Seattle was one of the last major cities in North America to install two-way radio systems in police patrol vehicles, and it wasn't until 1972 that portable radios were provided to the officers. Beat cops continued to use the 1890 vintage police call-box telephone system to 1972. And, although Extended 911 emergency telephone and mobile digital communications systems had been in use in American and Canadian Police Departments since the mid-sixties, the City of Seattle would not adopt these communication systems for their police until the 1990's.

[24] The Seattle Post Intelligencer, April 4, 1973. In 1972, the Seattle Police Department had a total complement of 1163 sworn officers (see City of Seattle Police Department Annual Report for 1972 pp. 17-19). Between 1970 and 1972, nearly 300 police officers were indicted by either a federal and/or a county grand jury in Seattle for one or more specific criminal offenses. Two hundred and thirty-one of these were named as "un-indicted co-conspirators," i.e., "involved in public corruption within the City of Seattle." The reader should keep in mind, however, that even though most of these officers would leave the force, few were ever convicted of a serious crime and less than a dozen would ever serve time in the county jail or within a state or federal penitentiary. However, the majority of these officers admitted to receiving, on a continuing bases, gratuities and/or outright payoffs from a variety of business firms within the city. These admissions were made either before one or more of the three grand juries assembled between 1970 and 1972 to investigate corruption within the police department, or before a Departmental Disciplinary Trial Board. These Boards, which were soon to be convened, followed the release of the findings of the Grand Jury.

Nearly two score officers, who were named as un-indicted co-conspirators in this police corruption scandal, appealed administratively to the Office of the Chief of Police their imminent dismissal from the Department. Each was granted the opportunity, along with their attorney, to discuss, with the Assistant Chief of Police for Staff Services, the charges reported out of the Grand Jury(s). When these discussions ended, at the direction of the Chief of Police, each officer was given the option:

(1). To resign from the force immediately, or

(2). To be dismissed.

With few exceptions, most of those officers identified as being involved in corrupt practices within the Department quietly resigned their commissions. Less than a dozen appealed their termination of employment through the Department's disciplinary procedures. However, none were successful in retaining their jobs though they pursued this internal process. One of the best examples of the continuing turmoil which existed within the Department at that time can be demonstrated by what happened to one patrolman caught up in this controversy. The accused officer, with the common last name of Stewart, instead of resigning as he agreed to during his interview with the then Chief of Staff (who was soon to be demoted himself), merely went back to work without further comment to anyone. His "good fortune," however, came to a quick end when he was accidently "discovered" by the new chief of police to be still working a year later, when the chief conducted a routine walk through inspection of the patrol bureau.

In another case, a high-ranking officer who was terminated sought support from the press in order to nullify his removal from office. Some members of the media vociferously condemned his dismissal from the Department and began a not too subtle campaign to remove the recently appointed Chief of Police; a campaign which received considerable behind the scenes support from the Office of the Mayor, for the "honey moon" of the current chief of police, George Tielsch, was past. Tielsch's downfall occurred when he had the impertinence to suggest that the mayor, members of the city council and the business community who orchestrated the pay-off system were just as culpable as were members of the police force. Although the Grand Jury accused a former mayor of illegally accepting bribes, and indicted the chairman of the public safety committee of the Council, subsequent to these charges there was evidence that payoff moneys had continued to flow into these offices. It soon became evident that the chief of police and those command officers who supported him in trying to end this scourge within the Department would not survive. Several key members of the command staff, who played leading roles in the disciplinary process following release of the Grand Jury findings and who were critical of the mayor's continuing manipulation of the Department for what was obviously political purposes, were demoted at the direction of the mayor to their tenured rank of police captain and reassigned to obscure jobs.

George Tielsch's forced resignation as Chief of Police was also soon to be accepted by the Mayor's Office with "regret."

[25] Steven Goldsmith, "Santos," Seattle Post Intelligencer, January 3, 1992, Section B, p. 2.

Chapter

15

Epilogue

Fortuitously, this writer has not only had the opportunity to live in both Vancouver and Seattle, but also to be closely associated with several of the key players in this story. Because of this, I have had the opportunity to observe first hand the good and the bad in public protection services offered by these two communities over a period of many years. I chose quite consciously to go beyond the mere collection of information about the single crime of robbery and murder portrayed in this story and have attempted to show the reader the interconnection between the visible and violent crime of the streets with that crime pursued by venal politicians and crooked cops when public corruption is a way of life in the community. I believe the issue of how we as residents of the northwestern U.S. and British Columbia got our communities into this type of difficulty, in which our police could not or would not meet a set of reasonable minimum standards of performance is critical to this story. And what about the future? What's in store for these communities if the police in our cities continue to perform as they have done in the past 50 years? The author has no crystal ball but, based upon the history of these two police departments, I believe it may be quite easy to predict the future.

But before doing so, we need to know a little more about the history of our two cities, and the plans and expectations of their law enforcement member professionals, as well as the people's plans for their police (i.e., what plans, if any, have the citizens of these two communities set in motion for their own future security?)

Our history books tell us that Seattle and Vancouver have experienced repeated occurrences of police and political corruption since their founding, Seattle in 1865 and Vancouver three years later. [See Murray Morgan's, *Skid Road*]. Seattle grew slowly from its first settlements along the shores of Puget Sound when a small group of travelers came by sea from San Francisco in 1852 and staked out land around Elliott Bay. But the Alaska-Yukon gold rush and World War I and II resulted in an accelerated growth as thousands of persons came to seek their fortune, and/or employment in this northwest city. The Cold War era also contributed to the rapid growth of the region, because of those seeking employment in the northwest's defense industries, until today Seattle's metropolitan area population exceeds two and one-half million people. Although less spectacular, Vancouver has grown from a small lumber town into the third largest city in Canada with a population of 457,000. Seattle in the 1950's, although a modern urban area, never reached the distinction of being one of the country's largest metropolitan cities.

Crime in Seattle at the time of the incident which I have narrated here, in stark contrast to Vancouver, was considered to be, by most police managers, at an "acceptable level," probably because of the marked reduction in crime following the war years 1942-1945, and this trend would continue for another few years. Yet in 1954, in comparison to the seventeen U. S. cities of 500,000 population and over, Seattle then, as it does today, had one of the highest crime rates in the U. S. In the intervening years, little has changed. In 1990, only six other major cities in the U. S. in this population group had a higher incidence of reported crime per 1000 population. It was no wonder, then, that when citizens looked at the police department they discovered the "bastard child" of city government. In 1955, Seattle's 1.56 per capita police employees per 1,000 population, was the lowest of the seventeen U.S. cities in their population group.[1] (That figure had increased substantially by 1992 to 2.31).

In the 1950's, Vancouver, unlike Seattle, was plagued by crime. Bank robberies were occurring almost daily, and the related drug wars in Vancouver were at a fever pitch. Forty years later little has changed in the city. And as we enter the 1990's, Vancouver, now nearly as large as Seattle with a population approaching one-half million people and a mushrooming metropolitan area, continues to be plagued by crime. In the 1950's, as now, it was in the comparison of the more serious crimes in the two cities where one found both a stark contrast and several similarities. In a community where the metropolitan population is still less than half of Seattle, and in a country which has some of the most restrictive firearms prohibitions, the rate of violent crime in Vancouver is considerably higher than in Seattle[2]. (In 1988, Vancouver reported 7399 cases per 100,000 population, and Seattle reported 6778.)[3] This suggests that Vancouver city fathers have a long way to go before they can claim that theirs is one of the more secure places to live in western Canada. (The author assumes that the reader recognizes that there is a direct relationship between the number of violent crimes occurring within a community and police performance, although many sociologists might suggest there is little or no correlation between the two).

The lack of exemplary leadership as exemplified by Chief Walter Mulligan and H. J. "Jimmie" Lawrence, which led to corruption and mismanagement within these organizations, as we have previously noted, has always been an issue within these two cities' police departments, but we have also seen that in both cities over the years this has not been of particular concern to the electorate. If one were to look closely, at the time there were several signs which would support this claim.

It was in police salaries in both agencies in the 1950's where the greatest neglect of the police services were evident. Police officer wages in these two cities, at the time of this crime at the Greenwood bank, can best be described as a disgrace. In Seattle, pay scales were more than 25 percent behind Los Angeles and San Francisco, and less than 50% of the salary of the average skilled tradesman within the city. (In one survey conducted in the fifties, over 60% of the police officers employed by the city worked two jobs to support their families).

In the 1950's, for large metropolitan police agencies in the U. S. and in Canada, police training was in its infancy and few departments could boast of operating a modern, up-to-date police academy. Seattle was no different. Thus, during this era, many new officers in the city and in other similar western cities continued to receive the on-the-job training experiences of whatever their "partner" was willing and/or able to provide during their regular tour of duty.[4]

A college education for police officers was considered entirely unnecessary. In some police circles, it was in fact a detriment to the officer in the field if he were unwise enough to mention the fact that he had graduated from a police administration course in one of the few educational institutions in the U. S. to offer such training.[5]

The 1968 Report of the President's Commission On Law Enforcement and the Administration of Justice, "The Challenge Of Crime In A Free Society," which identified the need to hire college-educated police officers, did much to turn this type of thinking around within the American police industry. This movement was given further emphasis when several college educators added their voice in support of this theory, "Police service may not be considered a profession . . . until training programs are provided for the police that are comparable to those that prepare persons for other professions. If police leaders want police service to attain professional standing, they must promote university training. Those who oppose it are saying, in effect, that the police service should not attain the status of a profession."[6]

It was not until after publication of The President's Crime Commission Report of 1968, however, that education of police officers was looked upon by the public as a necessity for improving the police services. At the recommendation of the Commission, the Law Enforcement Assistance Administration was created. Thus, a nationwide movement got underway in the U.S. to professionalize our state and local law enforcement personnel, and hundreds of thousands of young police officers embarked upon the road to improving their own education, supported by federal funds. Although the program received enormous support from the law enforcement community, the political leadership of the country soon found other uses for these funds and by 1980 the program, no longer funded by the U.S. government was finished. It is commonly believed by many professional police chiefs that, between the loss of these funds and the various affirmative action programs of this decade, which mandated the employment and/or promotion of unqualified women and minorities, some of whom were illiterate, over highly qualified and experienced professional police officers, both the opportunity and the emphasis for improving the professionalism of our police forces in America was lost. Thousands of young qualified professionals within the lower ranks of state and local police forces, who once pursued higher education for themselves along with their colleagues within their profession, after repeatedly being bypassed for promotion, no longer pursue higher education nor seek leadership roles within the service, thus the talent of a whole generation of potential professional leaders has been lost to the police service.

In Seattle, Frank C. Ramon (Chief of Police 1961-1969), must be given the credit for encouraging the continued education of Seattle police officers within the halls of higher education in the northwest during the decade of the sixties. But to do so, Ramon had to fight the resistance of the city's political leadership, many of whom feared a college educated cop would require payment of higher salaries. Surprisingly, however, the greatest resistance to educating and training police officers within educational institutions in the northwest came from the Federal Bureau of Investigation and the Washington Association of Sheriffs. Many in the Bureau saw college or university training programs as a threat to their leadership role in the police training arena. The federal government had just begun in the 1960's to fund that agency with substantial dollars to expand the FBI Academy for use by local law enforcement. The resistance encountered from the members of the Washington Sheriff's Association was instigated by a group of elected sheriffs who were better known for their political prowess than their law enforcement expertise. Their resistance appeared to be in response to "being content to live with the status quo" and, "to do nothing" which, in their myopic view of professional law enforcement, would be less threatening to the position of the constitutionally elected sheriff.

The uniformed police officer is frequently the only defense immediately available to local government in protecting our institutions, our citizens and in preventing the destruction of our way of life. Few would disagree that the continuing growth of serious crime in our two countries may well be reduced if our police officers were better educated, trained, and professionally managed, and if our political leaders were held strictly accountable for their failure to provide a high level of professional performance of not only the police, but also of those other law enforcement support agencies that make up our criminal justice system. Yet 34 years after the President's Crime Commission's recommendations were published, few police agencies in the U.S. require a college degree for entry into the service. By 1990, only 6 percent of local police agencies and 20 percent of state agencies required new recruits to have at least "some" college education.[7]

This writer is not so idealistic as to suggest that we live in a utopian world, but few cities can match Seattle (or Vancouver) for their earlier years of political puppetry by opportunistic politicians in their manipulation of police chief executives and their police agencies. Nor can a better example be found of public official and media irresponsibility for their failure to identify and hold accountable those business and political leaders who orchestrated repeated scenarios of scandalous behavior by political and business leaders, and for their tolerance of inept and corrupt police leaders.

Shortly before the turn of the century, Seattle city fathers and their colleagues in Vancouver passed ordinances designed to rid their cities of "gambling, prostitution and other vice activities." These ordinances created the foundation for several incompetent politicians to climb the ladder of success to top political jobs within city government, by using monies to finance their political campaigns from the city's vice operations. The vice crimes of a nation create huge sums of money, and the old adage that money is power comes to the forefront at the poles where venal politicians have shown a high degree of success in attaining political office. Thus, in the arena of vice crimes, little has changed in the last ninety years except that many vice activities which were frowned upon by the public at the turn of the century are now legal. During these years, members of the Seattle and Vancouver police departments have been torn between the reformers and the vice interests, and the frequent appointment of inept and/or iniquitously prone police chiefs added nothing toward creating a professional police service in either city.

The irresponsibility of the Seattle press in their continual support of deceitful politicians, while also ignoring the devious business practices carried on by some members of the local business community, was also very evident. Since the late 1800's, prostitution, operation of illegal liquor establishments and gambling of all types were common business enterprises operating throughout the city with the full knowledge and support of the news media, even though these activities were prohibited by law. Liquor "by the drink" in Seattle was prohibited by statute until 1949, yet "after-hour" clubs were freely advertised in the local press and operated visibly and outside the law for years. When it became legal to sell hard liquor over the counter, the "under the table" going price for a class "H" license, which allowed the sale of mixed drinks in hotels and restaurants, ranged up to $15,000.00 per location.

Prostitution operations flourished, aided by the media which carried daily advertisements of call-girl activities under the subterfuge of "escort services," with the press knowing full well that these were nothing more than fronts for prostitution. Gambling activities were no less prevalent. Prohibited by the state constitution, dozens of gambling establishments operated openly with the full blessing of the mayor and members of the city council under a city-wide gambling tolerance policy. High stakes gambling in fraternal lodges, churches and night clubs were common, and dozens of "after hour" no-limit card rooms flourished and were frequented by politicians and members of the media alike.

Further evidence of this irresponsibility of the press came to light in the Seattle police payoff scandals of the 1970's. Notwithstanding the fact that over 300 police officers of all ranks were indicted as a result of grand jury investigations during this period, accused, among other things, of accepting bribes from businessmen and of allowing prostitution and gambling activities to occur, although equally culpable in the eyes of the law, few businessmen were ever prosecuted for the criminal offense of bribing a public official. These clear violations of law by businessmen and malfeasance of politicians were ignored by the media and consequently by a majority of the public. However what the public did receive from the media was a better understanding of the hazards faced by anyone who sought the office of the chief of police in their city, for it did not go unnoticed that in the short 100-year history of this town, over 60 chiefs of police had come and gone. (In comparison with other city department heads it might be interesting to note that only 8 city light superintendents, 18 fire chiefs and 22 water department superintendents sat at the helm of these other operating departments of city government during this period).

Tenure for the office of chief of police, of course, does not guarantee that the citizen will receive professional service from its police force and, as a matter of fact, lengthy tenure in this office frequently accounts for a high degree of lethargy and poor performance so evident in many police departments. But the police cannot function effectively unless they are managed by professionals and judged solely on their performance. In the U.S., the state exercises control over, and sets standards for entry into the profession of architects, lawyers, engineers, nurses, electricians, veterinarians, etc., and a whole host of other professions, including physicians, but the state has not yet exercised its option to set minimum standards for those who hold the responsibility for managing our police agencies. "By 1975, forty states had established standards for the entry level officer; however, no state had established standards for law enforcement chief executives."[8] In commenting on this state of affairs in the attempts of our nation's police executives to improve law enforcement standards in the U. S., again from the bottom up, members of the Police Executive Research Forum (PERF) responded: "Clearly, this bottom up strategy of improving law enforcement and ignoring higher level officials is a rather unique approach."[9]

This writer believes it can be argued quite successfully that the state has the primary responsibility for the protection and welfare of our citizens and thus should establish minimum educational and performance standards for those who fulfill leadership roles, not only within these other professions, but in our local police forces as well.

Many of those who have studied this issue agree. The International Association of Police Chiefs in 1978 suggested that, "Every state, individually or in concert with one or more contiguous states, should enact legislation to establish executive programs for police chief executives' enrichment and development. Curricula and qualifications for enrollment should be established by each state or region. Certificates of achievement should be issued to those who attain specified qualification plateaus within the program.[10]

This failure on the part of the state to recognize the need to establish standards for its police chief executives has not gone unnoticed by those organizations who represent America's police leaders. It may be argued that, in a democracy, the control of the police properly rests with the elected executive managing the smallest unit of local government being served. However, federal intervention into the administration and operational practices of the police in the U.S. may, in the future, restrict the ability of locally elected officials to control the actions of the police, for there are renewed efforts to impose national operational standards through "voluntary" federally sponsored accreditation programs for law enforcement in the U.S.

A Commission on Accreditation for Law Enforcement Agencies was established in 1979 in the U.S. and in time this group may make some headway toward setting minimum standards for positions of leadership within this profession. This organization has issued over a thousand performance standards designed to increase performance and effectiveness of law enforcement agencies and to increase citizen confidence in the police in the U. S. These performance standards, however, have not been widely accepted within the police community. The only purpose they have served thus far has been to help a few local agencies in developing long overdue administrative and operational procedural standards. Yet here was a group of law enforcement chief executives who were given an abundant supply of federal law enforcement research funds to set performance standards and improve local law enforcement administration and management, from the top down, but instead chose to work from the bottom up. Thus little has been accomplished through their efforts and certainly no performance standards for the position of chief of police have been established to date.

The Police Executive Research Forum's (PERF) early efforts to professionalize America's police should also not go unnoticed by elected officials at the state and local levels of government. For they need not be too farsighted to understand the probable consequences, i.e. receipt of federal funding by the state, county or cities may well depend upon acceptable police performance standards at the local level. This may well usurp the authority of the locally elected executive responsible for the performance of the communities's police force.

Unfortunately however, it appears such performance standards or requirements are still years away, as the association of police chiefs, have been unable to reach a consensus on this issue, and thus have not been successful in establishing reforms which would set in motion the development of minimum standards for police chiefs. The reader should be aware that some of the larger police associations, i.e. the IACP, are controlled by a voting block of smaller agency chiefs of police and, in general, in these agencies there is little support for setting minimum professional standards for the position of chief of police. This, in part, accounts for the flight of many IACP association member chiefs, from the larger metropolitan police agencies, into the Police Executive Research Forum (PERF). Unable to move the IACP toward these goals, this splinter group from the larger departments established PERF. Its stated purpose is the "Professionalism of police executives and the promotion of public recognition for police management as a profession."[11]

However, because of this continued failure on the part of America's police executives and elected officials alike to address this most important issue of minimum standards for the office of chief of police, i.e. qualifications, tenure, training, and the professional relationship between the chief and the appointing authority, both the police and the community will suffer. Ignorant of professional police performance standards, politicians will fill this void and set the standard for appointment to the office of chief of police themselves, and no one should be surprised if the political background of prospective candidates for chief of police doesn't take precedence over professional competence. This is exactly what is occurring today in the western U.S., particularly at the state police level, but in many cities as well.

There are many examples of this political manipulation of the office of chief of police throughout the Western U.S., where state and city police management positions have been filled by candidates better known for their political skills than their professional police expertise. One only need look at the state police in Utah, California, Colorado, Oregon and Washington, and the police in cities such as Seattle, Portland and Denver to find examples of this. We can also find repeated instances where the candidate's race, sex, or religion, was more important to the appointing authority than the professional competence of the appointee. Glaring examples of this practice can be found throughout the American law enforcement community. Although the political leadership of effected communities frequently deny it, and members of the police profession refuse to discuss this issue publicly, the sex of the candidate was of primary concern in the selection process of the chiefs of police in Portland, Oregon, Houston, Texas and in several smaller communities. Race is and was the determining factor in Denver, Colorado and several other cities, and religion frequently is the primary delimitating factor in the selection of a chief of police to manage the largest departments in the state of Utah.

Today, in the western U.S., we also see the combining of multiple emergency units of local government into departments of public safety, with the professional police chief and fire chief being relegated to the position of secondary functionaries reporting not to the chief executive officer of the city or state, but to his or her political appointee. Nor is it unusual to find that the emphasis for the creation of this new layer of bureaucracy within the Office of the Director of Public Safety is based solely on the failure of elected officials to rid the city of an incompetent police chief, "frozen" in office due to incorrectly perceived civil service protection. Frequently this new appointee is no more than a former unemployed political hack of the chief executive's party. A recent example of this type of political manipulation of the state police occurred in Colorado when a politician, who had lost his bid for reelection as prosecuting attorney and had no police experience whatsoever, was appointed by the governor (from the same political party) as the head of the Department of Public Safety for the state.

Thus, in answer to this writer's opening comments about the future of policing in the west, unless the current leaders in the police profession, in cooperation with elected officials, address this most important issue of minimum standards and tenure for police chief executive officers, one does not need a crystal ball to predict that local and state police agencies will be destined to follow in the footsteps of America's elected sheriffs. Accordingly, the local police will follow a path of diminished responsibility, and the federal and state police shall usurp much of the local polices' enforcement role[12]. Although this country is blessed with many competent sheriffs, the seeds of the eventual failure of this well established law enforcement institution in the West are sown at the time of election. Those within the agency who do not support the elected head of their organization may, and often do, undermine the office, with the view to unseating the incumbent at the next election. This, of course, has been the history of the elected sheriff in the eastern States; thus we find the northeastern sheriff in the U.S. has been stripped of most of his enforcement authority and has been relegated to tax collector, custodial and process server duties.

If the police themselves do not soon address this issue of professionalization of our forces, and develop standards of qualifications, performance and tenure for the position of chief of police, in the future our communities will also not be provided with a reasonable expectation of security, and the events as described in this story will continue unabated in American (and in Canadian) communities. The author does not stand alone on this position, for many others more experienced have expressed similar beliefs, yet individual chiefs of police are still afraid, for good reason, to speak out against this system which places a premium on protecting the political administration in power, regardless of the cost, versus stepping up and publicly addressing the shortcomings within this political system that hamper an effective response to controlling crime within our communities.[13]

One only need turn to a study completed for the Department of Justice on the American law enforcement chief executive for a whole array of comments from chief executives of our nation's law enforcement agencies in support of this premise:[14] "Police chief executives fail to express their opinions on public issues for several reasons, including fear of being summarily removed, caution about gaining more public exposure than their superiors, lack of self-confidence, and inability to articulate their position as well as they would like."[15]

"While I was an appointed police chief, my superior let me know that I would be fired if I spoke out."[16] "Several police chief executives reported in interviews that their superiors had directed them not to express their opinions on public safety issues."[17]

Throughout this work the author has severely criticized the actions of both the police and political leadership of Canada and the U.S., in the 1950's; but this criticism was not unlike that which has been said by others who have looked at their own professions and realized that change was necessary at both the top and bottom of their organizations. Warren E. Burger, the Chief Justice of the United States Supreme Court was and is, to this day, probably one of the most respected jurists ever appointed to the Court. He was a hero to many in the business of trying to control crime in the U. S. because: "He frequently criticized Supreme Court rulings that he felt went too far in protecting an accused person's rights, and many of his decisions stressed the rights of society over the rights of persons accused of crime,"[18] a belief not dissimilar to that held today by many in the police management arena in the U.S. And when the Chief Justice suggested that one-half of the American lawyers who appeared before his court were incompetent and unqualified to practice law in the U.S., many in the police field were quick to agree with him. Yet in the law enforcement arena when one of their own suggests that this is also true in the ranks of America's police chiefs and sheriffs, our association leadership is quick to deny it. And many are just as quick to attack a colleague who would take such a public position. Their response, whenever this has occurred, has been to publicly demean the individual's character and if that doesn't work, ostracism of the individual chief within their constituency is the next best choice.

Our elected and appointed police officials must be held accountable for their actions. They determine the future course of law enforcement in a community, and the level of crime in that community is directly related to their performance. But, in a more personal vein, these leaders are also accountable for the lives and wellbeing of our police officers. And who are these faceless people in uniform? They are our sons and daughters. In the 1950's, most of them had already served their country honorably and with distinction in either World

War II or in Korea. They were good people. Even though they worked for low wages, at a task not highly respected by many, they were, for the most part honest and respectable members of their communities and they believed what they did would make a difference, and their countries would be a better place to live in as a result of their sacrifices. Then the reader may ask, what went wrong? Why were our police agencies so vilified at the time and why were they in such a state of disrepute? Was it because there was a complete absence of political leadership in our communities at the time or were the police solely responsible for this breakdown in law and order?

Notes

[1] 1955 Annual Report, Seattle Police Department, Seattle, Washington, p. 1.

[2] A comparison of reported serious offenses between the cities of Vancouver and Seattle, in the 1950's and today, is, as we will see, of interest. (The reader is cautioned that specific crimes are reported differently in several jurisdictions, and the criteria used for classification of offenses in Canada is not identical to that used by U.S. police agencies, and *no* specific comparisons should be made, yet some generalized comparisons and observations are made here to give the reader a view of crime in these two communities since 1954).

1954

	Seattle	Vancouver
Robbery Total	481	257
Serious Offenses Total	12682	16312

1990

	U.S.	Canada	B.C.
Murder, Rate/100,000	9.4	2.5	3.5
Robbery, Rate/100,000	257	106	126
Total Reported Crimes, Rate/100,000	5820.3	11,947	14,981

	Seattle	Vancouver
Total Crimes of Violence		
	7780	7417
Rate/100,000 Pop.		
	1507	1623

Vancouver Crime Trends	Canada Crime Trends
Robbery/Violence	Crimes of Violence*
1951 - 191	1962 - 41026
1952 - 177	1972 - 110468
1953 - 186	1982 - 168646
1954 - 257	1986 - 204917
1955 - 241	1990 - 269440
1988 - 1806	

*Total violent crime - Actual offenses; 1990 rate = 1013/100,000 population.

U.S. 1990 Violent Crime Rate/100,000 population = 732/100,000.
See Canadian Centre for Justice Statistics, Law Enforcement Program, Actual Number, Rate and Percentage Change of Violent Crime Offences and Rates, Canada, 1962 - 1986; Canadian Crime Statistics 1988, 1990 and 1991; U.S. Uniform Crime Reports - 1990; and Vancouver and Seattle Police Departments Annual Report - 1954, 1955.

[3] Canadian Centre For Justice Statistics, Crime in Canada, Statistics Canada Advisory Services, Pacific Region, Vancouver, B. C., Canada. 1988 Preliminary Crime Statistics, p. 41. Also see 1988 Annual Report, Seattle Police Department, Seattle, Washington, pp. 28-31. 1955 Annual Report, Seattle Police Department, Seattle, Washington, p. 1. Also see Crime in the United States, U.S. Department of Justice, Washington, D.C., 1990, pp. 51-58; and Canadian Crime Statistics, Canadian Centre for Justice Statistics, Ottawa 1990, pp. 26-36, and table no. 2-81-82.

[4] The Seattle Police Department, History of the Seattle Police Department, "Formal Training Begins," Seattle, Washington, 1987, p. 31.

"As far back as 1914, there had been a desire by various citizen groups as well as certain police officials for the establishment of a police training school. The old timers learned from the school of hard knocks and it was difficult to overcome the natural apathy many members of the Department had for formal law enforcement training.

Between 1928 and 1931, a very rudimentary training program for detective division personnel was conducted by Captain E. C. Collier. The council appropriated $3,000.00 for police training in the 1936 budget. Two plans were proposed in regard to police training. One was for the establishment of a local police school within the department; the other for a statewide law enforcement training program conducted by the University of Washington. A four-year course was proposed to operate in conjunction with the police department, where students were to obtain on-the-job experience as cadets. The statewide plan vanished in the bureaucracy of the new administration, and attention was turned to the establishment of an in-service training program within the Department.

Captain Emile Vallet founded the Seattle Police School in 1937 soon after his return from the FBI National Academy. The first classes were held on the fourth floor of the central fire station, but the school soon moved to new quarters in the old fire station on seventh and Columbia. By 1939, the school had developed something of an international reputation. Three Chilean officers were sent to Seattle to study and observe the operation of the police training school.

The training school moved to new quarters on the second floor when the present Public Safety Building was completed in 1952, and remained there until several years ago. The Academy was then moved to Providence Heights near Issaquah [Washington] and then to the temporary site at the Police Athletic Association Range. Training is currently conducted in cooperation with the Washington State Training Facility at Burien [a Seattle suburb].

[5] Unfortunately, by the 1990's, few of these institutions continue to offer a course of instruction directed at operating and managing a police agency. Some continue in name only, teaching the "sociology of policing," which is thought to be of little value to the street police officer. And few of these institutions, which now provide police education through their so-called criminal justice courses, are staffed with experienced police professionals. But their supporters say that such job-related professional staffing is entirely unnecessary, for police administration is not a science. It may not be, but when this issue is raised, it is appropriate to ask: who teaches the professional, i.e., lawyer, doctor, chemist, dentist etc? If the answer is "someone from within their own profession, then so it should be in the training of law enforcement professionals. In a recent conversation the author had with an officer-graduate of one of these schools, the officer had never heard of Sir Robert Peel, the famous British police administrator, organizational innovator and author of the Peelian Reform of the London Police of 1829. Nor had he heard of August Vollmer or Orlando W. Wilson, the two former police chief/educators who are considered by most law enforcement authorities to be the "fathers" of modern policing in America. The officer did not have the slightest understanding of the need nor did he have the knowhow to deploy police resources to meet both emergency and day-to-day workloads of the force, for he had no training or educational experiences in the strategic management of police resources.

[6] A. C. Germann, Police Executive Development, Charles C. Thomas Publishing Co., Op. Cit., Michael Johnson, pp. 4-10, Springfield, Il. P. 45.

[7] "Bureau of Justice Statistics - National Update," U.S. Department of Justice Washington, D.C., April 1992, Volume 1, No. 4, p. 5.

[8] Police Chief Executive, National Advisory Commission on Criminal Justice Standard and Goals, Washington, D. C. Government Printing Office, 1976, p. 28.

[9] Donald C. Witham, The American Law Enforcement Chief Executive: A Management Profile. Police Executive Research Forum, Washington, D. C., p. 46.

[10] J. J. Norton and G. C. Cowart, "Assaulting the Politics/Administration Dichotomy," Police Chief, 45:11 November 1978, p. 26.

[11] Standards for Law Enforcement Agencies, Commission on Accreditation for Law Enforcement Agencies, Inc. Fairfax, Virginia, 1984, p. Xi.

[12] This process of increasing the authority of the state and federal police while diminishing the responsibility of the local police, is well underway in the U.S. at the present time and is very noticeable when one reviews the rapid growth of the state and federal police services in the last several years. The Federal Bureau of Investigation and the various federal law enforcement services within the Departments of Justice and Treasury have more than doubled in size within the last 25 years. This is in stark contrast with what has occurred within our major cities in the U.S.

See 1980 "Crime in the United States," Section V. Law Enforcement Personnel, U.S. Government Printing Office, Washington, D. C. pp. 261-311 and 1988 Crime in the United States, Section V. Law Enforcement Personnel, pp. 231-297.

[13] "One study showed that 84 percent of law enforcement executives indicated that the lack of protection from arbitrary and unjustified removal [from office] either affected or would affect their ability to fulfill their responsibilities objectively and independently." See J. J. Norton and G. C. Cowart, "Assaulting the Politics/Administration Dichotomy," Police Chief, 45:11, November, 1978, p. 26.

[14] Police Chief Executive Report, Op. Cit., p. 124.

[15] Ibid.

[16] Ibid.

[17] Ibid.

[18] The World Book Encyclopedia, B, Volume 2. Field Enterprises Educational Corp. 1972 edition, p. 591.

Appendix

A

November 20, 1963

IN THE SUPREME COURT OF BRITISH COLUMBIA
NOTICE OF MOTION FOR A WRIT OF HABEAS
CORPUS AND SUBJICIENDUM

TAKE NOTICE that the Supreme Court of British Columbia will be moved before the Presiding Judge in Chambers at the Law Courts on Georgia Street, in the City of Vancouver, in the Province of British Columbia, on Friday, the 29th day of November, A.D. 1963 at the hour of 10:30 o'clock in the forenoon, or so soon thereafter as counsel may be heard, for an Order for and on behalf of John Wasylenchuk, directed to the Warden of Oakalla Prison Farm, directing him to show cause why a Writ of Habeas Corpus should not issue to have the body of John Wasylenchuk before a Judge in chambers in the Supreme Court of British Columbia at the City of Vancouver forthwith, pursuant to the Writ of Habeas Corpus to issue, to undergo and receive all and singular such matters and things as our said Court or Judge shall then and there consider of concerning him in this behalf; AND FURTHER an Order to show cause why a Writ of Certiorari should not issue to remove into this Court before the said Presiding Judge in Chambers a certain record of the Extradition Proceedings held before the Honorable Mr. Justice Hutcheson, acting as Commissioner under the Extradition Act and a Warrant of Committal issued thereunder, or directed to be issued thereunder, on Saturday, the 9th of November, A.D. 1963, whereby the said John Wasylenchuk was directed to be surrendered to the Authorities of the United States of America to be tried on charges of murder and robbery.

AND FURTHER TAKE NOTICE that upon the said hearing will be read the warrants of committal and the record of the proceedings had and taken before The Honourable Mr. Justice Hutcheson and at the time aforesaid a motion will be made for the discharge of the said John Wasylenchuk on the following amongst other grounds, namely:

1. That the Learned Commissioner, although directing his mind to his duties as a Magistrate sitting as though he were conducting a preliminary hearing, the said Commissioner did not apply his mind to the proper test involved when a Magistrate sits on a preliminary hearing.

2. That the Learned Commissioner should have found that there was no evidence, or alternatively, improper evidence to reach the conclusion that the accused was probably guilty.

3. That the Learned Commissioner should have found that he had no jurisdiction to issue his warrant.

4. That the Learned Commissioner should have found that the fugitive was not probably guilty.

5. That the Learned Commissioner should have found that the testimony of (Irvin) Teague was worthless and consequently there was no, or alternatively insufficient or alternatively improper evidence before him, on which to make a finding.

6. That the Learned Commissioner should have directed his mind to the whole of the evidence presented before him and if he had done so, he would have found that there was no prima facie cause of guilt, or alternatively that the fugitive was probably not guilty.

7. And upon the further ground that at law there was no evidence before the Learned Commissioner to warrant or justify a committal of the said John Wasylenchuk on the said charges, if the said John Wasylenchuk were being charged on the said charges at a preliminary hearing conducted in Canada.

8. And upon such further and other grounds as counsel may submit.

DATED at Vancouver, British Columbia this 20th day of November, A.D. 1963.

s/Thomas A. Dohm
Counsel for John Wasylenchuk

TO THE HONORABLE MR. JUSTICE HUTCHESON,
acting as an Extradition Commissioner
AND TO THE HONORABLE THE ATTORNEY
GENERAL OF THE PROVINCE OF BRITISH COLUMBIA
AND TO HUGH McGIVERN, ESQ.
Counsel for the United States of America
THIS Notice of Motion is filed for and on behalf of the said John Wasylenchuk by T.R. Braidwood, Esq., of the firm of Braidwood, Nuttall & MacKenzie, whose place of business and address for service is at 208 East Hastings Street, Vancouver, British Columbia.

334 • *Cops, Crooks & Politicians*

Appendix

B

April 17, 1964
Mr. Brockman Adams
140 Washington Building
Seattle, Washington 98101

Dear Mr. Adams:
With reference to a new ordinance which would grant Irvin Teague
a reward from the City of Seattle for his actions in the Greenwood
Bank murder case, please be advised that my request for such money
has been denied. As you are aware, on April 8th I met with Mr. Miller,
Chairman of the Finance Committee of the City Council and other
members of this committee. As a result of my application for
payment of the full reward offered by Ordinance No. 82843, Mr.
Harris, Chief Assistant, Corporation Counsel, stated that it was
impossible under the wording of that ordinance to pay any portion of
the reward inasmuch as there had been no conviction.

On April 16, I discussed with Mr. Miller the enactment of a new
ordinance which would pay Teague half of the reward for giving the
information that led to Wasylenchuk's arrest. After discussion and
consideration, this was denied. I regret that this closes the door to any
possibility of the city paying any reward money to Teague.

Assistant Chief C. A. Rouse has been discussing the employment of Teague in Houston, Texas by the Todd Shipyard Corporation with the appropriate people. On April 16, Mr. Zener, General
Manager, Todd's Shipyards, assured me that Todd will employ
Teague at Houston. Assistant Chief Rouse will continue his actions
to get this employment completely firmed up.

My understanding is that Teague may be paroled and placed
under the supervision of the United States Parole Office in whatever

area he is sent. I also understand that the Seattle First National Bank will make money available to Teague. It is my feeling that we should take no firm action on Teague unless and until the Department of Immigration has formally given approval for Teague remaining in the United States. When this approval is received, I would propose, upon Teague's parole, to purchase an airplane ticket with the money from the First National Bank to Houston, Texas, giving him the letter which would enable him immediately to go to work at Todd's and give him the balance of the money from the bank to support himself during the adjustment period.

Would you advise me if this proposed course of action is agreeable with you?

Best regards,

Yours very truly
F. C. RAMON
Chief of Police

BA:ms

UNITED STATES DEPARTMENT OF JUSTICE
UNITED STATES ATTORNEY
Western District of Washington
United States Court House
Seattle 4, Washington
May 12, 1964

Chief Frank Ramon
Seattle Police Department
Seattle, Washington

Re: *Irvin Lester Terrance Teague*

Dear Chief Ramon:

I am in receipt of your letter of April 17, 1964 for which I thank you. As I confirmed with you by telephone, we were very disappointed that the City Council of the City of Seattle has refused to cooperate in this matter.

We are very pleased to note that Chief C. A. Rouse is now of the opinion that employment can be obtained for Teague with Todd Shipyards, Houston, Texas. We have now cleared this matter with Immigration and Naturalization and I would appreciate your confirming with us that you have received the $1,000.00 from the Seattle First National Bank and that it is available to purchase an airplane ticket for Teague and to provide him with money with which to live until his employment takes effect in Houston.

As soon as you have confirmed this with us, we will write to Teague who is now an inmate at Sandstone, Minn. We will inform him that he should contact you by letter with regard to his release date so that you can make arrangements with him for transportation to Houston.

I want to thank you again for all of your cooperation in this matter.

Very truly yours,

WILLIAM N. GOODWIN
s/Brockman Adams
BROCKMAN ADAMS
Special Assistant to the
United States Attorney

THE CITY OF SEATTLE
DEPARTMENT OF
POLICE
Seattle 4, Washington

May 28, 1964

Mr. Douglas Fryer
Assistant United States Attorney
United States Courthouse
Seattle, Washington
Dear Sir:
    RE: IRVIN LESTER TEAGUE
The enclosed correspondence is being furnished for the purpose of programming the release of IRVIN LESTER TEAGUE at some as yet undetermined date.

We have the original correspondence which we can make available for transmittal to Mr. Teague for presentation at the Houston Division of Todd Shipyards for the purpose of obtaining employment as set forth in the letter.

We have funds in the amount of one thousand dollars ($1,000.00), which can be disbursed and furnished to provide transportation and living expenses for Mr. Teague while establishing himself on parole. We are awaiting advice from you with reference to making these funds available in any fashion which will provide him with the essential transportation and funds to maintain himself while getting established while on parole in Houston.

Two copies of the employment correspondence are being enclosed in the thought that you may want to transmit this information either to Teague or to parole officials with whom you may be discussing this situation.

Yours truly,
F. C. RAMON, Chief of Police
R. M. GREEN
Detective Division Chief

LESOURD & PATTEN
ATTORNEY AT LAW
1140 WASHINGTON BUILDING
SEATTLE, WASHINGTON 98101
Main 4-1040
June 4, 1964
  Mr. Irvin Terry Teague
  #5647-SS
  Federal Correctional Institution
  Box 1000
  Sandstone, Minnesota 55072
  Dear Terry:

I received your letter of May 31, 1964 and was disappointed to see that you had not heard the results of our efforts.

We have worked with the Immigration Service and you have been granted a parole into the United States. I am sending a copy of this letter to Douglas Fryer and he will confirm this with you.

We have also made arrangements for a job for you in Houston, Texas, through Chief Ramon of the Police Department and I am asking Doug Fryer to forward to you a letter giving you the specifics of the time and place of the job.

We have also completed arrangements for funds for you from Seattle and elsewhere and you will receive a letter from either Chief Ramon or Doug Fryer who will handle the details of this with the institution. I think you will find that you will be able to have your transportation paid for and have money to keep you until your job begins to carry you. I am asking Doug Fryer to work this out with the appropriate authorities here under the arrangements that we have made since he is in an official position and can make these arrangements more properly.

I am very pleased that you are going to be paroled on June 24th, and I have a great deal of faith in your ability to now be successful on the outside, and all of us, including particularly Doug, Dean and myself will certainly do what we can to help make your transition a successful one.

Please write me and confirm that you are aware of the arrangements we have made for you to remain in the country, have a job, and receive sufficient money to keep yourself until your employment is available so that I will know that you are all right.

With best regards,

Very truly yours,
Brockman Adams

cc: Chief Frank Ramon
   Douglas Fryer
   Dean Rolston
DMF:ms
50730

June 8, 1964

Mr. Irvin Lester Terrance Teague
#5647-SS
Federal Correctional Institution
Box 1000
Sandstone, Minnesota 55072
Dear Terry:

It gives me great pleasure to confirm the fact that we have now finalized the arrangements for your release and financial assistance. As you know, the Board of Parole has now approved your release on June 24, 1964. We have confirmed that this is not for deportation purposes only since you have been granted a six months parole extension by the Immigration & Naturalization Service. We are enclosing a copy of their letter confirming that action. The Immigration Service will require a review of your extension at the end of the six months period and they will then decide whether they will permit you to remain in the United States beyond that period. Since we assume everything will go well, we also assume that the extension will be granted at the end of the six month period.

This is also to confirm that fact that Seattle Police Department has made available a special fund of $1,000.00 to provide transportation and living expenses for you while establishing yourself on parole. We are enclosing a copy of a letter from the Seattle Police Department and also a copy of a letter from Todd Shipyard which assures you employment in Houston upon your arrival there. I will shortly forward to you a plane ticket from the point nearest Sandstone, Minn. to Houston and also a check in the amount of $200 to cover your immediate expenses. The balance of the money from the Seattle Police will be forwarded to Houston in care of L.E. Miggins, Chief Probation Officer, Houston, Texas who will turn it over to you as you need it in Houston.

We have also been advised by the FBI that they will make available to you an additional $1,000.00 for your assistance.

I will be in touch with you shortly to follow-up these matters.

Very truly yours,
WILLIAM N. GOODWIN
United States Attorney

DOUGLAS M. FRYER
Assistant United States
Attorney

cc w/o encl;
Brockman Adams
Jess Mincks
Robert Green

June 9, 1964

Mr. Douglas M. Fryer
Assistant United States Attorney
United States Courthouse
Seattle, Washington
Dear Sir:

RE: IRVIN LESTER TERRANCE TEAGUE

The enclosed airline ticket for IRVIN TEAGUE has been purchased from the funds which were made available to us, and we have also provided two cashier's checks in the amounts of $200.00 and $726.15 for transmittal to TEAGUE in accordance with our previous conversation.

The original copy of the letter from Assistant Treasurer, Mr. M. A. Flaten, in Seattle to Chief Ramon relative to TEAGUE'S employment in Houston is also enclosed in the event that it may be of value to you or assist in effecting this job placement.

Yours truly,

F. C. RAMON, Chief of Police
R. M. GREEN
Detective Division Chief

(Ticket $73.55)

Order Form

To order additional copies of:

COPS, CROOKS AND POLITICIANS

please send $17.95 plus $2.50 P&H, Washington residents
please include 8.2% sales tax (in Canada send $22.95 plus
$3.50 P&H). Make money order or check payable to:

THE DELAINE GROUP
10615 62nd Avenue South
Seattle, WA 98178

If you prefer to use VISA or MasterCard, please fill in your
card's number and expiration date. Please circle appropriate
card.

□□□□□□□□□□□□□□□□□

Signature_____Expiration date_____

Bulk purchase available by calling The Delaine Group at
(206) 722-1309.

_____Copies at $17.95 each_____

$2.50 P&H _____

Washington state residents add 8.2% tax _____

Total enclosed _____

Name_____

Address_____

City, State, Zip_____

Country_____